PERSPECTIVES ON EARLY CHILDHOOD PSYCHOLOGY AND EDUCATION

SPECIAL FOCUS

Helping Stakeholders Promote Behavioral Outcomes in Early Childhood

Volume 7, Issue 2
Fall 2022

ISBN: 978-1-935625-77-3
ISSN: 2471-1527

Member

CELJ

Council of Editors of Learned Journals

PERSPECTIVES on EARLY CHILDHOOD PSYCHOLOGY and EDUCATION

TABLE OF CONTENTS

Helping Stakeholders Promote Behavioral Outcomes in Early Childhood

Editor's Note

Maria Hernández Finch

This special issue focused on strategies to promote positive behavioral and academic outcomes in early childhood. The special issue includes articles on consultation and training techniques to improve early childhood educators' use of evidence-based strategies for classroom management. Several articles evaluate and discuss various interventions aimed at improving reading skills of early elementary students. Additionally, the importance of interdisciplinary practices in early childhood education is discussed, and an interdisciplinary training program for behavioral and mental health services is described. Trainers and researchers will appreciate the Behavior Analytic Multitiered Consultation Model for Early Childhood Educators for its practicality and integration of best practices.

We are asking for submissions for a special bridge issue for 8.1. We are encouraging articles and essays on future directions in research, teaching (Scholarship of Teaching and Learning, etc.), and training in areas or fields of study related to early childhood psychology and or education. Meta-analyses, systematic literature reviews, and general articles are also welcome, and will receive rapid review. Please email me through the portal with questions or to run an abstract, proposal, or idea by me. You will need to create a profile. Completed manuscripts should be submitted by February 6, 2023, for full consideration for publication in issue 8.1. Please access our submission portal here (click on submission link): https://press.pace.edu/perspectives-on-early-childhood-psychology-and-education/

Introduction to Special Focus: Helping Stakeholders Promote Behavioral Outcomes in Early Childhood

Kayla Bates-Brantley, Zachary C. LaBrot, and Sarah Wright Harry

Impact Statement: *Readers will gain information and insight into ten articles featured in PECPE's special issue dedicated to behavioral outcomes within early childhood settings.*

Abstract

Early childhood is often referred to as a sensitive period of development due to the critical nature of skills a young child is expected to acquire across a short period of time. It is a time when foundational social-emotional and academic skills can set the trajectory for later successful outcomes. It is also a time when the lack of critical skill development can increase a child's risk for future mental health and other long-term negative outcomes. Therefore, it is always pressing that early childhood institutions and stakeholders are abreast of evidence-based practices that promote the healthy development of a child's social-emotional and academic well-being. The focus of the second volume of this two-part special issue in Perspectives on Early Childhood Psychology and Education is aimed at providing effective practices to help relevant stakeholders promote positive pro-social outcomes throughout early childhood. This article will introduce volume two of the special issue. In addition, an overview of published manuscripts will provide readers with content-specific insight.

Keywords: *Early childhood; early childhood education; behavioral interventions; behavioral outcomes; early childhood academics*

Across the country, numerous programs (e.g., early childhood education, community-based programs, clinics, primary care, and ABA clinics) exist for early childhood learners. While these programs differ in design, structure, theoretical orientation, and other nuances, the basic goal of each of these programs is simple: increase foundational academic and social-emotional skills (Bakken et al., 2017; Gullo, 2013). What, in practice, might appear as a simplistic end goal is an incredible undertaking, with many early childhood educators struggling to meet the diverse needs of their students (McLeod et al., 2017). Considering early childhood is a period marked by rapid development, it is not surprising that research has indicated this as a sensitive period in which a number of critical skills are expected to develop (Juel, 1988; Scanlon & Vellutino, 1996; Willson & Hughes, 2009). Examples include academic, social-emotional, and behavioral skill acquisition. The development of these skills often marks the likelihood of success or failure across future outcome domains (Koller et al., 2022). This highlights the importance of additional training and support for our early childhood educators. This need was further amplified due to COVID-19. As we enter the post-pandemic era, the focal point of early childhood services should be to address children's limited opportunities to develop and practice certain social-emotional, behavioral, and academic skills (Ford et al., 2021; Gayatri 2020). Additionally, it is a time to address the critical needs of personnel responsible for providing vital services to these children (McCoy et al., 2021).

This special issue will highlight a number of the early childhood institutions and stakeholders that are addressing behavioral outcomes across young children ages 3-9 years old. From a reflection on clinical practice during COVID-19 to consultation practices in schools to academic interventions, each article addresses a critical need for additional evidence-based practice across behavioral domains.

The issue will open with conceptual and empirical articles about consultation and training techniques to improve early childhood educators' use of evidence-based classroom management practices. Smith et al. (2022) conducted a meta-analysis of consultation studies that examined the extent to which intervention implementation supports resulted in early childhood educators' generalized use of evidence-based practices. This study demonstrated the critical need for additional research in this area, with suggestions for future research. Additionally, this study provided practical recommendations for early childhood education consultants. In a conceptual article, LaBrot et al. (2022) describe a novel, data-based consultation model for early childhood educators. The existing literature base, recommendations for future research, implementation guidelines, and a case study are provided and thoroughly described. Beacham et al. (2022) continue this topic through an article dedicated to promoting the need for additional consultation training opportunities within infant and toddler settings. Specifically, the article describes an evidence-based consultation model validated in K-12 settings and discusses modifications that can be made to apply the method within early childhood settings to promote school readiness for infants and toddlers. Finally, Kemp and Whitcomb (2022) conducted a single-case design study at a Head Start investigating how to best align and integrate classroom management strategies and weekly social-emotional learning (SEL) curriculum. The findings suggest that through the use of professional development and weekly performance feedback, educators increased in their alignment with classroom management strategies to the weekly SEL lesson. The researchers also found strong levels of social validity reported through this consultation framework.

Academic skill acquisition is often overlooked as a behavioral outcome, but one most early childhood experts would argue is a key predictor of student success (Koller et al., 2022). The special issue will highlight three articles that evaluate early education academic support and interventions. Harry and colleagues (2022) discuss a summer academic intervention designed to reduce the risk of the "summer slide" for low SES students through a Tier 1 and Tier 2 model. Although mixed results were found across participants, most students exhibited some improvement with oral reading fluency through weekly intervention to help reduce the learning losses that typically occur over the summer break. The study discusses some limitations to summer remediation support (e.g., attendance) and future directions for further support in this pivotal academic area. Similarly, Billingsley-Ring (2022) and colleagues evaluated effective reading interventions, including listening passage preview and repeated reading in a group format. This study sought to evaluate the effectiveness and efficiency of each intervention in relation to student gains in reading fluency. Finally, Dillon et al. (2022) assessed the intervention fidelity for dialogic reading, which targets early academic skills of oral language, vocabulary, and print concepts. Two studies are highlighted in this manuscript, both using single-case design research methodology. The first study utilized an alternating treatment design comparing the use of scripts and checklists for fidelity, while the second study utilized a multiple baseline design looking at the effects from the supports and the subsequent impact on intervention fidelity.

To round out the second volume of this special issue, specific attention was given to additional stakeholders across early childhood. Kupzyk et al. (2022) discuss the importance of interdisciplinary practices within early childhood settings. Specifically, Kupzyk and colleagues describe a university-based training program in which school psychology, applied behavior analysis, and special education graduate students were provided interdisciplinary collaboration training across multiple facets of service provision to young children. Our final article featured how a state-run applied behavior analysis center adapted treatment during COVID-19 to ensure continuity of care for early learners with autism (Furlow et al., 2022). Taken together, this special issue offers significant insight into consultation practices, academic interventions, and behavioral support across multidisciplinary teams that intend to bridge the gap between evidence-based practice and early childhood stakeholders.

References

*Denotes articles included in Part II of the special issue

Bakken, L., Brown, N., & Downing, B. (2017). Early childhood education: The long-term benefits. *Journal of Research in Childhood Education*, 31(2), 255–269. https://doi.org/10.1080/02568543.2016.1273285

*Beacham, C., Perkins, C., Roach, A. T., Barger , B., Donehower, C., & Baggett, K. M. (2022). Building future capacity of school psychologists to address the demand for inclusive evidence-based consultation: Moving beyond K-12 to include school readiness frameworks. *Perspectives on Early Childhood Psychology and Education, 7*(2).

*Billingsley-Ring, M., Bates-Brantley, K., Ripple, H., Donald, M., Gadke, D., & Harry, S. W. (2022). An alternating treatment design comparing small group reading interventions across early elementary readers. *Perspectives on Early Childhood Psychology and Education, 7*(2).

*Dillon, C., & Newman, D. (2022). Supporting intervention fidelity of dialogic reading to support preschool children's early literacy skills. *Perspectives on Early Childhood Psychology and Education 7*(2).

Ford, T. G., Kwon, K. A., & Tsotsoros, J. D. (2021). Early childhood distance learning in the US during the COVID pandemic: Challenges and opportunities. *Children and Youth Services Review, 131*, 106297. https://doi.org/10.1016/j.childyouth.2021.106297

*Furlow, C. M., Barker, L. K., Brewer, R. R., Thomason, M. N., Brunner, A. G., & Huff, F. K. (2022). Perspectives for the delivery of early intervention services via telemedicine in rural states: Outcomes from the COVID-19 pandemic. *Perspectives on Early Childhood Psychology and Education, 7*(2).

Gayatri, M. (2020). The implementation of early childhood education in the time of COVID-19 pandemic: A systematic review. Humanities & Social Sciences Reviews, 8(6), 46-54. https://doi.org/10.18510/hssr.2020.866

Gullo, D.F. (2013). Improving instructional practices, policies, and student outcomes for early childhood language and literacy through data-driven decision making. *Early Childhood Education Journal, 41*, 413–421. https://doi.org/10.1007/s10643-013-0581-x

*Harry, S. W., Whitefield, B. L., Bates-Brantley, K., & McKinley, L. (2022). Avoiding the summer slide: Tier One and Two supports targeting early readers. *Perspectives on Early Childhood Psychology and Education, 7*(2).

Juel, C. (1988). Learning to read and write: A longitudinal study of 54 children from first through fourth grades. *Journal of Educational Psychology, 80*(4), 437-447. https://doi.org/10.1037/0022-0663.80.4.437

*Kemp, J. M., & Whitcomb, S. A. (2022). Aligning classroom management strategies with a social emotional learning curriculum in early childhood. *Perspectives on Early Childhood Psychology and Education, 7*(2).

Koller, K. A., Hojnoski, R. L., & Van Norman, E. R. (2022). Classification accuracy of early literacy assessments: Linking preschool and kindergarten performance. *Assessment for Effective Intervention.* https://doi.org/10.1177/15345084221081091

*Kupzyk, S., Bassingthwaite, B., Weaver, A. D., & Nordness , P. D. (2022). Interdisciplinary collaborative practice in early childhood. *Perspectives on Early Childhood Psychology and Education, 7*(2).

*LaBrot, Z. C., DeFouw, E. R., Lundy, M., McVay, K., Rozsa, A., & Dufrene, B. A. (2022). Towards a behavioral analytic multitiered consultation model for early childhood educators. *Perspectives on Early Childhood Psychology and Education, 7*(2).

McCoy, D. C., Cuartas, J., Behrman, J., Cappa, C., Heymann, J., López Bóo, F., & Fink, G. (2021). Global estimates of the implications of COVID-19-related preprimary school closures for children's instructional access, development, learning, and economic wellbeing. *Child Development, 92*(5). https://doi.org/10.1111/cdev.13658

McLeod, B. D., Sutherland, K. S., Martinez, R. G., Conroy, M. A., Snyder, P. A., & Southam-Gerow, M. A. (2017). Identifying common practice elements to improve social, emotional, and behavioral outcomes of young children in early childhood classrooms. *Prevention Science*, 18(2), 204-213. https://doi.org/10.1007/s11121-016-0703-y

Scanlon, D. M., & Vellutino, F. R. (1996). Prerequisite skills, early instruction, and success in first-grade reading: Selected results from a longitudinal study. *Mental Retardation & Developmental Disabilities Research Reviews*, 2(1), 54–63. https://doi.org/10.1002/(SICI)1098-2779(1996)2:1<54::AID-MRDD9>3.0.CO;2-X

*Smith, T. E., LaBrot, Z. C., Maxime, E., & Lawson, A. (2022). School-based consultation to promote generalization of early childhood educators' evidence-based practices: A meta-analysis. *Perspectives on Early Childhood Psychology and Education, 7*(2).

Willson, V. L., Hughes, J. N. (2009). Who is retained in first grade? A psychosocial perspective. *The Elementary School Journal, 109*(3), 251–266. https://doi.org/10.1086/592306

School-based Consultation to Promote Generalization of Early Childhood Educators' Evidence-based Practices: A Meta-analysis

Tyler E. Smith, Zachary C. LaBrot, Emily Maxime, and Abigail Lawson

Abstract

Early childhood educators are tasked with supporting young children's academic, behavioral, and social-emotional through the use of evidence-based practices (EBPs). Unfortunately, early childhood educators may struggle with consistent implementation of EBPs. When this occurs, school-based consultation may be beneficial in promoting early childhood educators' use of effective classroom management practices and interventions. A critical aspect of school-based consultation is ensuring that early childhood educators generalize strategies they have been trained to use through consultation. However, the extent to which early childhood educators generalize skills trained through consultation across settings, children, and other evidence-based practices is unclear. Therefore, the purpose of this meta-analysis was to synthesize the existing school-based consultation literature in early childhood settings to determine the extent to which early childhood educators generalize skills trained through consultation. A total of 12 studies including 39 educator consultees and 171 effects comprised our final sample. Three-level hierarchical models with robust variance estimation were used to pool both Log Response Ratios and Tau effect sizes for analyses. Overall results indicated school-based consultation had a positive and significant impact on educator generalization of EBPs (LRRi = 0.95; Tau = 0.79). Further, particular implementation supports (e.g., in situ training) significantly contributed to EBP generalization. These results suggest school-based consultation to be an effective means for promoting early childhood educator generalization of EBPs. Implications for research and practice and future research directions are discussed.

keywords: *school consultation, generalization, early childhood education, meta-analysis.*

Introduction

The National Center for Education Statistics estimates between 40% to and 86% of young children enroll in early childhood education programs (Hussar et al., 2020). As much as 30% of these children encounter difficulties, such as poverty, family discord, exposure to violence, and low parental education that place them at risk for developing long-term internalizing and externalizing difficulties (Wichstrom et al., 2012). Therefore, early childhood educators who have frequent contact with these children are in a unique position to play a vital role in buffering these risk factors. Specifically, early childhood educators' use of evidence-based practices (EBPs) has potential to enhance young children's social/emotional, behavioral, and cognitive development, leading to the prevention of problems and successful transition to elementary school (Carter et al., 2010).

Unfortunately, early childhood educators struggle to integrate EBPs into day-to-day classroom management practices (Floress et al., 2017; Odom et al., 1995). In fact, early childhood educators often report a significant need for professional development in EBP use with children who display challenging classroom behaviors (Reinke et al., 2011; Snell et al., 2012). This is concerning, as EBPs are only beneficial for promoting child outcomes if they are consistently implemented with high levels of treatment integrity (Gresham, 1989). As such, early childhood educators are clearly in need of supports to aid them in the adoption and implementation of EBPs in early education settings.

School-Based Consultation in Early Childhood Education

School-based consultation is an effective and preferred teacher training approach (Gutkin & Curtis, 2009) and can be used to improve early childhood educators' EBP implementation.

School-based consultation is an indirect service approach, in which a consultant with expertise in child behavior and development provides recommendations to aid educators in EBP delivery (Erchul & Sheridan, 2014). Unlike time-limited professional development trainings, school- based consultation is an ongoing support process aimed at addressing educators' needs (e.g., managing disruptive classroom behavior). If educators are unable to implement recommended practices and interventions, school-based consultants may provide various implementation supports (e.g., prompts, in situ training, performance feedback) to aid educators in EBP implementation.

Research consistently demonstrates that school-based consultation is effective for improving early childhood educators' EBP implementation, such as increasing behavior-specific praise (LaBrot et al., 2020, 2021), improving effective instruction delivery (Dufrene et al., 2012), promoting social interactions (Gomez et al., 2021), and implementing strategies to promote children's social-emotional competence (Hemmeter et al., 2015), among several others. School- based consultation plays a critical role in addressing deficits in early childhood educators' training and professional development, and promotes EBP delivery. Despite the importance and identified benefits of consultation, the extent to which early childhood educators generalize skills trained through consultation across settings, children, and other EBPs is unclear.

Generalization of Early Childhood Educators' Evidence-Based Practice Use

Generalization is the extent to which a trained behavior occurs in conditions where training did not occur. The success of behavioral training and interventions often depends on whether a learner generalizes what they have learned across time, settings, behaviors, and individuals (Cooper et al., 2020; Stokes & Baer, 1977). School-based consultation may be conceptualized in the same manner, in which success is determined by the extent to which educators generalize EBPs trained through consultation. In a school-based context, generalization of EBPs can be demonstrated through their implementation throughout the school year (i.e., time), across different activities or locations (i.e., setting), across other EBPs (i.e., behaviors), and with children who were not targeted in consultation (i.e., individuals).

However, many school-based consultation studies conducted in early childhood education settings fail to collect data on educators' generalized outcomes. This is problematic, as the collection of generalization data is important to determine the long-term effects (i.e., EBPs are sustained) and efficiency (i.e., EBPs spontaneously generalize across contexts) of school- based consultation techniques. Although some research has examined the extent to which early childhood educators generalize their use of EBPs trained through school-based consultation (e.g., Barton et al., 2018; LaBrot et al., 2021), there are no studies that have synthesized the school-based consultation generalization literature for early childhood educators. Therefore, research that synthesizes the literature and evaluates the extent to which early childhood educators generalize their use of EBPs trained through school-based consultation is needed.

The need to collect generalization data in school-based consultation research is not novel, as other scholars have acknowledged the importance of collecting these data. For example, Robinson and Swanton (1980) conducted a systematic review of the school-based consultation (termed "teacher training") literature to determine the extent to which this literature base collected generalization data and identified factors that lead to teachers' generalized outcomes. Only six single-case design studies published in the *Journal of Applied Behavior Analysis* between 1970 and 1978 were identified. Of note, only one study included early childhood educators as participants, while the remainder included elementary and secondary educators.

Across all six studies, only three demonstrated educators' generalization of intervention implementation following consultation.

Robinson and Swanton (1980) also noted that only half of the studies included sufficient data to determine whether teacher participants generalized intervention use. Notably, the only study that included early childhood educators did not contain sufficient data (i.e., at least three per study phase) or reliability data, and therefore could not experimentally demonstrate generalization. In general, results of this literature review highlight the need for experimentally rigorous studies that measure and promote educators' generalized use of EBPs following school-based consultation.

However, it is important to interpret the results of this systematic literature review in light of some limitations. Most notably, this review included studies that were published over 40 years ago. Since the time this review was published, many other school-based consultation studies have collected data on educators' generalized outcomes (e.g., Barton et al., 2018; LaBrot et al., 2021). Second, Robinson and Swanton (1980) only included published studies, which likely biased their research sample (sometimes referred to as the "file drawer effect"). As such, an updated review should make efforts to include unpublished literature such as theses and dissertations. Finally, the small sample size included in the Robinson and Swanton (1980) review did not allow for consultation outcomes to be systematically combined and analyzed across studies (i.e., meta- analysis). Beyond what is known from individual studies alone, evidence from a meta-analysis synthesizing data across multiple studies will help to determine if school-based consultation is an effective means of promoting educators' generalization of EBPs. Further, school-based consultation can also involve various components or strategies to foster educator use of EBPs (e.g., performance feedback, in situ training). Using meta-analytic methods, it is imperative to determine which specific components of consultation may be responsible for promoting educator use of EBPs.

Empirically determining effective consultation components is necessary to direct efficient and impactful school-based consultation efforts in the future.

Purpose

School-based consultation is likely influential in promoting early childhood educators' generalization of EBPs. However, the extent to which early childhood educators' EBP use generalizes across time, settings, other EBPs, and children is often overlooked in research and not well understood. Given the widespread use of school-based consultation (Gutkin & Curtis, 2009), limitations of past reviews in this area, and increased efforts focusing on education generalization, an updated synthesis of the literature is vital. Thus, the current meta-analysis aims to (a) provide novel insights into the effectiveness of school-based consultation for promoting early childhood educators' generalized use of EBPs, (b) serve as an updated evaluation of the effects of consultation for improving educator target outcomes, and (c) uncover which specific consultation components promote educator use of EBPs. In particular, the current meta-analysis was guided by the following research questions:

What are the effects of school-based consultation on (a) the generalization of early childhood educator EBPs (overall) and (b) educator generalization EBP subtypes (i.e., behavior specific praise, behavior analytic procedures, individual support plan, and instructional practices)?

What are the effects of school-based consultation on (a) educator target EBPs (overall) and (b) educator target EBP subtypes?

Which consultation components are most effective at promoting educator use of EBPs?

Method

The present study was part of a larger meta-analysis focused on the effects of school-based consultation for promoting educator use of EBPs. For purposes of the current meta-analysis, all included studies focused on *early childhood educators* and were identified and analyzed to answer our research questions. In the following section, we first describe methods and procedures from our larger meta-analysis, followed by selection and analyses of studies that focused on early childhood educators. Compilation of the current meta-analytic database included three steps: (1) literature search, (2) identification of studies, and (3) study coding. Further, between two and three individuals (i.e., study authors and trained graduate students) were involved at each stage of the process.

Literature Search Procedures

We used three central procedures in order to comprehensively search the relevant literature: electronic database searching, hand searching of journals, and reference list searching of previous relevant reviews. First, four electronic databases (*Academic Search Premiere, ERIC, APA PsychInfo, and APA PsychArticles*) were searched using multiple search term parameters and combinations. Specific search terms included a combination of search strings ("teacher*," "educator*," "school* staff," "school*, "consult*," "coach*," "behavior* manage*," strategy," "class* discipline," "generalization," "generalize," "maintenance," "maintain," and "fidelity"). Search parameters were limited to studies reported in English and those conducted from 1980 to 2020. The year 1980 was chosen as a starting point to build off the seminal work in this area by Robinson and Swanton (1980). In an attempt to capture grey literature, we also conducted searches through the online database *ProQuest: Dissertation & Theses* and Google Scholar. Second, we conducted hand searches of 15 different relevant journals focused on mental and behavioral health services in schools (e.g., *Journal of Behavioral Education, School Psychology Review, School Psychology*), teacher education and training (e.g., *Journal of Teacher Education, Teaching and Teacher Education*), and behavioral psychology (e.g., *Behavioral Interventions, Journal of Applied Behavior Analysis*). Third, as a secondary approach to identifying potential studies for inclusion, we searched reference lists of previously published relevant meta-analyses and large-scale reviews (e.g., Collier-Meek et al., 2018; Reddy et al., 2000).

Figure 1
Flowchart of Search and Screening Processes

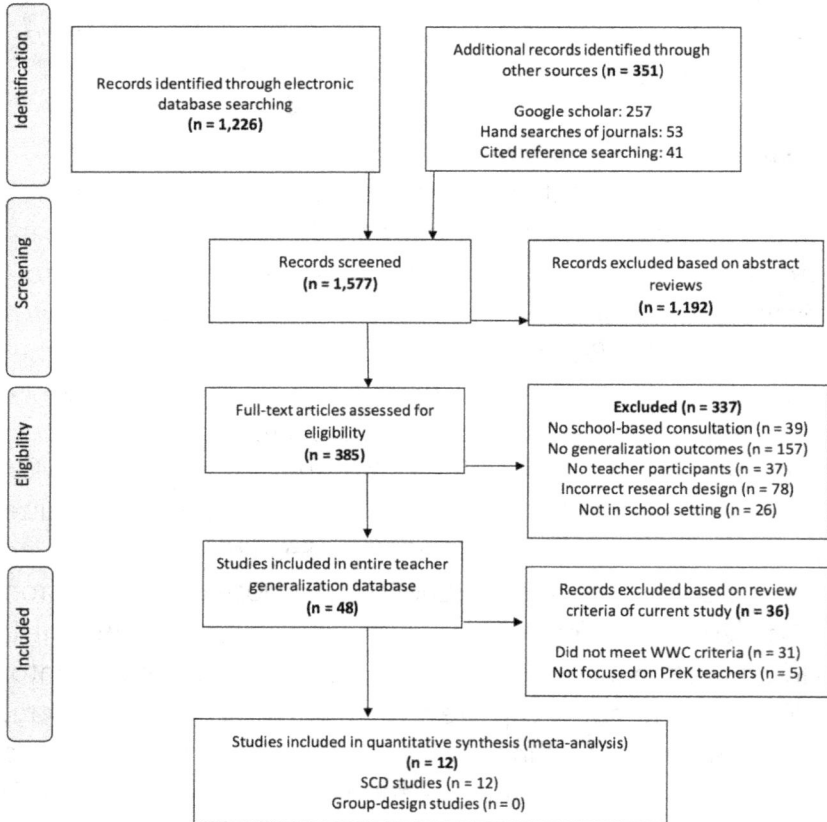

Study Identification

Search procedures yielded 1,577 journal articles, book chapters, and dissertations/theses to be reviewed (1,226 identified through electronic database searching and 351 records identified through other sources). See Figure 1 for an overview of search and screening processes at each stage of the study. Records located through our search procedures were then retained and reviewed for potential inclusion following a three-step approach with increasing specificity– abstract screening, full-text reviews, and reviewing WWC design criteria (for SCD studies only). This approach has been utilized by previous reviews of school-based interventions (e.g., Smith et al., 2022) and aims to be more inclusive at the abstract screening stage, as abstracts often do not include enough detail to make inclusion/exclusion determinations based on all study inclusion criteria. Details of screening and reviewing performed at each step are described below.

Abstract screening. First, all abstracts were independently screened by study authors based on two broad inclusion criteria: (1) the study must have assessed educator outcomes and (2) the study must have involved school-based consultation. Approximately 30% of all abstracts were double-screened and compared for inconsistencies during weekly research team meetings. When disagreements occurred about inclusion and exclusion criteria, the research team discussed determinations until consensus was reached. Inclusion/exclusion agreement was 94% for abstracts that were double-screened. At this stage, based on the two criteria described above, 385 articles were retained.

Full-text reviews. The second step of the identification process involved independent review by two research team members of full-text articles identified as potentially relevant during the abstract screening stage. Specifically, research team members were trained to ensure studies met the following criteria:

The study must have included consultation/coaching or training/professional development of school personnel aimed at indirectly supporting children's behavioral or social-emotional development (e.g., behavioral consultation with a school psychologist to address child disruptive behavior, educator training in classroom management practices);

Recipients of consultation/coaching or training/professional development must have been school-based personnel (including teachers, pre-service teachers, teacher aides, preservice clinicians [e.g., preservice behavior analysts], paraprofessionals, speech pathologists, before- and after-school staff, recess lunch monitors, classroom volunteers, or other school staff [e.g., secretaries]);

The study must have occurred in a school setting (e.g., hallways, classroom, playground, gym; Cole et al., 2000);

The study needed to include at least one outcome measurement assessing the generalization of school personnel practices (i.e., the ability to use and transfer practices across multiple participants [e.g., children], settings [e.g., different activities], and/or behaviors [e.g., praise, effective instruction];

The study must have included either a single-case experimental design (SCD) or group- design (i.e., experimental or quasi-experimental design) that compared groups receiving consultation/coaching or training/professional development with one or more control groups. At this stage, 48 SCD studies met our inclusion criteria.

Review based on WWC design criteria. Third, two research team members independently reviewed all 48 SCD studies for inclusion based on the Institute of Education Sciences What Works Clearinghouse (WWC) SCD standards (What Works Clearinghouse, 2020). Further, all studies were double-reviewed to ensure reliability. These standards were utilized to rule out threats to internal validity and included the following: (1) data are available in graphical display; (2) the independent variable was systematically manipulated with a researcher determining phase changes; (3) outcomes are measured by more than one observer for at least 20% of data points; (4) residual treatment effects are ruled out; and (5) each phase contained an adequate number of data points. Studies that did not *Meet Standards without Reservations* or *Meet Standards with Reservations* were excluded. At this stage, of the 48 SCD studies reviewed, 17 studies met inclusion criteria based on the WWC design standards.

Study Coding

Variable coding. All studies were coded by study authors to extract information pertinent to answering research questions. Study authors created and developed a codebook that included multiple sections designed to focus on study-, participant-, and outcome-level variables. The codebook was developed by creating initial codes, testing said codes, and revising codes as necessary. Once the codebook was developed, coders independently reviewed studies and met weekly to discuss disagreements and reach a consensus. Specifically, articles were coded based on consultee type (e.g., teacher, teacher aid, preservice teacher), consultant type (e.g., school psychologist, graduate students), consultation and implementation support characteristics (e.g., in situ training, behavioral skills training), and the form of generalization outcome measured (e.g., across settings, across children). Additionally, articles were coded for consultee characteristics, such as race/ethnicity, gender, age, number of years teaching, and education level. Further, all studies were double-coded and percent agreement was revealed to be 97%, indicating high agreement among reviewers.

Data extraction. Pertinent data were also extracted from each study in order to calculate effect size indices for meta-analysis. The data extraction tool, WebPlotDigitizer (Rohatgi, 2014) was used, as it has previously been shown to have high reliability and a high degree of usability (Moeyaert et al., 2016). Data were extracted for each baseline and intervention phase of relevant educator outcomes by uploading graphical images from studies into WebPlotDigitizer, calibrating axes, and manually clicking on data points to yield their XY coordinates. Two trained graduate students independently extracted data from included studies.

Approximately 25% of graphs were then randomly selected and double-reviewed by the first author and compared for intercoder reliability using proportional agreement (i.e., both coders' values being within 1% of the y-axis range). Proportional agreement was 94.9%, indicating a high level of agreement consistent with similar studies employing plot digitizing tools (e.g., Bruhn et al., 2022 Collins et al., 2020).

Once all studies were coded and relevant data were extracted to form our larger meta- analytic database, we selected and analyzed all studies focused on early childhood educators. This resulted in the final inclusion of 12 early childhood educator studies with 171 total effects (82 educator generalization outcomes, 89 educator target outcomes).

Data Analysis

Effect sizes. Selecting appropriate SCD effect sizes for application within meta-analytic methods continues to be a consistent challenge and widely debated topic (Zimmerman et al., 2018). For purposes of the current study, we chose to primarily use the Log Response Ratio (LRR; Pustejovsky, 2018) and supplement our main pooled effects with Tau (Parker et al., 2011) as a second effect size metric. These two indices were chosen given that LRR models change from baseline to intervention phases and Tau represents nonoverlap between baseline and intervention phases, both of which are key characteristics of single-case data (Kratochwill et al., 2010).

The LRR is particularly advantageous given that it is insensitive to how behavioral outcomes are measured and can be compared across different dimensional constructs (e.g., percentage durations, frequency counts). The LRR can also be translated directly to percentage change, which can provide a meaningful interpretation of treatment impacts for applied researchers and clinicians. Thus, the LRR served as the primary effect size index for the current study given these advantages and because the majority of our final sample included educator behavioral outcomes (e.g., observed classroom management practices) assessed through varying scoring procedures and on different dimensional characteristics. In particular, the increasing form of the LRR was calculated (i.e., LRRi), so that positive effect size values corresponded to improvement in educator behaviors (e.g., increased use of behavior specific praise). Raw data extracted from each outcome graph were used to calculate both LRRi and Tau indices with the online single-case effect size calculator SingleCaseES (Pustejovsky & Swan, 2018).

Meta-analysis. Basic meta-analytic methods typically involve one effect size estimate per study and assume different studies are independent from one another. However, LRR effect size estimates capture results at the level of the individual case as opposed to the study level.

Thus, we followed recommendations by Pustejovsky (2018) based on a proposed three-level, hierarchical model when synthesizing our LRRi effect size indices for meta-analysis (Van den Noortgate & Onghena, 2008). We also utilized robust variance estimation (RVE) techniques (Hedges et al., 2010) and applied small sample bias corrections (Tipton & Pustejovsky, 2015) when computing pooled effect sizes to account for data dependency issues and multiple effects per study. All analyses were conducted in R using the metafor (Viechtbauer, 2010) and clubSandwich (Pustejovsky, 2017) packages. For pooled main effects of consultation, we also converted LRRi effects and their 95% CIs to percentage change to help support interpretation.

Results

Description of Included Studies

In total, 12 studies including 39 educator consultees and 171 effects (82 educator generalization outcomes, 89 educator target outcomes) comprised our final sample. Seven studies (58.33%) were published journal articles and five (41.67%) were dissertations/theses. All but one study (91.67%) took place in the United States, with the other occurring in Turkey (8.33%). Four studies (33.33%) took place in inclusive classrooms, with four (33.33%) in Head Start/Early Head Start settings, two (16.67%) in regular classroom settings, and two (16.67%) in special education settings. In terms of specific types of generalization outcomes, seven studies (58.33%)

assessed generalization across activities/periods, followed by four (33.33%) across children, and one (8.33%) assessed generalization across a non-classroom setting. Regarding consultants, six studies (50%) included graduate students (e.g., school psychology doctoral trainees) as consultants, three studies (25%) included trained research personnel, and three (25%) used other personnel (e.g., school-based behavioral health providers). Regarding educator consultees, the vast majority were female (92.30%) and White (48.23%), followed by African American (39.45%), Latinx (6.47%), and Other (e.g., Asian-American; 5.85%). Most educator participants (69.23%) were classroom teachers, followed by preservice educators (17.95%), and teacher aides/assistants (12.82%). Of studies reporting educator age, ages ranged from 20 to 59 with an average of 31.77 years of age. The majority of educators had a Bachelor's degree (66.67%), followed by those with an Associate's degree (18.52%), and Master's degree (14.81%).

Effects of Consultation on Early Childhood Educator Generalization and Target Practices
Generalization Outcomes

To assess the effects of school-based consultation on educator generalization practices, we conducted six separate multi-level meta-analysis models summarizing effect size estimates (two models for educator generalization outcomes [overall] and four models for each educator generalization outcome subtype). See Table 1 for pooled effect size estimates including both LRRi and Tau, and Table 2 for LRRi estimates of each educator generalization outcome subtype. Each table additionally includes 95% confidence intervals produced from the robust standard errors, study-level variation, case-level variation, and corresponding percentage change when applicable.

For educator generalization outcomes (overall), the average LRRi estimate was 0.95 (95% CI [0.72, 1.18]), which corresponds to a 159% change from baseline levels (95% CI [105%, 225%]). For

Tau, the overall pooled effect for educator generalization outcomes (overall) was 0.79 (95% CI [0.59, 0.97]), suggesting that 79% of data did not overlap between baseline and intervention phases (see Table 1).

Table 1
Consultation Effects on Educator Generalization Outcomes (Overall)

	k	n	Estimate (SE)	CIs	% change	Study-level SD	Case-level SD
LRRi	12	82	0.95 (0.11)	0.72, 1.18	158.57	0.04	0.11
Tau	12	82	0.79 (0.15)	0.59, 0.97	--	0.02	0.08

Note: n = number of effect sizes; k = number of studies; SE = standard error; **CIs** = 95% confidence intervals; ** = p<0.01; *** = p <0.001

Regarding analyses for education generalization outcome subtypes, apart from individual support plans, all models revealed pooled effect size estimates significantly different from zero (see Table 2). For educator use of behavior specific praise, the average LRRi estimate was 0.82 (95% CI [0.34, 1.32]), which corresponds to an increase of 127% from baseline levels (95% CI [40%, 274%]). Regarding behavior analytic procedures, the average LRRi estimate was 1.22 (95% CI [0.84, 1.59]), which corresponds to an increase of 239% from baseline levels (95% CI [131%, 390%]). For instructional practices, the average LRRi estimate was 0.77 (95% CI [0.62, 0.92]), which corresponds to an increase of 116% from baseline levels (95% CI [86%, 150%]). With the exception of instructional practices which indicated nearly identical between-study and within-study variability, results for each of the other three behavior subtypes and for generalization outcomes (overall) indicate more within-study variability than between-study variability in effect sizes.

Target Outcomes

We additionally conducted six separate multi-level meta-analysis models summarizing effect size estimates to assess the impact of consultation on educator target outcomes. For educator target outcomes (overall), the average LRRi estimate was 0.99 (95% CI [0.73, 1.17]), which corresponds to a 169% change from baseline levels (95% CI [107%, 227%]). For Tau, the overall pooled effect for educator target outcomes (overall) was 0.86 (95% CI [0.71, 1.00]), suggesting that 86% of data did not overlap between baseline and intervention phases (see Table 3).

Table 2
Consultation Effects (LRRi) on Educator Generalization Outcome Subtypes

	k	N	LRRi (SE)	CIs	%change	t	Study-level SD	Case-level SD
Behavior specific praise	3	9	0.82 (0.21)	0.34, 1.32	127.05	3.94**	0.08	0.28
Behavior analytic procedures	4	23	1.22 (0.18)	0.84, 1.59	238.72	6.73***	0.06	0.10
Individual support plan	3	27	0.62 (0.28)	0.24, 1.19	85.89	3.30	0.16	0.41
Instructional practices	5	17	0.77 (0.07)	0.62, 0.92	115.98	11.02***	0.00	0.00

Note: n = number of effect sizes; k = number of studies; SE = standard error; ***CIs*** = 95% confidence intervals; ** = $p<0.01$; *** = $p <0.001$

Table 3
Consultation Effects on Educator Target Outcomes (Overall)

	k	n	Estimate (SE)	CIs	% change	Study-level SD	Case-level SD
LRRi	12	89	0.99 (0.10)	0.73, 1.17	169.12	0.06	0.16
Tau	12	89	0.86 (0.16)	0.71, 1.00	--	0.03	0.11

Note: n = number of effect sizes; k = number of studies; SE = standard error; ***CIs*** = 95% confidence intervals; ** = $p<0.01$; *** = $p <0.001$

Consistent with educator generalization outcomes, all models that estimated pooled effect sizes for educator target outcome subtypes were significantly different from zero with the exception of individual support plans (see Table 4). For educator use of behavior specific praise, the average LRRi estimate was 0.68 (95% CI [0.57, 0.78]), which corresponds to an increase of 97% from baseline levels (95% CI [77%, 118%]). Regarding behavior analytic procedures, the average LRRi estimate was 1.13 (95% CI [0.95, 1.28]), which corresponds to an increase of 210% from baseline levels (95% CI [158%, 259%]). For instructional practices, the average LRRi estimate was 0.81 (95% CI [0.63, 1.00]), which corresponds to an increase of 125% from baseline levels (95% CI [87%, 171%]). Results of all five models for educator target outcomes suggest more within-study variability than between-study variability in effect sizes.

Table 4
Consultation Effects (LRRi) on Educator Target Outcome Subtypes

	k	n	LRRi (SE)	CIs	%change	t	Study-level SD	Case-level SD
Behavior specific praise	3	10	0.68 (0.05)	0.57, 0.78	97.38	14.93***	0.00	0.01
Behavior analytic procedures	4	34	1.13 (0.09)	0.95, 1.28	209.56	10.90***	0.00	0.08
Individual support plan	3	19	0.49 (0.24)	0.30, 0.71	63.23	2.02	0.11	0.21
Instructional practices	5	33	0.81 (0.09)	0.63, 1.00	124.79	9.13***	0.03	0.17

Note: n = number of effect sizes; k = number of studies; SE = standard error; CIs = 95% confidence intervals; *** = $p < 0.001$

School-Based Consultation Component Analysis

To better understand the relevant components that relate to the effectiveness of school consultation, we calculated pooled treatment effects for four different consultation components (in situ training, performance feedback, behavioral skills training, and self-monitoring) for both educator target and generalization outcomes. We additionally coded three other consultation components (professional development, use of a treatment protocol, and video modeling); however, each of these three components was only used within one study, and thus could not be pooled for meta-analysis.

Results for the component analysis are provided in Table 3. Results indicated consistency among the components and their relationships to both educator target and generalization outcomes. That is, all four components were found to be significantly related to both educator target and generalization outcomes. Further, across both target and generalization outcomes, in situ training indicated the largest effects (i.e., 1.16; 1.05), whereas professional development indicated the smallest effects (i.e., 0.62; 0.72).

Table 5
Component Analysis for both Educator Target and Generalization Outcomes

Consultation component	k	n	LRRi (SE)	CIs	t	Study-level SD	Case-level SD
Generalization Outcomes							
In Situ	5	18	1.16 (0.19)	0.76, 1.55	6.15***	0.11	0.33
PF	3	17	0.96 (0.30)	0.35, 1.58	3.20**	0.23	0.49
BST	4	28	1.07 (0.27)	0.52, 1.63	4.36***	0.20	0.10
PD	2	31	0.62 (0.05)	0.52, 0.71	13.55***	0.00	0.00
Target Outcomes							
In Situ	5	23	1.05 (0.17)	0.70, 1.39	6.24***	0.12	0.07
PF	3	33	0.95 (0.35)	0.21, 1.69	2.73*	0.34	0.58
BST	4	43	0.90 (0.13)	0.65, 1.16	7.08***	0.03	0.19
PD	2	10	0.72 (0.08)	0.53, 0.91	8.51***	0.01	0.00

Note: n = number of effect sizes; k = number of studies; SE = standard error; CIs = 95% confidence intervals; ** = p <0.01; *** = p <0.001; PF = performance feedback; BST = behavioral skills training; PD = professional development

Discussion

Early childhood educators play a key role in supporting child development and mitigating factors that may place children at risk for developing long-term internalizing and externalizing concerns. Early childhood educator use of EBPs fosters optimal behavioral, social-emotional, and early learning for children during a vital period of development. School-based consultation has been shown to be a viable method to train educators to implement EBPs with fidelity. Unfortunately, less is known regarding how to train educators to generalize EBPs. This is problematic given that long-term, successful use of EBPs is dependent on educators' generalization of these skills. Individual studies have revealed that school-based consultation may be an important mechanism by which educators can be trained to generalize EBPs.

However, to our knowledge, no previous work has attempted to systematically combine and meta-analyze results across studies to determine the effects of school-based consultation in promoting educator use of EBPs. Thus, the current study offers a novel summary and quantitative synthesis regarding the available literature that included efforts to promote early childhood educator use of EBPs via school-based consultation. In particular, the current study both built from and aimed to address shortcomings previously discussed based on seminal work in this area (i.e., Robinson & Swanton, 1980).

Results revealed school-based consultation to be an effective means of promoting early childhood educator generalization of EBPs. This was found for early childhood educator outcomes (overall) along with three of the four early childhood educator generalization outcome subtypes (behavior specific praise, behavior analytic procedures, and instructional practices). This is an important finding, given that each of the three EBP subtypes are key educator practices that are imperative to supporting children's school outcomes. That said, the current study is part of a larger meta-analysis that is the first of its kind to link school-based consultation to the generalization of these practices through meta-analysis. Moving forward, future trainings and consultation practices should consider prioritizing these EBPs as areas of focus. Unexpectedly, the only early childhood educator outcome subtype found not to be significantly improved by school-based consultation was individual support plans. Individual support plans are often tailored to a specific student/classroom of interest, and thus can include a range of recommended EBPs that vary in intensity and resources required for implementation. This variability within individual support plans may account for the lack of significant impact across included studies.

The current study also explored the relative contributions of various components used within school-based consultation to support teacher use and generalization of EBPs. All four components (in situ training, performance feedback, behavioral skills training, and self- monitoring) were found to significantly drive the effects of school-based consultation for both educator target use and generalization of EBPs. Previous individual studies (e.g., LaBrot et al., 2021) have revealed consultation using specific components (e.g., in situ training) as effective for promoting educator generalization of EBPs; however, to our knowledge, this is the first study to evaluate these components on a larger scale via meta-analysis.

Implications for Practice and Research

The overall results of this meta-analysis indicate that implementation supports delivered via school-based consultation are effective for improving both target and generalization outcomes for early childhood educators. This finding is important, as many early childhood educators are not adequately prepared to integrate EBPs into day-to-day interactions with young children (Odom et al., 1995; Reinke et al., 2011; Snell et al., 2012). As such, school-based consultants can feel confident that implementation supports delivered via consultation often result in generalized EBP implementation.

This appears to be especially true when consultation involves in situ training and behavioral skills training, as these training techniques yielded the strongest effects for promoting target and generalized outcomes. These training practices may have the strongest benefits as they are often delivered in contexts in which early childhood educators are expected to deliver EBPs, and therefore may be more beneficial in promoting generalization (see Stokes &

Baer, 1977 for a more thorough description of promoting generalized outcomes). Therefore, consultants for early childhood education program should consider utilizing these training techniques when an EBP practice is clearly needed across multiple contexts (e.g., children exhibit disruptive behaviors throughout the day, multiple children would benefit from an intervention).

Conversely, professional development yielded the weakest effects for promoting early childhood educators' generalized use of EBPs. This is commensurate with previous research demonstrating that professional development is not as effective for promoting early childhood educators' use of EBPs in contexts in which trainings occurred (Dufrene et al., 2012), let alone promoting generalized outcomes. Given these effects, professional development should not be used as a standalone implementation support delivered through consultation, as it is not as likely to promote early childhood educators' target or generalized outcomes. Alternatively, if professional development trainings are utilized, they should be utilized as part of a continuum of consultation supports. That is, diligent data collection on early childhood educator and child outcomes should be collected to inform whether additional implementation supports (e.g., performance feedback, behavioral skills training, in situ training) should be delivered to bolster the effectiveness of professional development.

Regarding EBPs that were trained, results of this meta-analysis indicated that school- based consultation is not as effective for promoting early childhood educators' generalization of children's individual support plans when compared to other EBPs (e.g., behavior specific praise, effective instructions). This may be due to the fact that individual support plans often contain several different intervention components that are context specific, and therefore are not as easy to generalize. Conversely, other EBPs, such as behavior specific praise, are not as complex to learn as they contain fewer steps and may therefore be simpler to implement and generalize. Future research examining generalized outcomes for early childhood educators' implementation of individualized support plans should specifically program to promote generalization (see Stokes & Baer, 1977). Furthermore, future research should also examine the extent to which early childhood educators implement the individual components of individualized support plans, to determine if perhaps certain aspects of individualized support plans are more or less likely to generalize following school-based consultation.

Finally, only 12 experimentally rigorous studies that collected data on early childhood educators' generalized outcomes were identified. Given the wide range of school-based consultation studies that have been conducted in early childhood education settings, it is surprising that such a low number of educator generalization studies have been conducted. This is somewhat concerning, as there is currently limited evidenced that supports the effectiveness of school-based consultation for promoting early childhood educators' generalized use of EBPs.

Therefore, future research examining school-based consultation in early childhood settings should seek to collect data on educators' generalized outcomes.

Limitations and Future Directions

Although the results of this meta-analysis indicate that school-based consultation is effective for promoting early childhood educators' generalized use of EBPs, it is not without limitations. First, this meta-analysis was limited to early childhood educators. As such, the extent to which school-based consultation is beneficial for promoting these outcomes with other educators (e.g., elementary teachers, secondary teachers) is unclear. Moving forward, other meta-analyses should investigate the effects of school-based consultation across levels of child development, including exploring whether said effects may vary based on grade/developmental level.

Second, although we took made extensive efforts to search the available literature, we cannot say for certain that a truly exhaustive search of the literature was conducted. Thus, it is possible we may have missed some relevant studies. For one, it is worth reiterating that the current study represents a subsample of a larger meta-analysis project that is inclusive of PreK- 12th grade school populations. Throughout the larger study, our search procedures were meant to be exclusive to a broader school-based population, and thus we did not use search terms specific to early childhood populations. Additionally, studies were limited to those reported in English, which may systematically bias results by reducing findings to a particular region based on language (Smith & Sheridan, 2019). Finally, although we took some efforts to locate unpublished grey literature (i.e., searching *Google Scholar* and *ProQuest: Dissertations & Theses*), we did not contact prominent authors in this area to locate any unpublished relevant data. This is a recommended practice that can sometimes help to successfully locate relevant findings (e.g., Polanin et al., 2020). Future research in this area should consider efforts to use more targeted search terms, expand inclusion criteria beyond English only, and make additional efforts to locate grey literature by contacting authors.

Further, although we chose a primary effect size index (i.e., LRR) consistent with the structure of our data and used Tau as a secondary index, these choices are not without limitations. Neither LRR nor Tau account for possible trends in modeling SCD data. In cases in which time trends may have been present in our data, it is possible that some effect size may have produced biased estimates. Based on the current analyses, it is unknown whether trend issues impacted results. Additional research in this area should yield greater consideration to time trends and incorporate additional effect size indices meant to account for these issues (e.g., Tau-U).

Additionally, results of the current study are solely reliant on SCD experimental studies. Surprisingly, no group-design studies investigating the effects of school-based consultation on educator generalization outcomes were located. It is possible that our search procedures were not comprehensive enough to locate group-design studies; however, it seems more likely that educator generalization outcomes simply are yet to be investigated using rigorous large-scale research methodology (e.g., randomized controlled trials). Findings from the current study can hopefully provide a foundation to inform future school-based consultation practices that can be used to support educator delivery and generalization of EBPs within group-design research that is currently lacking. Finally, this study only examined rigorous single-case experimental designs that demonstrated strong effects. Additionally, researchers in these studies were often behavioral consultants or related personnel that likely had previously established relationships with participants. Given these factors, it is possible that our results were biased in favor of studies that were likely to obtain strong generalization effects. Therefore, future research should seek to address these limitations by examining the consultation literature more broadly (e.g., across other applied settings) and include research that does not necessarily meet rigorous research standards (e.g., What Works Clearinghouse).

References

References marked with an asterisk indicate studies included in the meta-analysis.

*Barton, E. E., Pokorski, E. A., Gossett, S., Sweeny, E., Qui, J., & Choi, G. (2018). The use of email to coach early childhood teachers. Journal of Early Intervention, 40(3), 212-228. https://doi.org/10.1177/1053815118760314

*Bose-Deakins, J. E. (2005). *Increasing early literacy instruction of Head Start teachers using videotape consultation* (Doctoral dissertation, The University of Memphis).

Bruhn, A., Gilmour, A., Rila, A., Van Camp, A., Sheaffer, A., Hancock, E., Fernando, J., & Wehby, J. (2022). Treatment components and participant characteristics associated with outcomes in self-monitoring interventions. *Journal of Positive Behavior Interventions, 24*(2), 156–168. https://doi.org/10.1177/1098300720946651

Carter, A. S., Wagmiller, R. J., Gray, S. A. O., McCarthy, K. J., Horwitz, S. M., & Briggs-Gowan, M. J. (2010). Prevalence of DSM-IV disorder in a representative, healthy birth cohort at school entry: Sociodemographic risks and social adaptation. *Journal of the American Academy of Child and Adolescent Psychiatry, 49*, 686–698. https://doi.org/10.1016/j.jaac.2010.03.018

Cole, C. L., Marder, T., & McCann, L. (2000). Self-monitoring. In E. S. Shapiro & T. R. Kratochwill (Eds.). *Conducting school-based assessments of child and adolescent behavior* (pp. 121-149). Guilford Press.

Collier-Meek, M. A., Fallon, L. M., & Gould, K. (2018). How are treatment integrity data assessed? Reviewing the performance feedback literature. *School Psychology Quarterly, 33*(4), 517-526. https://doi.org10.1037/spq0000239

Collins, T. A., Drevon, D. D., Brown, A. M., Villarreal, J. N., Newman, C. L., & Endres, B. (2020). Say something nice: A meta-analytic review of peer reporting interventions. *Journal of School Psychology, 83,* 89-103. https://doi.org/10.1016/j.jsp.2020.10.002

Cooper, J. O., Heron, T. E., & Heward, W. L. (2020). *Applied behavior analysis* (3rd ed.). Pearson.

Dufrene, B. A., Parker, K., Menousek, K., Zhou, Q., Harpole, L. L., & Olmi, D. J. (2012). Direct behavioral consultation in Head Start to increase teacher use of praise and effective instruction delivery. *Journal of Educational and Psychological Consultation, 22*(3), 159- 186. https://doi.org/10.1080/10474412.2011.620817

*Duncan, N. G., Dufrene, B. A., Sterling, H. E., & Tingstrom, D. H. (2013). Promoting teachers' generalization of intervention use through goal setting and performancefeedback. *Journal of Behavioral Education, 22*(4), 325-347. https://doi.org/10.1007/s10864-013-9173-5

Erchul, W. P., & Sheridan, S. M. (2014). *Handbook of research in school consultation.* Taylor & Francis.

Floress, M. T., Berlinghof, J. R., Rader, R. A., & Riedesel, E. K. (2017). Preschool teachers' use of praise in general, at-risk, and special education classrooms. *Psychology in the Schools, 54*(5), 519-531. https://doi.org/10.1002/pits.22014

*Frantz, R. J. (2017). *Coaching teaching assistants to implement naturalistic behavioral teaching strategies to enhance social communication skills during play in the preschool classroom* [Doctoral dissertation]. University of Oregon.

Gomez, L., Barton, E. E., Winchester, C., & Locchetta, B. (2021). Effects of email performance feedback on teachers' use of play expansions. *Journal of Early Intervention, 43*(3), 235- 254. https://doi.org/10.1177/1053815120969821

*Gouvousis, A. (2012). *Teacher implemented pivotal response training to improve communication in children with autism spectrum disorders.* (Publication No. AAI3456462). [Doctoral dissertation, East Carolina University]. ProQuest.

Gresham, F. M. (1989). Assessment of treatment integrity in school consultation and prereferral intervention. *School Psychology Review, 18*(1), 37-50. https://doi.org/10.1080/02796015.1989.12085399

Gutkin, T. B., & Curtis, M. J. (2009). School-based consultation: The science and practice of indirect service delivery. In T. B. Gutkin & C. R. Reynolds (Eds.), *The Handbook of School Psychology* (4th ed., pp. 591-635). Wiley.

Hedges, L. V., Tipton, E., & Johnson, M. C. (2010). Robust variance estimation in meta-regression with dependent effect size estimates. *Research Synthesis Methods, 1*(1), 39– 65.

*Hemmeter, M. L., Hardy, J. K., Schitz, A. G., Adams, J. M., & Kinder, K. A. (2015). Effects of training and coaching with performance feedback on teachers' use of Pyramid Model practices. *Topics in Early Childhood Special Education, 35*(3), 144-156. https://doi.org/10.1177/02711214155949

Hussar, B., Zhang, J., Hein, S., Wang, K., Roberts, A., Cui, J., Smith, M., Mann, F. B., Barmer, A., & Dilig, R. (2020). The condition of education 2020. NCES 2020-144. *National Center for Education Statistics.*

Kratochwill, T. R., Hitchcock, J., Horner, R. H., Levin, J. R., Odom, S. L., Rindskopf, D. M., & Shadish, W. R. (2010). *Single-case designs technical documentation.* Retrieved from https://ies.ed.gov/ncee/wwc/Docs/ReferenceResources/wwc_scd.pdf

*LaBrot, Z. C., Dufrene, B. A., Olmi, D. J., Dart, E. H., Radley, K., Lown, E., & Pasqua, J. L. (2021). Maintenance and generalization of preschool teachers' use of behavior-specific praise following in situ training. *Journal of Behavioral Education, 30*(3), 350-377.

LaBrot, Z. C., Dufrene, B. A., Whipple, H., McCargo, M., & Pasqua, J. L. (2020). Targeted and intensive consultation for increasing Head Start and elementary teachers' behavior-specific praise. *Journal of Behavioral Education, 29*(4), 717-740. https://doi.org/10.1007/s10864-020-09375-5

Moeyaert, M., Maggin, D., & Verkuilen, J. (2016). Reliability, validity, and usability of data extraction programs for single-case research designs. *Behavior Modification, 40*(6), 874- 900. https://doi.org/10.1177/0145445516645763

Odom, S. L., McLean, M. E., Johnson, L. J., & Lamontagne, M. J. (1995). Recommended practices in early childhood special education: Validation and current use. *Journal of Early Intervention, 19*(1), 1-17. https://doi.org/10.1177/105381519501900101

Parker, R. I., Vannest, K. J., & Davis, J. L. (2011). Effect size in single-case research: A review of nine nonoverlap techniques. *Behavior Modification, 35*, 303–322. https://doi.org/10.1177/0145445511399147.

*Peck, C. A., Killen, C. C., & Baumgart, D. (1989). Increasing implementation of special education instruction in mainstream preschools: Direct and generalized effects of nondirective consultation. *Journal of Applied Behavior Analysis, 22*(2), 197-210. https://doi.org/10.1901/jaba.1989.22-197

*Pellecchia, M., Connell, J. E., Eisenhart, D., Kane, M., Schoener, C., Turkel, K., ... & Mandell, D. S. (2011). We're all in this together now: Group performance feedback to increase classroom team data collection. *Journal of School Psychology, 49*(4), 411-431. https://doi.org/10.1016/j.jsp.2011.04.003

Polanin, J. R., Espelage, D. L., Grotpeter, J. K., Valido, A., Ingram, K. M., Torgal, C., El Sheikh, A, & Robinson, L. E. (2020). Locating unregistered and unreported data for use in a social science systematic review and meta-analysis. *Systematic Reviews, 9*(1), 1-9. https://doi.org/10.1186/s13643-020-01376-9

Pustejovsky, J. E. (2017). *clubSandwich: Cluster-robust (sandwich) variance estimators with small-sample corrections.* https://cran.r-project.org/package=clubSandwich

Pustejovsky, J. E. (2018). Using response ratios for meta-analyzing single-case designs with behavioral outcomes. *Journal of School Psychology, 68,* 99-112. https://doi.org/10.1016/j.jsp.2018.02.003

Pustejovsky, J. E., & Swan, D. M. (2018). *Effect size definitions and mathematical details.* https://cran.r-project.org/web/packages/ SingleCaseES/vignettes/Effect-size-definitions.html

*Rakap, S. (2017). Impact of coaching on preservice teachers' use of embedded instruction in inclusive preschool classrooms. *Journal of Teacher Education, 68*(2), 125-139. https://doi.org/10.1177/0022487116685753

Reddy, L. A., Barboza-Whitehead, S., Files, T., & Rubel, E. (2000). Clinical focus of consultation outcome research with children and adolescents. *Special Services in the Schools, 16*(1-2), 1-22. https://doi.org/10.1300/j008v16n01_01

Reinke, W. M., Stormont, M., Herman, K. C., Puri, R., & Goel, N. (2011). Supporting children's mental health in schools: Teacher perceptions of needs, roles, and barriers. *School Psychology Quarterly, 26*(1), 1-13. https://doi.org/10.1037/a0022714

Robinson, V., & Swanton, C. (1980). The generalization of behavioral teacher training. *Review of Educational Research, 50*(3), 486-498. https://doi.org/10.3102/00346543050003486

Rohatgi, A. (2014). *WebPlotDigitizer user manual version 3.4.* https://automeris.io/WebPlotDigitizer/userManual.pdf https://automeris.io/WebPlotDigitizer/userManual.pdf

*Shepley, C.N. (2019). *Training teachers in inclusive preschool classrooms to monitor child progress and make data-based decisions through direct behavioral observation* [Theses and Dissertations]. University of Kentucky.

Smith, T. E., & Sheridan, S. M. (2019). The effects of teacher training on teachers' family engagement practices, attitudes, and knowledge: A meta-analysis. *Journal of Educational and Psychological Consultation, 29,* 128-157. https://doi.org/10.1080/10474412.2018.1460725

Smith, T. E., Thompson, M. A., & Maynard, B. R. (2022). Self-management interventions for reducing challenging behaviors among school-age students: A systematic review. *Campbell Systematic Reviews.* https://doi.org/10.1002/cl2.1223

Snell, M. E., Berlin, R. A., Voorhees, M. D., Stanton-Chapman, T. L., & Hadden, S. (2012). A survey of preschool staff concerning problem behavior and its prevention in Head Start classrooms. *Journal of Positive Behavior Interventions, 14*(2), 98-107. https://doi.org/10.1177/1098300711416818

Stokes, T. F., & Baer, D. M. (1977). An implicit technology of generalization. *Journal of Applied Behavior Analysis, 10*(2), 349-367.

Tipton, E., & Pustejovsky, J. E. (2015). Small-sample adjustments for tests of moderators and model fit using robust variance estimation and meta-regression. *Journal of Educational and Behavioral Statistics, 40*(6), 604-634. https://doi.org/10.3102/1076998615606099

Van den Noortgate, W., & Onghena, P. (2008). A multilevel meta-analysis of single-subject experimental design studies. *Evidence-Based Communication Assessment and Intervention, 2*(3), 142-151. https://doi.org/10.1080/17489530802505362

Viechtbauer, W. (2010). Conducting meta-analyses in R with the metafor package. *Journal of Statistical Software, 36*(3), 1-48. https://doi.org/10.18637/jss.v036.i03

What Works Clearinghouse (2021). What Works clearinghouse standards handbook, version 4.1.Retrieved from https://ies.ed.gov/ncee/wwc/Docs/referenceresources/WWC-Standards-Handbook-v4-1-508.pdf

Wichstrom, L., Berg-Nielsen, T. S., Angold, A., Egger, H. L., Solheim, E., & Sveen, T. H. (2012). Prevalence of psychiatric disorders in preschoolers. *Journal of Child Psychology and Psychiatry, 53*(6), 695-705. https://doi.org/10.1111/j.1469-7610.2011.02514.x

*Wimberly, J. K. (2016). *Generalization of teachers' use of effective instruction delivery following in situ training* [Doctoral dissertation]. The University of Southern Mississippi.

Zimmerman, K. N., Pustejovsky, J. E., Ledford, J. R., Barton, E. E., Severini, K. E., & Lloyd, B.P. (2018). Single-case synthesis tools II: Comparing quantitative outcome measures. *Research in Developmental Disabilities, 79*, 65-76. https://doi.org/10.1016/j.ridd.2018.02.001

Towards a Practical Behavior Analytic Multitiered Consultation Model for Early Childhood Educators

Zachary C. LaBrot, Emily R. DeFouw, Marshall Lundy, Kayla McVay, Andrew Rozsa, and Brad A. Dufrene

Impact statement: *This paper delineates an effective and potentially more efficient model for implementing behavioral consultation. This paper is meant to serve as a call-to-action for consultation researchers to further evaluate the effectiveness, efficiency, and feasibility of this model with early childhood education professionals.*

Abstract

Early childhood educators are in a critical position to support young children's social-emotional, behavioral, and learning development, which can be accomplished through consistent use of evidence-based practices delivered in day-to-day interactions. However, early childhood educators may require support for implementing evidence-based practices. The purpose of this paper is to introduce a novel form of behavioral consultation for early childhood educators. Specifically, a behavior analytic multitiered consultation model in which implementation supports become increasingly more intensive is described. Rationale, implementation, evidence base, and implications for practice and research are described. Finally, this paper concludes with an empirical case study to illustrate this model's implementation. This paper is also meant to serve as a call-to-action for researchers and practitioners to replicate this consultation model.

Keywords: *Early childhood consultation; multitiered consultation; behavioral consultation*

Introduction

Early childhood is a period of rapid development, which can be enhanced by positive family interaction, community engagement, and participation in early childhood education programs (Bick & Nelson, 2017; McWayne et al., 2004). However, pervasive risk factors that many families experience, such as poverty, family conflict, violence, and low parental education, can place young children at risk for developing internalizing and externalizing difficulties (Carter et al., 2010; Egger & Angold, 2005; Wichstrom et al., 2012). Because approximately 86% of young children attend some form of an early childhood education program (Hussar et al., 2020), early childhood educators play a critical role in promoting social-emotional and behavioral development that may serve to buffer young children from the various risk factors they experience. Additionally, social-emotional and behavioral skills fostered in the course of early childhood education often mediate successful transition into elementary education (Carter et al., 2010).

Given the vital role early childhood educators play in promoting young children's social-emotional and behavioral development, supports to aid these educators are often needed. That is, early childhood educators may encounter behavioral difficulties in the classroom they are not adequately equipped to address (Reinke et al., 2011; Snell et al., 2012). When this occurs, early childhood educators, or the program itself, may seek assistance from a consultant with expertise in behavior, development, and educational systems (Collier-Meek et al., 2017b). Consultants often recommend the use of educator-implemented, evidence-based classroom interventions to address presenting concerns. However, early childhood educators may encounter several barriers to intervention implementation, such as having several responsibilities throughout the classroom, inadequate intervention training, high levels of stress/burnout, and an inconsistent reinforcement history with intervention implementation (Allen & Warzak, 2000; Collier-Meek et al., 2017b;

Sanetti & Kratochwill, 2009a). Therefore, consultants may also provide implementation supports throughout the consultation process to aid early childhood educators in intervention delivery to promote high levels of integrity (i.e., extent to which interventions are delivered as intended; Gresham, 1989; Sanetti & Kratochwill, 2009a).

Various implementation supports, such as prompts (LaBrot et al., 2022; Markelz et al., 2021), performance feedback (Barton et al., 2020; Gomez et al., 2021), modeling (LaBrot et al., 2020), and in situ training (Dufrene et al., 2012; LaBrot et al., 2016, 2021b), to name a few, are effective for promoting early childhood educators' intervention implementation. These supports vary in intensity and resources required for implementation, with limited empirical guidance that delineates their systematic delivery (Collier-Meek et al., 2017b). Furthermore, early childhood education programs historically have limited access to mental and behavioral health consultation and supports (Ali et al., 2018; Grace et al., 2006; National Center for Education Statistics [NCES], 2020). As such, a conceptual and empirically based model to guide school-based consultants in the systematic delivery of implementation supports for early childhood educators is needed.

Such a model should be effective and efficient, in which intensive consultation resources are conserved for those educators who require a greater amount of support. Further, such a model should be feasible in implementation to facilitate consultants' access to a greater number of programs and classrooms. Therefore, the purpose of this paper is to describe a multitiered consultation model for supporting early childhood educators' intervention implementation. This paper will first define this model and provide an empirical rationale for its use. Second, this paper will describe the application and adaptations of this model for early childhood education programs and educators. Third, current research, implications for applied practice, and future directions are discussed. Finally, this paper concludes with an empirical case study that demonstrates this model's application and effectiveness.

For the purposes of this paper, consultation refers to the overarching process in which consultants work with educators, and implementation supports are the specific strategies used within consultation (e.g., prompts, performance feedback) to target educators' intervention implementation.

Multitiered Consultation Model

Previous research has emphasized the importance of ensuring high levels of treatment integrity when addressing student concerns (Sanetti & Kratochwill, 2009a). Often, educators are the implementers delivering these interventions and supports. However, educational background and training is often inconsistent across educators (Freeman et al., 2014). As such, delivering implementation supports through consultation on a systematic continuum may be an effective and efficient approach to address early childhood educators' unique training needs.

Similar to the Pyramid and Multi-tiered Systems of Support (MTSS) models that support children's social-emotional, behavioral, and academic needs (Fox et al., 2010; Marsh & Mathur, 2020), a multitiered consultation framework can be also applied to support educators' intervention implementation (Sanetti & Collier-Meek, 2015). Multitiered consultation is a three-tiered framework that provides universal, targeted, and individualized support strategies to increase educators' implementation of various interventions (Fallon et al., 2018; LaBrot et al., 2020; McKenney et al., 2019; Myers et al., 2011). This model of consultation is grounded in behavioral consultation, in which consultants (e.g., school psychologists, behavior analysts, mental health professionals) guide consultees (e.g., educators, center staff) through a collaborative and problem-solving process to address the needs of clients (i.e., children). Specifically, this model follows behavioral consultation's four-stage problem-solving process (i.e., problem identification, problem analysis, plan implementation, and plan evaluation) (Dufrene et al., 2016).

Within a multitiered consultation model, Tier 1 implementation supports can be universally delivered to all educators. For example, a common Tier 1 implementation support is individual or universal professional development trainings (e.g., Collier-Meek et al., 2017a; Fallon et al., 2018; LaBrot et al., 2021a). These trainings often involve the consultant introducing the intervention, modeling the intervention, providing an opportunity to practice, and delivering feedback (Sterling-Turner et al., 2002). Although professional development trainings are widely utilized, they may not be enough to adequately improve early childhood educators' intervention implementation (e.g., Dufrene et al., 2012). Consequently, educators may require additional and more targeted Tier 2 implementation supports that specifically address implementation barriers (e.g., knowledge, beliefs, skills, training, stress/burnout) that cause low or declining levels of treatment integrity (See Sanetti & Kratochwill, 2009a for an overview of treatment integrity barriers). Tier 2 implementation supports generally involve more direct one-to-one work between a consultant and educator, but can be less direct in implementation (e.g., automatically delivered emailed prompts; Fallon et al., 2018). However, educators' implementation that does not reach desired levels may require more intensive and individualized Tier 3 supports. Similar to the Pyramid and MTSS models, Tier 3 implementation supports are individualized, more frequent, and require more time and personnel support (Sanetti & Collier-Meek, 2015). For example, performance feedback can be tailored to an educator's intervention implementation and requires consistent progress monitoring and delivery.

Although the multitiered consultation model has garnered promising evidence for improving implementers' treatment integrity (e.g., LaBrot et al., 2020; Myers et al., 2011; Sanetti & Collier-Meek, 2015; Simonsen et al., 2014; Thompson et al., 2012), implementation supports utilized within Tiers 2 and 3 vary. For example, Myers et al. (2011) evaluated a multitiered consultation model for increasing middle school teachers' behavior specific and general praise rates. Tier 2 involved in-person weekly performance feedback meetings and Tier 3 involved in-person daily performance feedback (i.e., consequent-based supports for both tiers). Similarly, LaBrot et al. (2020) utilized this consultation model to increase preschool and elementary school teachers' rates of behavior specific praise. Tier 2 involved weekly emailed performance feedback with video models (i.e., consequent-based support) and Tier 3 involved a teacher wearing a device that provided tactile prompts (i.e., antecedent-based support). Results of these studies indicated that teachers' rates of behavior specific praise increased, although both may have used unnecessary time and resources (e.g., continuous monitoring and data collection to provide performance feedback) for lower-level tiers, when less resource-intensive strategies (e.g., brief prompts) may have sufficed. Therefore, a conceptual model that guides which implementation supports are delivered within each tier is needed.

Behavior Analytic Conceptualization of a Multitiered Consultation Model

One solution for a multitiered consultation model that may effectively and efficiently allocate consultative resources and help differentiate Tier 2 from Tier 3 strategies is a behavior analytic application of implementation supports (Collier-Meek et al., 2017b). Through the lens of Applied Behavior Analysis (Baer et al., 1968), socially important behavior (i.e., intervention implementation) is evoked by antecedents (e.g., intervention prompts) and maintained through consequences (e.g., implementation feedback) (Collier-Meek et al., 2017b). Given this logic, the range of various implementation supports may be conceptualized as either antecedent-based, consequent-based, or combined.

Antecedent-based implementation supports involve proactively providing instructions or reminders to evoke intervention implementation (Collier-Meek et al., 2017a). Conversely, consequent-based implementation supports are delivered in response to intervention implementation and involve providing positive and corrective feedback to function as positive reinforcement (i.e., teachers engage in intervention implementation to increase desired child behaviors) or negative reinforcement (i.e., teachers engage in intervention implementation to remove supports) for treatment integrity (Collier-Meek et al., 2017a).

Although both antecedent- (e.g., prompts) and consequent-based (e.g., performance feedback) implementation supports have evidence demonstrating their effectiveness for improving treatment integrity (Collier-Meek et al., 2017a; Duchaine et al., 2011; Fallon et al., 2018; O'Handley et al., 2018), educators' response to these supports can be variable (e.g., LaBrot et al., 2020, 2021a). This may be due to the fact that more traditional consultation models, such as behavioral and direct behavioral consultation, tend to continuously deliver a single implementation support regardless of approach (antecedent or consequent) and ideographic educator response (e.g., Dufrene et al., 2012; LaBrot et al., 2016, 2021b).

Thus, a data-based model that conceptualizes intervention implementation from a behavior analytic standpoint and includes a continuum of implementation supports could be an effective and efficient option for maintaining treatment integrity. Within a behavior analytic multitiered consultation framework, lower-level tiers consist of antecedent-based supports (e.g., professional development trainings at Tier 1, prompting at Tier 2) to evoke intervention implementation (Collier-Meek et al., 2017b). To the degree that educators fail to consistently increase treatment integrity in response to antecedent-based supports, consequent-based supports (e.g., performance feedback at Tier 3) are added to both evoke and maintain educators' treatment integrity.

Fallon et al. (2018) utilized a behavior analytic multitiered consultation model to increase three elementary teachers' treatment integrity of group contingency implementation. In this study, didactic training (i.e., Tier 1) resulted in variable and low increases in treatment integrity. Following didactic training, Fallon and colleagues delivered emailed prompts (i.e., Tier 2) that described intervention steps which resulted in increased, albeit variable, treatment integrity. Finally, emailed performance feedback (i.e., Tier 3) was implemented, which resulted in treatment integrity levels above those in the emailed prompt phase for all three elementary teachers. Additionally, participants rated this model of implementation supports as feasible, understandable, and effective (Fallon et al., 2018). Results of this study provide evidence for the effectiveness and feasibility of behavior analytic multitiered consultation. However, conceptual guidance for its implementation with early childhood educators is necessary to guide use in early childhood settings.

Behavior Analytic Multitiered Consultation for Early Childhood Educators

In early childhood education programs, the behavior analytic multitiered consultation model follows the same behavior analytic conceptualization, in which antecedent-based supports are delivered in Tiers 1 and 2 and consequent-based supports are delivered at Tier 3. Similarly, this model also follows the same four-stage problem-solving process as behavioral consultation (i.e., problem identification, problem analysis, plan implementation, plan evaluation; Dufrene et al., 2016). However, data collected, variables assessed, and targeted interventions vary in early childhood education settings, as these settings are markedly different from elementary and middle schools.

It is important to note that there are currently no established standards for foundational knowledge and resources necessary to implement this model of consultation. However, this model is a derivation of behavioral consultation as implemented in educational settings (See Erchul & Martens, 2012). Therefore, at minimum, consultants should have knowledge of the behavioral consultation process (delineated below), which includes interviewing relevant individuals and systematic and ongoing data collection. Furthermore, this model would be best implemented in conjunction with both educators and center administrators to ensure a consolidated plan is being implemented. See Figure 1 for a visual representation of the behavior analytic conceptualization of a multitiered consultation model.

Figure 1
Visual Representative of the Behavior Analytic Multitiered Consultation Model

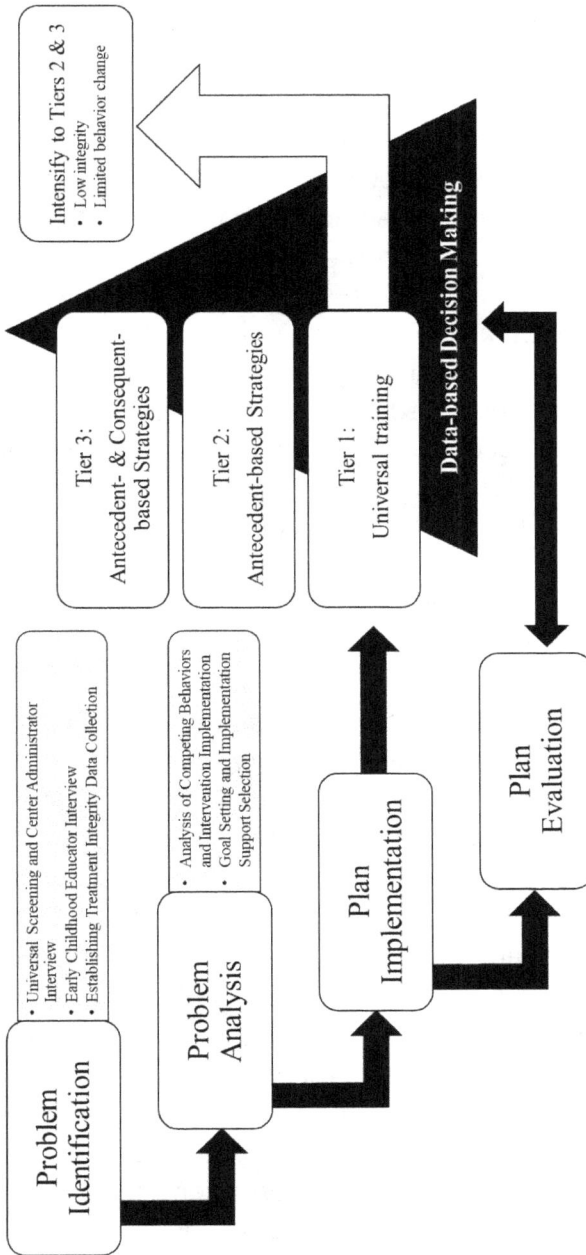

Problem Identification

The first step of the behavior analytic multitiered consultation model involves universal screening and interviews with administrators and early childhood educators. The goal of these interviews is to identify potential underlying problems (e.g., lack of training in effective classroom management strategies) associated with educators' poor intervention implementation (Dufrene et al., 2016). Through the Problem Identification process, multiple variables are assessed related to the referral concern. Objectives of Problem Identification include goal specification, performance assessment, and procedural specification. Although the following sections outline the type of data to be collected during the problem identification process, readers should also reference the Planning Realistic Implementation and Maintenance by Educators (PRIME) Problem-solving Consultation Guide to inform other forms of data that may be collected during the Problem Identification process (Sanetti et al., 2014), which is a freely available online resource for consultants and researchers.

Universal Screening and Center Administrator Interview

Upon receiving a referral for services, data on classroom and educator needs should be gathered via universal screening. That is, early childhood education centers that already collect data on classroom management practices can aid consultants in determining training needs. For example, the Preschool-Wide Evaluation Tool (Pre-SET) is a standardized assessment of program-wide positive behavior supports with strong psychometric properties (Steed & Webb, 2013) that can be utilized to identify center-wide supports that are inconsistently implemented across an early childhood education center. Inconsistently implemented center-wide supports (e.g., enriched environment with engaging activities, charts that demonstrate classroom expectations; Hemmeter et al., 2007) can be targeted through large or small group professional development trainings (i.e., Tier 1 consultation/training supports).

Following review of universal screening data, the formal consultation process should begin with an interview with the early childhood education center director. The purpose of interviewing an administrator is to determine the extent to which program staff have received previous training in classroom management. It is possible that center staff have not received adequate instruction or training in evidence-based classroom management practices (e.g., LaBrot et al., 2022). In this case, a universal, Tier 1 training on classroom management practices may be more efficient in addressing referral concerns. Paired with universal screening data, center administrator knowledge regarding educators' skill sets, strengths, and weaknesses could inform effective Tier 1, professional development trainings on effective classroom management practices. Additionally, universal screening data from previous years, in conjunction with center administrator input, can be used to inform beginning-of-the-year professional development trainings.

Early Childhood Educator Interview

In addition to universal screening and center administrator interviews, classroom teachers should also be interviewed to gain more specific feedback and insights regarding referral concerns (Dufrene et al., 2016). During the teacher interview, it is important to assess teachers' history with intervention implementation in the classroom. Specifically, consultants should inquire about interventions that have previously been implemented unsuccessfully (i.e., did not affect child outcomes) and how these interventions were implemented. It could be that previously utilized classroom management interventions were not implemented with integrity, and could be more effectively implemented with consultant-provided instructions and modeling (i.e., reiteration of Tier 1 supports). Furthermore, it is important to determine the extent to which educators have been consistent in previously implementing other classroom interventions, as a history of inconsistent intervention implementation could be indicative of teachers who struggle to follow consultant recommendations (Allen & Warzak, 2000; Collier-Meek et al., 2017b). If this is the case, it is important to assess and account for barriers to previous intervention implementation when developing a new plan. For example, inquiring about previous intervention complexity, educators' perceived competence in intervention delivery, and resources available for intervention implementation can aid consultants in developing an appropriate plan (Sanetti & Kratochwill, 2009a, 2009b).

Similarly, classroom management practices teachers are currently implementing should be assessed to determine if consultant-provided instructions and modeling may aid in more effective implementation. Relatedly, relevant antecedents and consequences to children's behavior should be assessed during the teacher interview. This will aid consultants in developing implementation supports that prepare teachers to identify and alter contingencies for children's behaviors (e.g., delivering behavior specific praise for appropriate behavior vs. reprimands for attention-maintained disruptive behaviors). Furthermore, other contextual variables that impact child behavior, such as the structure of the day, format of instructional time, amount of free play activities, and small vs. large group instructions should be assessed to identify targets for teacher behavior change (e.g., modification of instruction time).

Given the importance of family involvement in early education settings (Fox et al., 2015; Hemmeter et al., 2007), consultants should also inquire about the extent of parent-teacher collaboration. Limited parent-teacher collaboration can be addressed through Tiers 1 and 2 implementation supports by prompting teachers to make regular contact with children's family members. Furthermore, strategies to collaborate with families can be disseminated. As such, this variable is essential to assess to ensure comprehensive supports are being provided.

Establishing Treatment Integrity Data Collection

The final step in the Problem Identification phase should include establishing treatment integrity data collection. The type of treatment integrity data collected should be directly informed by data from the universal screening, center administrator interview, teacher interview, and direct observation. That is, the intervention trained via multitiered consultation should be operationally defined and broken into measurable steps. Treatment integrity data can be collected by an educator (i.e., self-report), via permanent product, or through consultant observation (Collier-Meek et al., 2018). Regardless of the method, regular collection of treatment integrity data is essential to the behavior analytic multitiered consultation model, as transitions between the tiers of implementation supports are primarily based on educators' treatment integrity.

Problem Analysis

The primary objective of the Problem Analysis phase of multitiered consultation is to analyze early childhood educators' treatment integrity as well as the implementation environment via a behavior analytic framework. That is, educators' intervention implementation, or competing behaviors, can be evoked by antecedents (e.g., prompts, visual aids) and maintained by consequences (e.g., praise from center director, improved child behavior) (Collier-Meek et al., 2017b). For example, intervention implementation (target behavior) can be evoked by visual aids (e.g., scripts, signs; antecedents) and maintained by improved child behavior (i.e., positive reinforcement; consequence). Relatedly, an educator may have a child removed from the classroom for disruptive behavior (competing behavior) instead of implementing an intervention (target behavior) during an instructional period which results in not having to manage difficult behavior (negative reinforcement) (Collier-Meek et al., 2017b).

Analysis of Competing Behaviors and Intervention Implementation

To begin the Problem Analysis phase, it is important to clarify and define any behaviors that interfere with effective intervention implementation. For example, educators' use of reprimands, sending children out of the room, and removing/avoiding child task demands can result in reinforcement for these behaviors by way of eliminating difficult child interactions, but actively prevent intervention implementation. Once identified, competing behaviors should be operationally defined such that they are quantifiable and observable (Collier-Meek et al., 2017b). Similarly, potential antecedents and consequences to teachers' target behaviors (i.e., intervention implementation) and competing behaviors should also be clarified and operationally defined. Hypothesized competing behaviors and their respective environmental variables to be observed can be gathered during the Problem Identification stage. However, the Problem Analysis stage is used to verify and clearly define these.

Following an objective and measurable description of competing behaviors and environmental variables, direct observations should be conducted. Systematic direct observations of educators' competing behaviors can result in the development of hypotheses about environmental variables that maintain competing behaviors and prevent intervention implementation. Antecedent-behavior-consequence (ABC) continuous recording allows consultants to record the occurrence of competing behaviors in addition to relevant environmental stimuli using interval-based recording (Cooper et al., 2020). These data can allow consultants to calculate conditional probabilities (i.e., extent to which antecedents, behaviors, and consequences are related; Eckert et al. 2005). These data make it possible to identify patterns of antecedents that evoke competing behaviors and consequences that maintain them (Collier-Meek et al., 2017b).

This assessment should also occur for developmentally appropriate classroom management practices, such as behavior specific praise, effective instruction delivery, differential attention, precorrection delivery, and emotion labeling, to name a few (Dufrene et al., 2012; Hemmeter et al., 2007; Stormont et al., 2007). Conducting ABC conditional probabilities analyses for these practices can help identify antecedents that prevent their occurrence (e.g., lack of visual reminders) and consequences that suppress their use (e.g., behavior specific praise delivery resulted in increased disruptive behavior). Conversely, analyzing environmental variables associated with evoking intervention implementation (e.g., verbal reminders from consultant to prompt implementation) and maintaining its use (e.g., when effective instructions are used, children are more likely to comply) can provide important information on variables that can be capitalized on during consultation. Following systematic observation, hypotheses about functions of competing behaviors can be developed. This information should be used to develop implementation supports that alter those environmental variables that influence competing behaviors (Collier-Meek et al., 2017b).

Goal Setting and Implementation Support Selection

The final stage of Problem Analysis is to identify a treatment integrity goal and implementation support. The treatment integrity goal should be evidence-based and supported by empirical research. That is, goals for increasing treatment integrity should be based on educators' baseline rates of a given skill. For example, it may not be practical to require an educator to implement an intervention with 100% integrity if their baseline rates of intervention implementation are near zero. In this scenario, the treatment integrity goal should be gradually increased over time as the educator has opportunities to practice intervention implementation and be reinforced (e.g., slightly improved child behavior, praise from center director/ consultant) for implementation (Allen & Warzak, 2000; Collier-Meek et al., 2017b). Notwithstanding, treatment integrity goals should also be supported by the literature. For example, some research indicates that an educator's behavior specific praise rate of about one praise statement per two minutes, on average, is sufficient for promoting improved behavior in young children (LaBrot et al., 2020, 2021). Of particular importance is using research literature to make empirically informed decisions about selecting target treatment integrity levels that result in improved child outcomes.

Additionally, implementation supports to be utilized should be selected prior to Plan Implementation. In a behavior analytic multitiered consultation framework, initial implementation supports are antecedent-based procedures. For example, supports such as behavioral skills training, intervention manuals/scripts, and prompting are ideal supports, as they can be feasibly implemented and be broadly applied across more than one educator (Collier-Meek et al., 2017b). However, the decision to utilize one of these supports should include educator input. Allowing educators an opportunity to choose the implementation supports they receive can result in increased intervention adherence (Dart et al., 2012). Furthermore, educator-chosen supports may be more salient to educators given their preference for those supports, and therefore more effective and promoting intervention implementation.

Plan Implementation and Plan Evaluation

Once an implementation support is selected, educators should be adequately prepared in its use. Assuming Tier 1 supports (i.e., professional development trainings) have not been effective for promoting treatment integrity, consultants should ensure that educators have the necessary resources to implement an intervention and can identify intervention components. As such, a brief meeting/training session may be held in which a consultant trains an educator in intervention implementation utilizing evidence-based teaching methods (e.g., behavioral skills training; LaBrot et al., 2022). If data determine that Tier 1 supports are ineffective, consultants should prepare educators to receive Tier 2 supports by thoroughly explaining (1) how the implementation support will be delivered and (2) exactly how educators should respond to them. For example, if an educator and consultant agree that receiving emailed prompts is the most appropriate support, the educator should be informed how often emailed prompts will be sent, when they will be sent, what they will consist of, and how often they should be viewed (LaBrot et al., 2022). After ensuring that educators understand the intervention and implementation supports, the supports should then be systematically delivered.

A vital component of the behavior analytic multitiered consultation model is monitoring educators' intervention implementation. Assessment of intervention implementation should be feasible but should also occur with enough regularity that consultants can make effective and efficient decisions to either withdraw or intensify supports. Ideally, data collection should involve direct observation of educators' intervention implementation. This can be done in vivo (i.e., consultant observes during ongoing classroom activities; LaBrot et al., 2020) or via audio- or visual-recording (e.g., LaBrot et al., 2021a). That said, audio- and visual-recording allow consultants more feasibility in data collection and therefore allow them to engage in other consultative activities. However, if audio- and/or visual-recordings are utilized, educators should be trained how and when (i.e., during time in which intervention implementation is expected) to record treatment integrity data. Additionally, there are likely ethical issues related to inadvertently recording child data which should be controlled for if possible. If this is not possible, audio- and visual-recording may not be possible.

Data-based Decision Making

The central tenet of the behavior analytic multitiered consultation model is data-based decision making. Data-based decision making allows consultants to determine whether implementation supports should be (1) continued, (2) intensified or changed, or (3) withdrawn. Careful consideration should be given to the threshold by which decisions are made. That is, data should be collected in such a way that changes in implementation supports can be made quickly to promote educators' rapid acquisition of interventions skills. This may also prevent the worsening of children's problem behavior.

Following a referral concern, data should first be collected on educators' implementation of interventions trained during Tier 1. In many cases, this serves as a baseline given that all educators have received universal, professional development (i.e., this condition exists across all educators within an early childhood education center) (e.g., LaBrot et al., 2020, 2021a). Following baseline data collection on educators' treatment integrity after Tier 1 training, a criterion for moving to more intensive training should be established. Previous multitiered consultation research in early childhood education settings shifted from lower to higher tiers contingent upon not meeting a criterion for five consecutive observations (LaBrot et al., 2020). However, LaBrot et al. (2020) noted that this criterion may be too stringent and could result in educators receiving Tier 2 supports for a prolonged period of time with only variable treatment integrity and lack of improvement in child behavior. Alternatively, less stringent thresholds for transitioning to more intensive implementation supports (e.g., not meeting criterion three times nonconsecutively; LaBrot et al., 2021) should be strongly considered to prevent degradation in treatment integrity and child behavior.

Using this data-based decision-making approach, consultants can make objective decisions in changes between tiers. Following data collection after Tier 1 supports that indicate a clear pattern of low or inconsistent intervention implementation, educators should be transitioned to Tier 2 supports. Tier 2 supports should include antecedent-based implementation supports (See Table 1). As discussed previously, data gathered during the Problem Analysis phase should be taken into careful consideration as the consultant selects an antecedent-based implementation support. For example, educators who seem to perform skills well, but less frequently than needed, may benefit from daily prompts to perform a skill. Alternatively, educators that seem to struggle with understanding how and when to implement an intervention may benefit from more direct antecedent-based implementation supports (e.g., in situ training; Dufrene et al., 2012; LaBrot et al., 2016, 2021b). If an educator's treatment integrity improves with Tier 2 supports (i.e., meets the criterion previously established), they should be transitioned back to Tier 1 supports (i.e., no additional implementation supports provided beyond the regularly scheduled professional development). The criterion to switch an educator from Tier 2 back to Tier 1 supports should more stringent (e.g., five consecutive observations of meeting criterion) than the criterion to switch from Tier 1 to 2, to ensure educators adequately and consistently maintain a skill overtime. This may also ensure that an effective implementation support is not prematurely withdrawn before an educator has mastered intervention implementation.

Alternatively, if educators fail to meet a predetermined criterion during Tier 2, they should then be transitioned to Tier 3. Tier 3 implementation supports should consist of both antecedent- and consequent-based supports (See Table 1). Following implementation of Tier 3 supports, data should continue to be collected to determine whether the educator meets the predetermined criterion. If the criterion is achieved, the educator should be transitioned back to Tier 2 supports and then monitored to determine if the criterion continues to be met. Then, if the criterion is again met, the educator should be transitioned to Tier 1 supports (i.e., removal of all implementation supports). We recommend a stepwise transition from Tier 3 to Tier 1, so implementation supports are gradually faded to help maintain educators' intervention implementation (LaBrot et al., 2021a). Additionally, transition to Tier 3 should include a less stringent criterion than transferring from Tier 3 to 2. As previously stated, a less stringent criterion to transition to higher tiers may help prevent degradation in treatment integrity, while a more stringent criterion to switch from Tier 3 to 2, and so on, may promote educator mastery of intervention implementation.

Table 1
Empirically Based Implementation Supports

Implementation Support	Description	Studies	Delivery of Support	Hypothesized Mechanism of Action
Intervention manual	Intervention overview and steps for implementation provided in a detailed, written manner	Lawton & Kasari, 2012*	Prior to implementation	Antecedent
Test driving interventions	Implementer tries various interventions before selecting the most acceptable intervention for ongoing implementation	Dart et al, 2012**; Johnson et al, 2013**	Prior to implementation	Antecedent
Direct training	Training activities including an introduction to the intervention, consultant modeling, implementer practice, and feedback	Baker et al., 2010*; Tiano & McNeil, 2006*	Prior to or during implementation (as needed)	Antecedent
Treatment planning protocol	Three-step standardized process to define an intervention, develop intervention integrity assessment, and create an intervention integrity self-assessment form	Sanetti & Kratochwill, 2009**	Prior to implementation	Antecedent
Implementation planning	Detailed logistical planning related to intervention implementation (i.e., Action Planning) and problem-solving approach to address potential implementation barriers	Sanetti, Fallon, & Collier-Meek., 2013**; Sanetti et al., 2014*	Prior to or during implementation (as needed)	Antecedent
Intervention scripts	Implementer provided with written instructions and language to use during implementation	Ehrhardt, et al, 1996*	Prior to implementation	Antecedent
Role play	Consultant models the intervention and allows the implementer to practice using actual intervention scenarios followed by feedback	Trevisan, 2004	Prior to or during implementation (as needed)	Antecedent
Participant modeling	Consultant models the intervention within the implementation setting and provides the implementer with support during independent practice	Tschannen-Moran & McMaster, 2009**	Prior to or during implementation (as needed)	Antecedent
Self-monitoring	Implementer completes checklist during or after implementation	Simonsen et al., 2013***	During implementation	Antecedent
Prompts	Consultant provides proactive reminders to implement components of an intervention	LaBrot et al, 2022*	During implementation	Antecedent
Instructional coaching	Intensive, differentiated strategies conducted by a skilled and empathic listener/coach to support implementers	Knight, 2007	Prior to or during implementation (as needed)	Antecedent (e.g. training) / Consequence (e.g. feedback)
Video support	Video recorded during implementation to self-monitor by the implementer and provide consultant feedback	Downer et al., 2011*	During implementation	Consequence
Performance feedback	Feedback (i.e., verbal, graphic) provided on actual implementation behavior. May be combined with practice, prompting, or self-monitoring components	Kaufman et al., 2013*; Sanetti, Luiselli, & Handler, 2007*	During implementation	Consequence

Note. All studies without a superscript are general overviews. * PreK-K Teachers   ** Elementary Teachers   ***Middle School Teach

Current Research, Practical Implications, and Future Directions

Current Research

Although a multitiered consultation model is largely conceptual at this point in time, there are four known published studies that have evaluated this model with early childhood educators. It is important to note that these studies do not explicitly state that they followed a multitiered consultation model. Rather, these studies were identified through a systematic search, and demonstrated similar methodology; that is, there were multiple tiers of implementation supports in which switching to higher tiers was contingent upon not meeting a specific criterion in a lower tier. These studies provide the groundwork for this model in terms of practical applications and future research needs.

Gerencser et al. (2018) evaluated a multitiered consultation model for training paraprofessionals in three preschool special education classrooms to implement discrete trial instruction (DTI) with children with various neurodevelopmental disabilities (e.g., developmental delay, autism spectrum disorder). Tier 1 support involved paraprofessionals individually engaging in an interactive computer training on DTI implementation, Tier 2 involved use of a checklist to remind paraprofessionals of DTI steps, and Tiers 3 and 4 involved provision of remotely delivered performance feedback. Data indicated that all paraprofessionals required at least three tiers of support to increase DTI implementation to adequate levels, with evidence that DTI skills maintained over time and generalized to novel skills taught via DTI. No child data were collected in this study. Of note, this is the only study of the four that implemented a behavior analytic multitiered consultation framework, in that initial consultation tiers (Tiers 1 and 2) involved antecedent-based supports (i.e., training, checklists) and the more intensive tiers (Tiers 3 and 4) involved consequent-based supports (i.e., various forms of performance feedback).

LaBrot et al. (2020) evaluated a non-behavior analytic multitiered consultation framework for increasing four educators' (two Early Head Start teachers, two elementary teachers) rates of behavior specific praise and decreasing reprimands. Tier 1 involved large group professional development, Tier 2 involved performance feedback, and Tier 3 involved tactile prompting. Results indicated that only Tier 2 was necessary to increase the two early childhood educators' rates of behavior specific praise to adequate levels that maintained over time, with concomitant increases in children's appropriate behaviors and decreases in disruptive behaviors. No meaningful decreases in early childhood educator reprimands were observed and no data on generalized outcomes were collected. Ennis et al. (2020) evaluated a multitiered consultation model with three early childhood educators for increasing rates of behavior specific praise, choice giving, and precorrections. Like LaBrot et al. (2020), Tier 1 involved large group professional development. However, Tiers 2 and 3 involved coaching (i.e., prompts, performance feedback, examples) and self-monitoring, respectively. Results indicated that only one educator required all three tiers to increase rates of all dependent measures, while the other two educators only required Tier 2 supports. No generalization, maintenance, or child data were collected.

Finally, Markelz et al. (2021) tested the effectiveness of a multitiered consultation framework for increasing three early childhood educators' rates of behavior specific praise. Tier 1 included individual educator training and goal setting, Tier 2 included self-monitoring, and Tier 3 included tactile prompting. Results of this study indicated that all three early childhood educators' rates of behavior specific praise increased to adequate levels after receiving all three tiers of supports, which resulted in generalization of behavior specific praise across children. Child data indicated improved on-task behavior; no maintenance data were collected. Collectively, these four studies demonstrate initial evidence for the effectiveness of a multitiered consultation model for early childhood educators. Methods and results of these studies offer important information for this model's application.

Implications

First, the majority (three of four) of these studies involved training early childhood educators to implement relatively simple strategies, such as behavior specific praise (Ennis et al., 2020; LaBrot et al., 2020; Markelz et al., 2021), choice giving, and precorrections (Ennis et al., 2020). Although only demonstrated in LaBrot et al. (2020), these strategies are often effective for improving young children's behavior in early childhood education settings (Dufrene et al., 2012; Gorton et al., 2021; LaBrot et al., 2021; Stormont et al., 2007). As such, use of a multitiered consultation model for training early childhood educators to implement simple and effective universal behavior management strategies is encouraged.

Alternatively, Gerencser et al. (2018) evaluated a behavior analytic multitiered consultation model for teaching early childhood paraprofessionals a relatively complex intervention (i.e., DTI), which may have resulted in all participants requiring each tier of consultation support. Additionally, implementation supports utilized in initial tiers were indirect in nature; that is, interactive computer training (Tier 1) and checklists (Tier 2) did not involve direct teaching or rehearsal in the environment in which DTI would occur. This also may have contributed to all participants requiring Tiers 3 and 4 (one participant), which involved providing performance feedback on direct skill use. Therefore, it is possible a behavior analytic multitiered consultation model to teach more complex interventions should involve more direct training techniques at each tier. For example, behavioral skills training and in situ training delivered in the environment in which early childhood educators are expected to perform the intervention being trained (e.g., Dufrene et al., 2012; LaBrot et al., 2016, 2021) could serve as Tiers 1 and 2, respectively. Furthermore, Tier 3 could involve in situ training in which both prompts and performance feedback are delivered in real-time.

Similarly, another implication for this model involves the types of implementation supports delivered within Tier 1. That is, Tier 1 supports across all four studies included some form of professional development that involved instructions (Ennis et al., 2020; Gerencser et al., 2018; LaBrot et al., 2020; Markelz et al., 2021), modeling (Gerencser et al., 2018), rehearsal/role-playing (Ennis et al., 2020; Gerencser et al., 2018; Markelz et al., 2021), and performance feedback (Gerencser et al., 2018; Markelz et al., 2021). Although these training components were delivered inconsistently across studies, it may be beneficial to ensure all of these are incorporated into Tier 1 supports to bolster the potential effectiveness of this support.

Furthermore, two studies (i.e., LaBrot et al., 2020; Markelz et al., 2021) included antecedent-based supports (i.e., tactile prompting) at the Tier 3 level. This may indicate that if these had been implemented as Tier 2 supports, early childhood educator participants could have improved intervention integrity sooner. This also would have been commensurate with a behavior analytic multitiered framework, in which antecedent-based supports precede consequent-based supports. Of course, the antecedent-based supports delivered during Tier 3 may have been effective, in part, due to multiple treatment interference (i.e., more than one intervention impacting behavior) and order effect (i.e., particular order of tiered supports resulted in behavior change). Regardless, researchers and practitioners are encouraged to adopt the behavior analytic multitiered consultation model as the delivery of potentially effective antecedent-based interventions may negate the need for further implementation support, which may save times and resources.

Finally, results of these studies highlight ideal consultation interactions in which participants generally implemented interventions trained through consultation. However, it can often be the case that barriers such as uncooperative early childhood educators, educator turnover, or extended educator absences impact effective, ongoing consultation. In these instances, consultants may consider delivering electronic universal supports (e.g., emailed prompts; LaBrot et al., 2022) to all educators and staff involved with a given child or classroom, to ensure all are prepared to deliver necessary evidence-based practices. Furthermore, if educators are uncooperative with the consultation process, strategies such as motivational interviewing (e.g., LaBrot et al., 2016) and educator-led goal setting (e.g., Cohrs et al., 2016) may result in improved adherence to consultation and subsequent intervention implementation.

Future Directions

Because only four known studies have evaluated the effectiveness of multitiered consultation with early childhood educators, there are several areas of future research that should be explored. First, data on early childhood educators' maintenance and generalized outcomes should be collected in future multitiered consultation studies. These data are important to collect to determine the long-term effectiveness (i.e., intervention implementation is sustained) and efficiency (i.e., intervention implementation spontaneously generalizes without additional support) of the multitiered consultation model. Second, data on early childhood educators' outcomes have been limited to DTI, behavior specific praise, choice giving, and precorrections. While these are important interventions that impact young children's social-emotional, behavioral, and learning development, they are limited in scope. As such, additional research should evaluate the effectiveness of a multitiered consultation model for promoting other educator-implemented interventions (e.g., effective instruction delivery, group contingencies).

Third, future studies evaluating this model should seek to collect child outcome data. These data are important to collect to determine the extent to which educators' improved intervention implementation results in improved child outcomes. Fourth, more research is needed to evaluate the effectiveness of a behavior analytic multitiered consultation model. The behavior analytic multitiered consultation model has the potential to be effective and potentially more efficient than a multitiered model in which supports are non-systematically delivered. As such, future research should seek to specifically evaluate this model's efficiency in terms of time, resources, cost-effectiveness, and social validity. Finally, although this model is proposed as an approach to better ensure efficiency in consultation, no data on barriers and difficulties with this model have been collected. Therefore, future research should seek to collect data on consultants' and teachers' perceived barriers and difficulty with this model (e.g., consultation intensity, teacher stress/burnout), to determine future steps to improve this model's implementation.

Case Study

The following case study took place in a suburban university-based child development center in a mid-sized city in the southeastern USA. The child development center housed nine classrooms with children grouped by age, ranging from 3 months to 5 years. A licensed psychologist faculty member and two doctoral-level graduate students served as consultants for this case study. Data in the following case study were collected during the course of contractual consultation between a doctoral school psychology program and the described child development center. As part of our formal agreement with this agency, educators, staff, and administrators were aware that clinical data collection could be used for teaching and research purposes. In addition, the teacher participant in this case study provided verbal consent to allow de-identified data collected during consultation for this manuscript and other teaching purposes.

Problem Identification

Upon receiving a referral for consultative services by this child development center, a consultant met with the center administrator.

The center administrator indicated that several teachers in the center had not received formal behavior or classroom management training. However, some had previously received brief professional development trainings from the faculty supervisor on strategies such as behavior specific praise, planned ignoring, effective instruction delivery, and precorrections as strategies to prevent problem behavior. The center administrator provided a list of teachers who would benefit from consultation to improve their classroom management strategies. At the time of this case study, no formal universal screening was in place.

One of the teachers who was referred for consultation was a lead teacher, Ms. Mary (pseudonym). Ms. Mary was a 28-year-old White female who held a bachelor's degree in Child and Family Sciences and was currently in her third year of teaching. Upon receiving her name as a referral, a consultant conducted a brief interview with Ms. Mary. Children's ages in Ms. Mary's classroom ranged from 2 to 3 years old and consisted of three White males, one African American male, and one Caucasian female. Additionally, one child was diagnosed with autism spectrum disorder. Ms. Mary indicated that the most common problem behaviors she experienced in her classroom included low rates of compliance, tantrums, and leaving designated areas. Moreover, she noted that these behaviors most often occurred during art activities. Art activities consisted of painting, drawing, and coloring. Child expectations during art activities included staying seated, keeping materials on the table, and complying with teacher instructions. During each art activity, Ms. Mary sat with the children and facilitated the activity and managed disruptive behavior.

Problem Analysis

After the brief interview with Ms. Mary, a consultant observed the art activity. The consultant noted that Ms. Mary delivered an adequate amount of behavior specific praise during the activity, but sometimes these praise statements were not directed towards "rule-following" behavior (i.e., praised for using brush correctly, but not praised for following instructions). Ms. Mary was not observed to remind children of expectations before, during, or after the art activity. When children did not follow instructions or engaged in disruptive behavior, Ms. Mary was observed to deliver reprimands (i.e., competing behavior), which appeared to function to terminate disruptive behavior (i.e., negative reinforcement for competing behavior). As such, the consultation team (i.e., consultants, teacher, faculty supervisor) determined that increasing Ms. Mary's rate of precorrections was the most appropriate intervention, given that she was not observed to implement this strategy and she was already delivering adequate rates of praise. The consultants further hypothesized that precorrections might function to increase compliance expectations for art activities, which would facilitate behavior specific praise delivery for "rule-following" behavior.

Precorrections were defined as vocal statements directed towards a single child or group of children to specify appropriate, expected behaviors before an activity and/or during the activity (e.g., "Remember to keep materials on the table," "Remember to stay in your seat during art time," "Remember to follow directions during art time"). Consultants set a preliminary goal to increase Ms. Mary's use of precorrective statements to approximately three per 10 min on average, which has some derivation from empirical research (Ennis et al., 2020). Observations to monitor treatment integrity were ten minutes in duration and occurred between two to three days per week. Observers recorded Ms. Mary's rate of precorrection statements during 10 sec intervals, which was converted to a rate-based measure by dividing the total number of pre-corrective statements by 10 (i.e., length of observation in minutes). For all observations, observers sat in an unobtrusive location in the classroom and used a digital audio cueing device that prompted the beginning and end of each observation interval.

Ms. Mary indicated she was motivated to improve children's behavior and would be open to consultants selecting the implementation supports to be used. Given Ms. Mary's high level of motivation and demonstrated skills with other intervention use (i.e., good behavior specific praise), the consultants decided to implement goal setting (Tier 2) and provide performance feedback (Tier 3) because these strategies are effective, simple, and minimally invasive.

Plan Implementation

As previously stated, some teachers in the early childhood development center (including Ms. Mary) had received professional development training on effective classroom management practices (Tier 1). Tier 1 universal training involved teaching individual teachers to use behavior-specific praise, planned ignoring, effective instruction delivery, and precorrections to management classroom behavior. Ms. Mary had received this training approximately two months prior to this case study.

Goal setting (Tier 2) began with a consultant asking Ms. Mary how many precorrective statements she would like to try to implement during the 10 min art activity, to which she selected three. Additionally, the teacher selected three distinct pre-corrective statements that would be most relevant to the task. These statements included "Remember to stay in your seat during art time," "Remember to keep materials on the table," and "Remember to follow directions during art time." On days in which the consultant was in the center, they briefly reminded Ms. Mary of her goal.

The Tier 3 implementation support consisted of goal setting with the addition of performance feedback. In addition to reminding Ms. Mary of the precorrective statement goal, feedback was provided regarding precorrective statement rate. If Ms. Mary met or exceeded the precorrective statement delivery goal, the consultant provided praise. If Ms. Mary did not meet the precorrective statement delivery goal, the consultant provided a reminder of the goal and encouragement to increase pre-corrective statement delivery for the next observation.

Plan Evaluation

Results for Ms. Mary's rate of precorrective statements are displayed graphically in Figure 2. During baseline data collection, Ms. Mary's precorrection statement rates remained low and stable ($M = 0$ statements per minute). During goal setting (Tier 2), Ms. Mary's rate of precorrections reflected an immediate level increase with high variability and an increasing trend at the conclusion of the phase ($M = .26$ statements per minute). Due to the variability of the data, and some cases in which the goal was not met, the consultation team agreed to begin providing performance feedback (Tier 3). During Tier 3 implementation supports, Ms. Mary's rate of precorrection statements stabilized, albeit with a decreasing trend ($M = .47$ statements per minute). Because the end of the program semester was quickly approaching and because Ms. Mary indicated she believed she could maintain precorrective statement use at her current rate, the consultation team agreed to terminate all implementation supports and monitor for maintenance. However, the ideal situation would have been to implement Tier 2 supports for at least a short period of time (e.g., one to two days). During maintenance, Ms. Mary's rate of precorrection statements demonstrated moderate variability ($M = .33$ statements per minute), but were generally consistent with the previously established goal. Unfortunately, social validity data assessing Ms. Mary's perceptions of this model were not collected.

Figure 2
Ms. Mary's Rate of Precorrection Statements

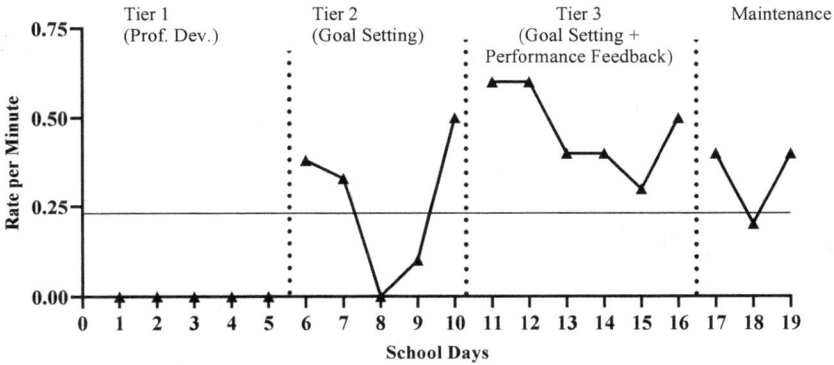

Summary and Conclusions

This case study generally follows the proposed guidelines of a behavior analytic multitiered consultation model. First, consultants met with the lead center administrator to gather background information related to the needs of center teachers and staff as a whole. This led to an interview with Ms. Mary, in which relevant data were collected such as Ms. Mary's previous experience with learning about and implementing evidence-based strategies (e.g., behavior specific praise), her willingness and motivation to implement new strategies, and child problem behaviors and other relevant barriers to intervention implementation. Collecting these data allowed consultants to select an appropriate evidence-based strategy (i.e., precorrective statements) and a Tier 2 implementation support (i.e., goal setting). Goal setting may have also aided in teacher compliance with consultation procedures, as Ms. Mary was allowed to select not only her precorrective statement rate but the most relevant types of precorrective statements. This level of input is often beneficial for teacher buy-in.

Following implementation of goal setting, data suggested that Ms. Mary's implementation of precorrections were variable. As such, a data-based decision to implement Tier 3 supports (i.e., goal setting with performance feedback) was made. Although Ms. Mary's overall use of precorrective statements increased above baseline levels during Tier 2, a decision to move to Tier 3 was made as inconsistent use of an intervention can be just as detrimental as lack of intervention implementation. Following a consistent increase in precorrective statements during Tier 3, the consultation team decided to move Ms. Mary to maintenance. Although we recommend that educators be gradually transitioned to lower level supports to facilitate fading, it is sometimes appropriate to shift away from use of implementation supports given qualitative data. In Ms. Mary's case, this included her high-level of motivation, verbal indication she no longer needed support to implement this strategy, and the fact that there was not enough time to fade from Tier 2 to maintenance before the conclusion of the program. Taken together, results of this case study highlight the use and effectiveness of the behavior analytic multitiered consultation model. However, this should not be considered an experimental demonstration of this model's effectiveness; rather, it is our hope that this case study serves as a guide for practitioners and researchers.

References

Ali, M. M., Teich, J., Lynch, S., & Mutter, R. (2018). Utilization of mental health services by preschool-aged children with private insurance coverage. *Administration and Policy in Mental Health and Mental Health Services Research, 45*(5), 731-740. https://doi.org/10.1007/s10488-018-0858-x

Allen, K. D., & Warzak, W. J. (2000). The problem of parental nonadherence in clinical behavior analysis: Effective treatment is not enough. *Journal of Applied Behavior Analysis, 33*(3), 373-391. https://doi.org/10.1901/jaba.2000.33-373

Baer, D. M., Wolf, M. M., & Risley, T. R. (1968). Some current dimensions of applied behavior analysis. *Journal of Applied Behavior Analysis, 1*(1), 91-97. https://doi.org/10.1901/jaba.1987.20-313

Baker, C. N., Kupersmidt, J. B., Voegler-Lee, M. E., Arnold, D. H., & Willoughby, M. T. (2010). Predicting teacher participation in a classroom-based, integrated preventive intervention for preschoolers. *Early Childhood Research Quarterly, 25*(3), 270–283. https://doi.org/10.1016/j.ecresq.2009.09.005

Barton, E. E., Velez, M., Pokorski, E. A., & Domingo, M. (2020). The effects of email performance-based feedback delivered to teaching teams: A systematic replication. *Journal of Early Intervention, 42*(2), 143-162. https://doi.org/10.1177/105381511987245

Bick, J., & Nelson, C. A. (2017). Early experience and brain development. *Wiley Interdisciplinary Reviews: Cognitive Science, 8*(1-2), 1-12. https://doi.org/10.1002/wcs.1387

Carter, A. S., Wagmiller, R. J., Gray, S. A. O., McCarthy, K. J., Horwitz, S. M., & Briggs-Gowan, M. J. (2010). Prevalence of DSM-IV disorder in a representative, healthy birth cohort at school entry: Sociodemographic risks and social adaptation. *Journal of the American Academy of Child and Adolescent Psychiatry, 49,* 686–698. https://doi.org/10.1016/j.jaac.2010.03.018

Cohrs, C. M., Shriver, M. D., Burke, R. V., & Allen, K. D. (2016). Evaluation of increasing antecedent specificity in goal statements on adherence to positive behavior-management strategies. *Journal of Applied Behavior Analysis, 49*(4), 768-779. https://doi.org/10.1002/jaba.321

Collier-Meek, M. A., Fallon, L. M., & DeFouw, E. R. (2017a). Toward feasible implementation support: Emailed prompts to promote teachers' treatment integrity. *School Psychology Review, 46,* 379-394. DOI: 10.17105/SPR-2017-0028.V46-4

Collier-Meek, M. A., Fallon, L. M., & Gould, K. (2018). How are treatment integrity data assessed? Reviewing the performance feedback literature. *School Psychology Quarterly, 33*(4), 517-526. https://doi.org/10.1037/spq0000239

Collier-Meek, M. A., Sanetti, L. M. H., & Fallon, L. M. (2017b). Incorporating applied behavior analysis to assess and support educators' treatment integrity. *Psychology in the Schools, 54*(4), 446-460. https://doi.org/10.1002/pits.22001

Cooper, J. O., Heron, T. E., & Heward, W. L. (2020). *Applied behavior analysis* (3rd ed.). Pearson.

Dart, E. H., Cook, C. R., Collins, T. A., Gresham, F. M., & Chenier, J. S. (2012). Test driving interventions to increase treatment integrity and student outcomes. *School Psychology Review, 41*(4), 467-481. https://doi.org/10.1080/02796015.2012.12087500

Downer, J. T., Pianta, R. C., Fan, X., Hamre, B. K., Mashburn, A., & Justice, L. (2011). Effects of Web-Mediated Teacher Professional Development on the Language and Literacy Skills of Children Enrolled in Prekindergarten Programs. NHSA Dialog, 14(4), 189–212. https://doi.org/10.1080/15240754.2011.613129

Duchaine, E. L., Jolivette, K., & Fredrick, L. D. (2011). The effect of teacher coaching with performance feedback on behavior-specific praise in inclusion classrooms. *Education and Treatment of Children, 34,* 209-277. DOI: 10.1353/etc.2011.0009

Dufrene, B. A., Parker, K., Menousek, K., Zhou, Q., Harpole, L. L., & Olmi, D. J. (2012). Direct behavioral consultation in Head Start to increase teacher use of praise and effective instruction delivery. *Journal of Educational and Psychological Consultation, 22*(3), 159-186. https://doi.org/10.1080/10474412.2011.620817

Dufrene, B. A., Zoder-Martell, K. A., Dieringer, S. T., & LaBrot, Z. (2016). Behavior analytic consultation for academic referral concerns. *Psychology in the Schools, 53*(1), 8-23. https://doi.org/10.1002/pits.21885

Eckert, T. L., Martens, B. K., & DiGennaro, F. D. (2005). Describing antecedent-behavior-consequence relations using conditional probabilities and the general operant contingency space: A preliminary investigation. *School Psychology Review, 34*(4), 520-528. https://doi.org/10.1080/02796015.2005.12088013

Egger, H. L., & Angold, A. (2006). Common emotional and behavioral disorders in preschool children: Presentation, nosology, and epidemiology. *Journal of Child Psychology and Psychiatry, 47*(3), 313-337. https://doi.org/10.1111/j.1469-7610.2006.01618.x

Ehrhardt, K. E., Barnett, D. W., Lentz Jr., F. E., Stollar, S. A., & Reifin, L. H. (1996). Innovative methodology in ecological consultation: Use of scripts to promote treatment acceptability and integrity. *School Psychology Quarterly, 11*(2), 149-168. https://doi.org/10.1037/h0088926

Ennis, R. P., Flemming, S. C., Michael, E., & Lee, E. O. (2020). Using a tiered approach to support early childhood educators' use of behavioral strategies. *Education and Treatment of Children, 43*(3), 265-277. https://doi.org/10.1007/s43494-020-00027-x

Erchul, W. P., & Martens, B. K. (2012). *School consultation: Conceptual and empirical bases of practice* (3rd ed.). Springer.

Fallon, L. M., Collier-Meek, M. A., Kurtz, K. D., & DeFouw, E. R. (2018). Emailed implementation supports to promote treatment integrity: Comparing the effectiveness and acceptability of prompts and performance feedback. *Journal of School Psychology, 68,* 113-128. https://doi.org/10.1016/j.jsp.2018.03.001

Fox, L., Carta, J., Strain, P. S., Dunlap, G., & Hemmeter, M. L. (2010). Response to intervention and the pyramid model. *Infants & Young Children, 23*(1), 3-13. DOI: 10.1097/IYC.0b013e3181c816e2

Fox, L., Corso, R., Binder, D., Simonsen, B., George, H., Freeman, J., & Sugai, G. (2015). Program-wide PBS and school-wide PBIS crosswalk. Retrieved December 28, 2022 from chrome-extension://efaidnbmnnnibpcajpcglclefindmkaj/https://nceln.fpg.unc.edu/sites/nceln.fpg.unc.edu/files/resources/pyramid_and_swpbis_crosswalk.pdf

Freeman, J., Simonsen, B., Briere, D. E., & MacSuga-Gage, A. S. (2014). Pre-service teacher training in classroom management: A review of state accreditation policy and teacher preparation programs. *Teacher Education & Special Education, 37*(2), 106-120. https://doi.org/10.1177/0888406413507002

Gerencser, K. R., Higbee, T. S., Contreras, B. P., Pellegrino, A. J., & Gunn, S. L. (2018). Evaluation of interactive computerized training to teacher paraprofessionals to implement errorless discrete trial instruction. *Journal of Behavioral Education, 27*(4), 461-487. https://doi.org/10.1007/s10864-018-9308-9

Gomez, L., Barton, E. E., Winchester, C., & Locchetta, B. (2021). Effects of email performance feedback on teachers' use of play expansions. *Journal of Early Intervention, 43*(3), 235-254. https://doi.org/10.1177/1053815120969821

Gorton, K., Allday, R. A., Lane, J. D., & Ault, M. J. (2021). Effects of brief training plus electronic feedback on increasing quantity and intonation of behavior specific praise among preschool teachers. *Journal of Behavioral Education,* 1-21. https://doi.org/10.1007/s10864-020-09427-w

Grace, C., Shores, E. F., Zaslow, M., Brown, B., Aufseeser, D., & Bell, L. (2006). *Rural disparities in baseline data of the early childhood longitudinal study: A chartbook.* Mississippi State University Early Childhood Institute.

Gresham, F. M. (1989). Assessment of treatment integrity in school consultation and prereferral intervention. *School Psychology Review, 18*(1), 37-50. https://doi.org/10.1080/02796015.1989.12085399

Hemmeter, M. L., Fox, L., Jack, S., & Broyles, L. (2007). A program-wide model of positive behavior support in early childhood settings. *Journal of Early Intervention, 29*(4), 337-355. https://doi.org/10.1177/105381510702900405

Hussar, B., Zhang, J., Hein, S., Wang, K., Roberts, A., Cui, J., Smith, M., Mann, F. B., Barmer, A., & Dilig, R. (2020). The condition of education 2020. NCES 2020-144. *National Center for Education Statistics.*

Johnson, L. D., Wehby, J. H., Symons, F. J., Moore, T. C., Maggin, D. M., & Sutherland, K. S. (2013). An analysis of preference relative to teacher implementation of intervention. *The Journal of Special Education, 48*(3), 214–224. https://doi.org/10.1177/0022466913475872

Kaufman, D., Codding, R. S., Markus, K. A., Tryon, G. S., & Kyse, E. N. (2013). Effects of verbal and written performance feedback on treatment adherence: Practical application of two delivery formats. *Journal of Educational and Psychological Consultation, 23*(4), 264-299. https://doi.org/10.1080/10474412.2013.845494

LaBrot, Z. C., DeFouw, E. R., & Eldridge, M. (2021a). Examination of a tiered training model to increase school psychology graduate students' behavior specific praise. *Education and Treatment of Children, 44*(4), 233-248. https://doi.org/10.1007/s43494-021-00048-0

LaBrot, Z. C., Dufrene, B. A., Olmi, D. J., Dart, E. H., Radley, K., Lown, E., & Pasqua, J. L. (2021b). Maintenance and generalization of preschool teachers' use of behavior-specific praise following in situ training. *Journal of Behavioral Education, 30*(3), 350-377. https://doi.org/10.1007/s10864-020-09375-5

LaBrot, Z. C., Dufrene, B. A., Whipple, H., McCargo, M., & Pasqua, J. L. (2020). Targeted and intensive consultation for increasing head start and elementary teachers' behavior-specific praise. *Journal of Behavioral Education, 29*(4), 717-740. https://doi.org/10.1007/s10864-019-09342-9

LaBrot, Z. C., Johnson, C., Maxime, E., Cato, T., Butt, S., & DeFouw, E. R. (2022). Emailed prompt package to promote maintenance and generalization of early childhood educators' behavior specific praise. *Journal of Behavioral Education*, 1-21. https://doi.org/10.1007/s10864-022-09475-4

LaBrot, Z. C., Pasqua, J. L., Dufrene, B. A., Brewer, E. A., & Goff, B. (2016). In situ training for increasing Head Start after-care teachers' use of praise. *Journal of Behavioral Education, 25*(1), 32-48. DOI: 10.1007/s10864-015-9233-0

Lawton, K., & Kasari, C. (2012). Teacher-implemented joint attention intervention: Pilot randomized controlled study for preschoolers with autism. *Journal of Consulting and Clinical Psychology, 80*(4), 687–693. https://doi.org/10.1037/a0028506

Markelz, A., Riden, B., & Hooks, S. D. (2021). Component analysis of training and goal setting, self-monitoring, and tactile prompting on early childhood educators' behavior-specific praise. *Journal of Early Intervention, 43*(2), 99-116. https://doi.org/10.1177/1053815120927091

Marsh, R. J., & Mathur, S. R. (2020) Mental health in schools: An overview of multitiered systems of support. *Intervention in School and Clinic, 56*(2), 67-73. https://doi.org/10.1177/1053451220914896

McKenney, E. L., Page, V., Lakota, J., Niekra, N., & Thompson, S. J. (2019). Supporting integrity of discrete trial teaching via tiered consultation: A pilot study. *Journal of Applied School Psychology, 35*(1), 52-74. https://doi.org/10.1080/15377903.2018.1493555

McWayne, C. M., Fantuzzo, J. W., & McDermott, P. A. (2004). Preschool competency in context: An investigation of the unique contribution of child competencies to early academic success. *Developmental Psychology, 40*(4), 633-645. https://doi.org/10.1037/0012-1649.40.4.633

Myers, D. M., Simonsen, B., & Sugai, G. (2011). Increasing teachers' use of praise with a response-to-intervention approach. *Education and Treatment of Children, 34*(1), 35-59. DOI: 10.1353/etc.2011.0004

National Center for Education and Statistics. (2020). *Prevalence of mental health services provided by public schools and limitation in schools' efforts to provide mental health services.* Use, availability, and perceived harmfulness of opioids among youth (n. d.). Retrieved December 16, 2021 from https://nces.ed.gov/programs/coe/indicator/a23/school-mental-health-services#:~:text=The%20majority%20of%20schools%20(54,professionals%20as%20a%20major%20limitation.

O'Handley, R. D., Dufrene, B. A., & Whipple, H. (2018). Tactile prompting and weekly performance feedback for increasing teachers' behavior-specific praise. *Journal of Behavioral Education, 27*(3), 324-342. https://doi.org/10.1007/s10864-017-9283-6

Reinke, W. M., Stormont, M., Herman, K. C., Puri, R., & Goel, N. (2011). Supporting children's mental health in schools: Teacher perceptions of needs, roles, and barriers. *School Psychology Quarterly, 26*(1), 1-13. https://doi.org/10.1037/a0022714

Sanetti, L. M. H., & Collier-Meek, M. A. (2015). Data-driven delivery of implementation supports in a multi-tiered framework: A pilot study. *Psychology in the Schools, 52*(8), 815-828. https://doi.org/10.1002/pits.21861

Sanetti, L. M. H., Collier-Meek, M. A., Long, A. C. J., Kim, J., & Kratochwill, T. R. (2014). Using implementation planning to increase teachers' adherence and quality to behavior support plans. *Psychology in the Schools, 51*(8), 879–895. https://doi.org/10.1002/pits.21787

Sanetti, L. M. H., Fallon, L. M., & Collier-Meek, M. A. (2013). Increasing teacher treatment integrity through performance feedback provided by school personnel. *Psychology in the Schools, 50*, 134 – 150. https://doi.org/10.1002/pits.21664

Sanetti, L. M. H., & Kratochwill, T. R. (2009a). Toward developing a science of treatment integrity: Introduction to the special series. *School Psychology Review, 38*(4), 445-459.

Sanetti, L. M. H., & Kratochwill, T. R. (2009b). Treatment integrity assessment in the schools: An evaluation of the Treatment Integrity Planning Protocol. *School Psychology Quarterly, 24*, 24-35. https://doi.org/10.1037/a0015431

Sanetti, L. M. H., Kratochwill, T. R., Collier-Meek, M. A., & Long, A. C. J. (2014). PRIME: Planning realistic implementation and maintenance by educators. University of Connecticut. https://implementationscience.uconn.edu/wp-content/uploads/sites/1115/2014/12/PRIME_quickguide_problem-solving_consultation.pdf

Sanetti, L.M. H., Luiselli, J. K., & Handler, M. W. (2007). Effects of verbal and graphic performance feedback on behavior support plan implementation in a public elementary school. *Behavior Modification, 31*, 454 – 465. https://doi.org/10.1177/0145445506297583

Simonsen, B., MacSuga-Gage, A. S., Briere, D. E., Freeman, J., Myers, D., Scott, T. M., & Sugai, G. (2014). Multitiered support framework for teachers' classroom management practices: Overview and case study of building the triangle for teachers. *Journal of Positive Behavior Interventions, 16*(3), 179-190. https://doi.org/10.1177/1098300713484062

Simonsen, B., MacSuga, A. S., Fallon, L. M., & Sugai, G. (2013). The effects of self-monitoring on teachers' use of specific praise. *Journal of Positive Behavior Interventions, 15*(4), 231-241. https://doi.org/10.1177/1098300712440453

Snell, M. E., Berlin, R. A., Voorhees, M. D., Stanton-Chapman, T. L., & Hadden, S. (2012). A survey of preschool staff concerning problem behavior and its prevention in Head Start classrooms. *Journal of Positive Behavior Interventions, 14*(2), 96-107. https://doi.org/10.1177/1098300711416818

Steed, E. A., & Webb, M. Y. L. (2013). The psychometric properties of the preschool-wide evaluation tool (PreSET). *Journal of Positive Behavior Interventions, 15*(4), 231-241. https://doi.org/10.1177/1098300712459357

Sterling-Turner, H. E., Watson, T. S., & Moore, J. W. (2002). The effects of direct training and treatment integrity on treatment outcomes in school consultation. *School Psychology Quarterly, 17,* 47-77. https://doi.org/10.1521/scpq.17.1.47.19906

Stormont, M. A., Smith, S. C., & Lewis, T. J. (2007). Teacher implementation of precorrection and praise statements in Head Start classrooms as a component of program-wide system of positive behavior support. *Journal of Behavioral Education, 16*(3), 280-290. DOI: 10.1007/s10864-007-9040-3

Thompson, M. T., Marchant, M., Anderson, D., Prater, M. A., & Gibb, G. (2012). Effects of tiered training on general educators' use of specific praise. *Education and Treatment of Children, 35*(4), 521-546. DOI: 10.1353/etc.2012.0032

Tiano, J. D., & McNeil, C. B. (2006). Training Head Start teachers in behavior management using Parent-Child Interaction Therapy: A preliminary investigation. *Journal of Early and Intensive Behavior Intervention, 3*(2), 220-233. https://doi.org/10.1037/h0100334

Trevisan, M. S. (2004). Practical training in evaluation: A review of the literature. *American Journal of Evaluation, 25*(2), 255-272. https://doi.org/10.1177/109821400402500212

Tschannen-Moran, M., & McMaster, P. (2009). Sources of self-efficacy: Four professional development formats and their relationship to self-efficacy and implementation of a new teaching strategy. *The Elementary School Journal, 110*(2), 228-245. https://doi.org/10.1086/605771

Wichstrom, L., Berg-Nielsen, T. S., Angold, A., Egger, H. L., Solheim, E., & Sween, T. H. (2012). Prevalence of psychiatric disorders in preschoolers. *The Journal of Child Psychology and Psychiatry, 53*(6), 695-705. https://doi org/10.1111/j.1469-7610.2011.02514.x

Aligning Classroom Management Strategies with a Social Emotional Learning Curriculum in Early Childhood

Jessica M. Kemp and Sara A. Whitcomb

Abstract

Traditionally, school-based preventative frameworks have been implemented in isolation with little consideration of alignment and integration of practices throughout the school day. The present study aims to address this gap by increasing school psychologists' preventative involvement with consultation in early childhood school settings. Using an integrated approach through a multiple baseline design, four Head Start educators were trained in classroom management practices, to increase opportunities throughout the day for teaching, prompting, and reinforcing key skills taught through the *Second Step Early Learning (SSEL)* social emotional learning curriculum. Findings suggest that a brief professional development session (1-hour) followed by weekly performance feedback (15 minutes) largely increased educator use of aligning classroom management strategies with weekly *SSEL* lessons (ES = .94, p-value = <.000). Effects on challenging behavior were limited, although two classrooms demonstrated an overall decrease in challenging behavior (ES = -.20). Results further indicate this intervention increased feelings of teacher self-efficacy and was a socially valid approach; educators reported the aligned strategies were acceptable, sustainable, and beneficial to children. Limitations and implications of this study are further discussed with suggested directions for future research.

Keywords: Childhood, Classroom Management, Social-Emotional Learning, Consultation, Performance Feedback

Aligning Classroom Management Strategies with a Social Emotional Learning Curriculum in Early Childhood

A Need for Prevention in Early Childhood

Effective early childhood school settings include preventative systems of support, enabling educators to foster positive learning environments ripe for developing child social-emotional competencies (Hemmeter et al., 2015; McLeod et al., 2017). By strengthening the implementation of universal prevention programs, schools have the potential to cultivate resiliency and decrease the number of children requiring more intensive services (Durlak et al., 2011). Moreover, prosocial interactions between children and educators have been identified as a catalyst for facilitating the connection between instruction and optimized learning, rendering development of social competencies relevant for all children (Elias & Haynes, 2008). Children with under-developed social and emotional competencies tend to demonstrate challenges connecting with educators and peers, often resulting in a negative perception of self and a failure to develop prerequisite skills needed to navigate a school environment (Gunter et al., 2012). Further, research estimates that roughly 10-20% of children have at least one diagnosable mental health disorder and that nearly half of all of children will display symptoms or be diagnosed with a disorder by the age of 21 (Kessler et al., 2005; O'Connell et al., 2009).

Social Emotional Learning and Second Step

Social and Emotional Learning (SEL) refers to a child-centered strengths-based approach aiming to foster a core set of competencies including self-management, self-awareness, relationship skills, social awareness, and responsible decision making (Collaborative for Academic, Social, and Emotional Learning [CASEL], 2008; Durlak et al., 2011). Recognized as one of the most popular SEL curriculums, *Second Step* is a universal intervention aimed at increasing social emotional competencies for students in Pre-K-12th grade (Committee for Children, 1991; 1992a; 1992b; 1997). In a meta-analysis of the *Second Step* curriculum (Moy & Hazen, 2018), 5 of the 24 studies involved a Pre-K population, with outcomes including medium effect sizes for increasing prosocial behaviors (Beisly, 2011) and small effect sizes for reductions in antisocial behavior (McCabe, 2000; McMahon & Washburn, 2003) and increases in social-emotional knowledge (Neace & Muñoz, 2012).

Attempting to further bolster early childhood outcomes, a new version of *Second Step, Second Step Early Learning (SSEL;* Committee for Children, 2011*)* was developed. This SEL curriculum includes short Pre-K SEL lessons designed to be implemented daily, additionally targeting executive functioning competencies. In a two-year randomized trial with 31 Head Start and community preschool classrooms, results suggested significant improvements in children's executive functioning skills for those in the *SSEL* condition as compared to the *Creative Curriculum*, as well as smaller but significant effect sizes indicated for children's prosocial problem solving and emotion knowledge (Upshur et al., 2017). Supplemental follow-up studies with the *SSEL* curriculum found that the program continued to have significant and direct impact on executive functioning but no significant impact on social emotional skills (Upshur et al., 2019; Wenz-Gross et al., 2018). Although the *SSEL* curriculum is widely used, it has not been extensively studied and its effects on challenging behavior are unclear.

Proactive Classroom Management in Early Childhood

In addition to promoting children's social-emotional competencies, educators are charged with creating healthy classroom environments. Primary prevention strategies targeted at the classroom level can be utilized to support all children in the facilitation of prosocial interactions and reduction of challenging behaviors (Hemmeter et al., 2006). While SEL curricula tend to be child-centered, proactive classroom management practices implemented within a positive behavioral support model are often educator-centered with a focus on teaching skills, prompting, and acknowledging behaviors. Prosocial behaviors are taught and reinforced, while maladaptive behaviors are responded to consistently and preventatively (Sugai & Horner, 2006). Proactive classroom management strategies are described as effective and evidence-based for students with and without disabilities (Collins et al., 2018; Myers et al., 2017). Strategies such as modeling, multiple opportunities to respond, error corrections, behavior specific praise, and tangible reinforcement are successfully implemented in inclusive early childhood classrooms to decrease disruptive behaviors and increase prosocial skills (McLeod et al., 2017).

Facilitating Integration of SEL and Classroom Management Strategies

A growing body of research suggests that when SEL and positive behavioral classroom management strategies are implemented in combination, student mental health outcomes are bolstered, as compared to implementing one framework alone (Bradshaw et. al., 2014; Cook et. al., 2015; Reinke et. al., 2012). In an early childhood context, the Pyramid Model is a prominent framework that has provided an avenue for the integration of proactive classroom management practices and SEL (Fox, et al., 2003; Hemmeter, et al., 2006). The Pyramid Model largely aligns with the three-tiered Positive Behavior Interventions and Supports (PBIS) framework, utilizing evidence-based practices to promote social and emotional competencies for children 0-5 years. The Pyramid Model organizes evidence-based practices that include universal interventions for all children, more focused strategies for children who need targeted social-emotional supports, and individualized behavior support strategies for children with significant social skill deficits or persistent challenging behavior (Hemmeter, et al., 2006).

In classrooms where the Pyramid Model has been implemented, research has found significant improvements in the overall social skills of children with persistent behavioral challenges, as well as decreases in challenging behavior (Hemmeter, Fox, & Snyder, 2013; Hemmeter, et al., 2016). While the Pyramid Model framework is often utilized in early childhood settings, the framework itself does not include a specific social-emotional learning curriculum, and dozens of suggested evidence-based practices can leave some teachers feeling overwhelmed. In general, educators in Pre-K-12 classrooms tend to report inadequate preparation in classroom management and behavior in their college coursework and prior training (Hemmeter et al., 2015; Reinke et al., 2012; Simonsen et al., 2014). Moreover, an abundance of studies articulate the importance of extending past the time-limited professional development session to include a form of on-going follow-up support with educators (Fallon et al., 2015; Hemmeter et al., 2016). To enhance implementation, behavioral consultation with performance feedback has been shown to expedite educator behavior change and increase implementation fidelity of social-emotional and behavior practices in early childhood settings (Baughan, et al., 2019; Dufrene et al., 2012; Hemmeter et al., 2015). Moreover, the added benefits of graphic visual representation of performance feedback coupled with verbal feedback have been consistently documented (Collins et al., 2018; Fox et al., 2014; Simonson et al., 2010).

Current Study

The current study adds to the literature by conceptualizing outcomes of a brief educator training and weekly performance feedback, designed to align relevant SSEL lessons with specific positive behavioral classroom management strategies. This study focuses on the effects of this intervention on educator aligned intervention, social validity, and levels of children's challenging behavior. This research further aims to support implementation of primary practices of the Pyramid Model, drawing from research integrating SEL and PBIS at the elementary level with on-going consultation and performance feedback (Bradshaw, 2014; Cook et al., 2015; Reinke et al., 2012).

Method

Setting and Participants
Educator Participants

Participants included full-day Head Start educators (n = 4) and their classrooms from an urban setting in Western Massachusetts. Educator 1 was 39 years old, Caucasian, had 21 years of teaching experience, and had 6 students with Individualized Education Programs (IEPs). Educator 2 was 30 years old, Caucasian, had 5 years of teaching experience, and had 1 student with an IEP. Educator 3 was 23 years old, identified as Hispanic/Latina, had 3 years of teaching experience, and 6 students with IEPs. Educator 4 was 42 years old, also identified as Hispanic/Latina, had 17 years teaching of experience, and 10 students with IEPs. Of note, all the educators had less than 3 years experience in the current Head Start setting. While educators had some exposure implementing *SSEL*, implementation and alignment of the *SSEL* curriculum with other preventative classroom management practices had been identified as a need by the program director for these four classrooms in particular. All educators were provided $200 in compensation for their participation in the study.

Child Participants

Children (n = 73) included those in the four full-day low-income Head Start classrooms with educators participating in the current intervention. The four classrooms were comprised of approximately 17-20 children ages 3-5 years. These full-day classrooms have been determined to have the highest level of need within the Head Start program either due to a higher number of children with special education classification or higher reported problem behaviors. Children's ethnicity was 56% Hispanic, 22% African American, 14% biracial, and 8% Caucasian.

Design
 The current study employed a multiple-baseline design (MBL) over four months. The first three educators in the study were introduced concurrently, while the fourth educator was non-concurrent and entered the baseline phase four weeks behind the others. Baseline data collection occurred twice per week with at least five baseline data points used to conduct a within-phase analysis. To begin the intervention phase, at least three consecutive baseline data points related to teacher behavior needed to remain stable or demonstrate a downward trend (Kratochwill et al., 2010). In the intervention phase, when at least three data points indicated a clear alteration in level, trend, or variability for educator behavior, the next educator with the lowest stable baseline data began the intervention phase. Given the nature of the MBL design, each educator received the intervention phase for a slightly shorter period than the prior educator. Due to the study timeframe, educator baseline stability of aligned classroom management was used to determine introduction of the intervention phase, rather than also requiring maintenance of stability for child behavior.

Dependent Variables
Aligned SSEL Classroom Management Strategies
 As a primary dependent variable, the six specified classroom management strategies were operationally defined and listed under one of three categories: Anticipate, Remind, or Reinforce. This framework is consistent with another current early childhood SEL curriculum for promoting generalization of social emotional competencies (Whitcomb & Damico, 2016). In particular, aligned classroom management strategies were defined as strategies specifically related to the current *SSEL* skill of the week, or the *SSEL* skill from the previous week. For instance, if "Identification of happy and sad feelings" was the skill of the week, and "Asking for what you need or want" was the skill from the previous week,

any classroom management strategies related to these two skills were considered to be aligned.

Aligned SSEL Anticipate strategies included:
1. Modeling: Educator demonstrates or has a peer demonstrate, a skill to promote learning aligned with relevant *SSEL* skill.
2. Precorrections: Educator makes statement explaining desired behavior before starting a task or entering a new setting related to relevant *SSEL* skill.

Aligned *SSEL* Remind strategies included:
3. Opportunity to Respond: Educator provides opportunity and prompts child to attend and practice relevant *SSEL* skill.
4. Validation and redirection: Educator conveys understanding of emotion and states expected behavior after challenging behavior has occurred related to relevant *SSEL* skill.

Aligned SSEL Reinforce strategies included:
5. Behavior specific praise: Educator provides verbal comment indicating approval of relevant *SSEL* skill.
6. Tangible reinforcement: Educator provides tangible reward as a result of child demonstrating relevant SSEL skill.

Examples of aligned classroom management strategies with *SSEL* lessons were sent to educators ahead of time via email. One practice example included: "Show me a thumbs up if you think the girl in the story is feeling happy, or a thumbs down if you think she is feeling sad" while reading a story (Opportunity to Respond). The way to create a group contingency for children practicing the relevant *SSEL* skill was also shared with educators as an example (tangible reinforcement).

Challenging Behaviors

The presence of challenging behaviors within the entire classroom was assessed with the classroom observation form.

To maintain consistency in comparison of challenging behaviors, each educator was observed at the same time each day, primarily during a part of the school day identified by the educator as most challenging. The observers collecting data positioned themselves in an area where all children could be seen and heard in the classroom, moving as necessary to ensure consistent observation. Specific challenging behaviors coded included (a) taking materials from another child; (b) yelling; (c) hitting; (d) refusing to comply with head teacher direction after 2 requests; (e) spitting; (f) teasing; (g) swearing; (h) throwing objects; (i) kicking; (j) crying; (k) refusing to let another child play with them; (l) running around classroom; (m) putting hands on another child and/or pushing; (n) blurting out during a lesson. Operational definitions of each challenging behavior were given to observers during a 1-hour training where observers practiced coding videos of children, as well as during the actual observations.

Measures
Classroom Observation Form
The classroom observation form was specifically designed for this study to assess the occurrence of classroom management strategies aligned with *SSEL* lessons, as well as challenging child behaviors. Over a 30-minute time period, this study used a combined recording method of partial interval with a frequency count during 1-minute intervals to indicate the frequency of children's challenging behaviors. For aligned classroom management strategies, a similar frequency count within partial interval was employed using 1-minute intervals. This form tracked the activity, as well as the current and previous week's *SSEL* lesson. In addition, educator use of strategies related to *SSEL* lessons in general (beyond the current lessons) was also accounted for via frequency count, with qualitative indication of the referenced lesson. Classroom observations were conducted twice a week for 30 minutes during a predetermined time period in each classroom, and were

modeled after procedures utilized in a similar early childhood study (Stormont, 2007).

Inter-Observer Agreement (IOA)

Inter-observer agreement (IOA) was calculated using Cohen's Kappa (Uebersax, 1982) to discern the level of agreement between raters. Surpassing the guidelines suggested by What Works Clearinghouse (Kratochwill, et. al., 2010), interobserver observations were conducted by graduate students trained in study observation procedures for approximately 33 percent of observations in each educator's baseline and intervention phase. When rating educators' use of aligned strategies, Cohen's Kappa (κ) ranged from 0.73 to 0.86 across all classrooms, indicating substantial agreement between raters. Regarding observation of challenging behaviors, Kappa ranged from 0.62 to 0.78, also falling in the substantial range of rater agreement. These results suggest that interpretations drawn from the data collected can be discerned with a substantial level of certainty (Viera & Garrett, 2005).

Educator Self-Efficacy and Social Validity

To assess educator self-efficacy and general social validity, questions were administered with response options on a five-point Likert scale from (1) strongly disagree to (5) strongly agree and included questions targeting the following: Does consultation and performance feedback increase feelings of educator efficacy for classroom management? Do educators believe alignment and increased implementation will promote positive child outcomes as compared to implementing *Second Step* alone? Do educators believe these aligned practices are sustainable? At the end of all weekly performance feedback sessions, educators also rated their sense of self-efficacy on the same five-point Likert scale related to the following question, "This performance feedback session made me feel increased efficacy around my classroom management skills."

Intervention Components
Selection of SSEL Lessons
Eight *SSEL* lessons were chosen for the current intervention based on general relevance to the majority classroom population, the likelihood of ability to use/reinforce skills multiple times per day, and their breadth across the multiple domains of the SEL curriculum. All four educators implemented the selected *SSEL* lessons in the following order: focusing attention; following directions; asking for what you need; identifying happy and sad feelings; caring and helping; managing anger; managing waiting; fair ways to play. Educators were asked to implement the *SSEL* lessons, intended to be implemented daily, starting at the beginning of the week to ensure that at least one lesson had been taught before the first weekly observation was conducted.

Educator Professional Development Session
Following at least three stable baseline observations and prior to beginning weekly performance feedback consultation sessions, educators participated in a 1-hour, one-on-one professional development session with the primary investigator. At the beginning of the training session, educators were asked to report on their current implementation of *SSEL* lessons and any perceived barriers to implementation. The primary investigator then provided explicit instruction on how to align behaviorally oriented classroom management strategies with *SSEL* lessons. Given the current Head Start program's endorsement of the Pyramid Model and previous educator trainings, all educators had some familiarity with the given strategies. Using an Anticipate, Remind, Reinforce framework, the following aligned classroom strategies were described and demonstrated: (a) modeling; (b) pre-correction; (c) opportunities to respond; (d) validation and redirection; (e) behavior specific praise; (f) tangible reinforcers. These classroom management strategies have been commonly identified in the early childhood literature and rated by experts in the field as either useful or essential for improving social, emotional, and behavioral

outcomes in the classroom (Fox et al., 2003; McLeod, et al., 2017). The training session included (a) an overview of study purpose and procedures; (b) description of Anticipate, Remind, Reinforce framework; (c) definition of classroom management strategies; (e) skill steps; (f) multiple examples and non-examples including videos of strategies shown aligned with *SSEL* lessons; (g) numerous practice opportunities for teachers to identify aligned strategies in classroom videos with corrective feedback provided as necessary.

Performance Feedback Sessions

Derived from a behavioral consultation framework, performance feedback sessions began shortly after the professional development session had occurred (2-5 days). Performance feedback sessions were conducted weekly for approximately 15 minutes immediately following one of the two weekly classroom observations. Sessions were structured as follows:

1. Problem identification: visual feedback reviewing graph of aligned classroom management implementation and challenging behavior.
2. Verbal feedback on progress toward goals: identifying three specific strengths and three areas for improvement.
3. Problem analysis: discussing rationale for low skill implementation and strategies to increase implementation.
4. Plan development: weekly goal setting and modeling of strategies.
5. Answering any questions.
6. Completing fidelity checklist for consultation session.
7. Rating of self-efficacy regarding classroom management skills.

This format is relatively consistent with a recent study that used educator consultation to facilitate delivery of *SSEL* in a Head Start setting (Upshur, et al., 2017). Prior to the next observation, educators were sent an email with the current and previous week's *SSEL* lesson, their individualized goal, and several example scripts of how they could align all six classroom management strategies with the weekly *SSEL* lessons.

Results

Visual analysis indicates that for all four educators, the training plus performance feedback intervention was successful in increasing use of aligned classroom management strategies with weekly *SSEL* lessons. Data suggest this intervention had limited effects on challenging classroom behaviors. Visual analysis included acknowledging changes in level, trend, and variability as well as immediacy of effect, consistency, and overlap of data across phases. Tau-U analysis was further applied to demonstrate effect sizes between study phases, allowing for supplemental objectivity and precision beyond visual analysis. Results pertaining to each of the four educators follows, below.

Educator 1

During baseline, educator 1 demonstrated aligned classroom management strategies at a significantly low level with a few instances of aligned strategy use (non-significant), approaching the intervention phase. Regarding challenging behaviors for educator 1, while the trend of behaviors is generally stable in the baseline phase, there was an insignificant increase in trend mid-way through baseline observations.

In the intervention phase, educator 1's use of aligned classroom management strategies showed an immediate yet gradual increase in trend, followed by a pattern of decreasing and then increasing trend. The percentage of intervals, as well as the frequency in which aligned strategies were observed, increased during the intervention phase with no overlap between phases. Challenging behaviors indicated a gradual decrease in trend and level with increases in trend mid-intervention. Of note, although challenging behaviors showed a large amount of variability over the intervention phase, these increases in behavior were generally seen when aligned strategy use was low. Lowest levels of challenging behaviors were observed during times the teacher implemented the largest amount of aligned classroom management strategies. Overall, educator 1 exhibited a significant increase in their use of aligned classroom management strategies and a significant reduction was observed in classroom behaviors (Aligned strategy use Tau-U phase contrast = 1; Challenging behaviors Tau-U phase contrast = -0.70). See Figure 1, *Percent of Intervals Observed with Aligned Classroom Management Strategies and Challenging Behaviors*, for data on all four educators.

Educator 2

Observations from implementation of aligned classroom management strategies in baseline for educator 2 indicated some variability during the first few weeks of data collection. However, approaching the intervention phase, educator use of aligned strategies demonstrated more of a flat and consistent trend. Challenging behaviors showed a general increase in trend throughout baseline.

In intervention phase, educator 2 demonstrated an immediate positive trend in aligned strategy use with a notable increase in level. Although variability is rather high regarding aligned strategy use in the intervention condition, all intervention observations indicated higher aligned strategy use as compared to the baseline phase with no overlapping data points. Of note, the observed routine for educator 2 often included direct instruction, perhaps providing increased opportunities to facilitate child responses, as compared to routines observed with the other educators. Challenging behaviors observed in the intervention condition were highly variable with significant increases and decreases in trend. Although there was a slight increase in challenging behaviors, this is not considered significant as it was equal to one challenging behavior across a 30-minute observation period. Overall, this educator demonstrated a large significant increase in aligned strategy use with no observed decrease in children's challenging behaviors (Aligned strategy use

Tau-U phase contrast = 0.98; Challenging behaviors Tau-U phase contrast= 0.10).

Educator 3

Baseline data indicate that educator 3 demonstrated low aligned strategy use overall, with some variability in the beginning of baseline data collection. However, prior to approaching the intervention phase, the level of strategy use was more consistent with less variability. The level of challenging behaviors during baseline observations was high with large amounts of variability throughout and no apparent trend.

In the intervention phase, aligned strategy use showed an immediate increase in trend followed by a period of stability. This then decreased to near baseline levels at the end of intervention. Of note, average increase in trend regarding aligned strategy use throughout the intervention phase is significant. Challenging behaviors during the intervention phase showed high variability with no apparent trend. The frequency of challenging behaviors observed during intervention were similar to those observed during the baseline phase (e.g. high overlap in data) with a minor decrease in overall level. Overall, educator 3 demonstrated an increase in aligned strategy use. Although challenging behaviors did show a slight increase, this was not considered clinically significant (Aligned strategy use Tau-U phase contrast = .80; Challenging behaviors Tau-U phase contrast = .11).

Educator 4

During educator 4's baseline observations, data indicate generally low levels of aligned classroom management implementation with one observed instance of higher strategy use on the second observation. Level of challenging behaviors was high during baseline and indicates a large amount of variability throughout the initial phase. Given this variability, baseline data were corrected with Tau-U analysis.

When the intervention was introduced, data demonstrate a clear and immediate increase in trend and level for aligned strategy use. Challenging behaviors generally show a gradual decrease in trend and nearly half the level observed during baseline. Two instances of overlap in baseline and intervention phase data are indicated. Overall, educator four demonstrated a significant increase in aligned strategy implementation, indicating a large effect size, and a moderate reduction in challenging behaviors (Aligned strategy use Tau-U phase contrast = 1; Challenging behaviors Tau-U phase contrast = -.39).

Treatment Integrity

Fidelity of professional development and performance feedback sessions were evaluated using self-report integrity checklists completed by the school consultant. All professional development sessions were rated with 100% implementation fidelity, with minor adjustments made to the level of skill description based on the teacher's familiarity with the skill. Fidelity of individual teacher performance feedback sessions ranged from 94-97% implementation, with overall 95% implementation. At times, only one or two areas of educator strength or improvement were identified during performance feedback sessions, instead of the designated three. Moreover, in the few instances where visual feedback was not immediately reviewed due to the context of the environment (i.e., outside) these graphs were emailed to the educator with a brief description for interpretation. In general, visual, and verbal feedback were consistently provided in addition to problem analysis and plan development.

Social Validity

Employing formative measurement, during each performance feedback session in the intervention phase, all educators reported that they "agreed" or "strongly agreed" that the current intervention made them feel increased self-efficacy regarding their classroom management skills every week. Educators also completed a self-report social validity scale at the conclusion of the study regarding their belief that their classroom benefited from receiving the intervention. All educators indicated they "agreed" or "strongly agreed" with questions related to the current intervention's significance for positive child outcomes, feasibility, and sustainability. All educators also indicated they "agreed" or "strongly agreed" that they liked the procedures used in the intervention, that it was beneficial, and that alignment and increased implementation of classroom management strategies with the *SSEL* lessons would promote more positive student outcomes, as compared to implementing *SSEL* lessons alone. Moreover, three of the four educators reported they "strongly agreed" aligning classroom management strategies to *SSEL* lessons reduced challenging behaviors. When asked for suggestions for future improvements, some educators indicated a desire for additional lessons and a few acknowledged that certain lessons were dense with information.

Discussion

There is a critical need to support young children at-risk for early school failure due to behavioral and emotional challenges. Although the menu of evidence-based interventions for SEL and proactive classroom management continues to grow, a notable gap exists regarding the factors that ensure sufficient training and implementation fidelity (Hemmeter et al., 2015). The current study adds to the literature by using consultation with performance feedback to align classroom management strategies with the *SSEL* curriculum in a Head Start program. In addition, it aims to expand the role of the school psychologist to facilitate integrated preventative practices in preschool settings. The purpose of this research was to understand the effects of a brief professional development session and weekly performance feedback on educator implementation of aligned *SSEL* lessons and classroom management practices, on children's challenging behaviors, as well as its social validity.

Figure 1

Percent of Intervals Observed with Aligned Classroom Management Strategies and Challenging Behaviors

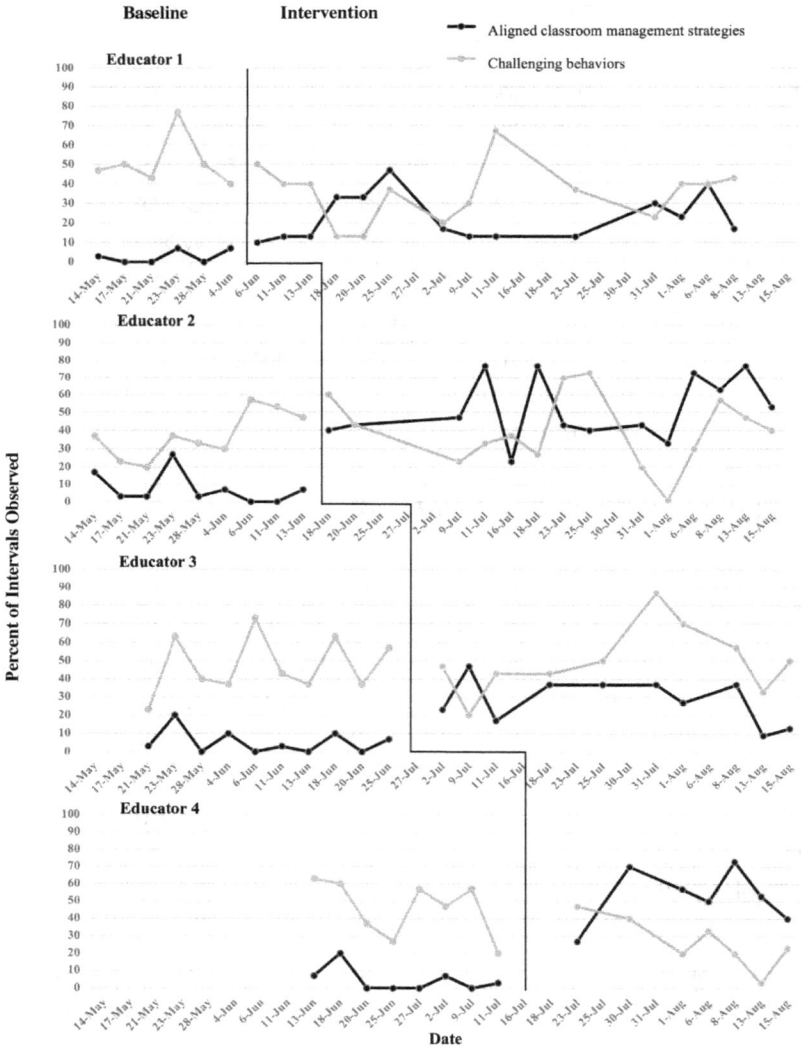

Table 1

Frequency of Second Step Early Learning (SSEL) Strategy Use

	Pre - Average frequency (#) of aligned strategies implemented per 30-minute observation	Post - Average frequency (#) of aligned strategies implemented per 30-minute observation	Pre – Average frequency of other *SSEL* lessons referred to outside of current week's lessons per 30-minute observation	Post - Average frequency of other *SSEL* lessons referred to outside of current week's lessons per 30-minute observation
Educator 1	0.83	10.36	6.67	11.57
Educator 2	3.22	34.36	7.33	18.21
Educator 3	1.90	13.00	2.70	6.56
Educator 4	2.00	36.86	3.13	15.00

Table 2

Tau-U Analysis

	Within phase aligned strategy use	Phase contrast aligned strategy use	Within phase challenging behaviors	Phase contrast Challenging behaviors
Educator 1	0.20	1.00	-0.13	-0.70
Educator 2	-0.25	.98	0.36	0.10
Educator 3	-0.11	0.80	0.11	0.11
Educator 4	-0.18	1.00	-0.46	-0.39
Tau-*U* effect size		0.94*		-0.20
Confidence Interval (95%)		.67 – 1.00		.48 - .07

**p $< .01$

Table 3
Social Validity Results

1 = Strongly disagree, 2=Disagree, 3=Neither agree nor disagree, 4=Agree, 5= Strongly agree					
	Educator 1	Educator 2	Educator 3	Educator 4	Mean
This consultation model (professional development session and performance feedback) was an acceptable intervention for aligning classroom management skills with *SSEL* lessons.	5	5	5	5	5
This consultation model made me feel increased efficacy around my classroom management skills.	5	5	5	4	4.75
Integrating prevention efforts, such as aligning classroom management strategies with *SSEL* lessons, is important.	5	5	5	5	5
I liked the procedures used in the consultation model.	5	5	5	5	5
Aligning classroom management strategies with *SSEL* lessons increases children's generalization of social emotional competencies.	5	5	4	5	4.75
Aligning classroom management strategies to *SSEL* lessons reduced challenging behaviors in my classroom.	5	5	3	5	4.5
I believe alignment and increased implementation of classroom management strategies with the *SSEL* lessons will promote more positive child outcomes as compared to implementing *SSEL* lessons alone.	5	5	4	5	4.75
This invention was meaningful for the children in my classroom.	5	5	4	5	4.75
I believe these aligned classroom management strategies are sustainable.	5	4	4	5	4.5
Overall, the consultation model was beneficial.	5	5	5	5	5

Interpretation of Findings

Overall findings suggest that a 1-hour professional development session followed by weekly consultative support with performance feedback significantly increased educator use of classroom management strategies aligned with the relevant *SSEL* social emotional learning lessons of the week. This functional relationship between direct observation and performance feedback on educator strategy use further indicated a relatively immediate impact with aligned strategy use, increasing within two weeks after the intervention was introduced. It was observed that children received explicit *SSEL* lessons and were also encouraged to practice, were redirected, and were praised for using recently learned social emotional skills multiple times throughout the week. Results further suggest that educators increased their use of language related to all *SSEL* lessons in general. Recognizing implementation barriers associated with the larger Pyramid Model framework (Hemmeter et al., 2016), increasing implementation of key preventative practices within this model may be most efficient and advantageous to facilitate teacher behavior change. Many early childhood educators have also expressed desire to receive implementation support of preventative practices (Fox et al., 2003; Hemmeter, 2006). Acknowledging the importance of educator self-efficacy in the reduction of burn-out (Reinke, 2012), the current educators' formative and summative reports of increased self-efficacy around their classroom management skills is encouraging.

Regarding the intervention's effectiveness on children's challenging behaviors, two out of four classrooms had an average reduction in challenging behavior, although this change was not at the level of significance to establish that the intervention was effective in reducing student challenging behaviors. Moreover, variability during baseline allows for limited conclusion of results. Reasons for this finding of minimal effects on challenging behaviors could vary. Although there are numerous benefits to conducting research in preschool settings for children with and without disabilities, this universal intervention was not intended to provide support to remediate all challenging behaviors, such as those for which individualized education plans may be needed. In addition, given the measurement of classroom behaviors as a whole, it is difficult to discern if classroom behaviors would have decreased more significantly if behaviors were calculated based on a selection of a few children in the classroom, rather than the classroom in its entirety. Of note, although visual and Tau-U analysis imply minimal reductions in behaviors, social validity data from three educators conversely suggests that the educators' believed the current intervention did lead to a reduction in challenging behaviors in their classroom. This could be a reflection of increased efficacy regarding their classroom management skills.

Limitations

While these outcomes suggest several promising implications, they are not without limitations. A first limitation involves reactive experimental arrangements. Although direct observation and performance feedback are often salient methods to facilitate increased implementation, serious consideration must be given to reactivity that occurs in educator behavior as a result of being observed and provided feedback on a regular schedule. Selection bias may also be present in this study due to a few educators being increasingly familiar with *SSEL* lessons or classroom management strategies over others.

A second limitation of the current study is the use of only one dependent variable related to aligned classroom management strategies in determining stability in trend or level prior to beginning the intervention phase. Due to the limited timeframe of the study that often exists in school settings, it was not feasible to also require stability in both challenging behaviors and aligned classroom management strategies. This limitation impacts the interpretation of changes in challenging behaviors as a result of the current intervention, as two of the educators' classrooms were exhibiting a downward trend in the frequency of challenging behaviors just prior to the intervention.

A third limitation involves ambiguity around the amount of classroom management skill use needed to observe a change in challenging behaviors. There is minimal research and lack of professional standards on the optimal rate of using each behavioral skill to measure meaningful child behavior change (Simonsen et al., 2010). Likewise, variability may exist among the *SSEL* lessons to be incorporated into the general classroom context. Although all educators followed the same lesson sequence, each educator began receiving the intervention phase during a different *SSEL* lesson.

Future Research

Given the preliminary nature of this study, additional research should investigate similar questions while ensuring implementation fidelity of all lessons in the *SSEL* curriculum. A comparable study with a longer duration of intervention may further facilitate positive changes in child challenging behavior, as a result of increased exposure to the social emotional curriculum and aligned classroom management strategies. Moreover, for long-term feasibility purposes, after educators have achieved a consistently high rate of aligned classroom management practices with the weekly *SSEL* lessons, it may be beneficial to fade on-going consultative support. Supplemental research is also needed regarding the type of measure that may be most appropriate for measuring short-term and long-term prevention outcomes associated with many SEL curriculums. Current standardized measures of behavior may not fully capture all intended outcomes over time and the extent of the effectiveness of the program; for instance, many SEL curricula do not have their own assessment measures beyond that of emotion knowledge (Greenberg & Abenavoli, 2017).

Additional research is further warranted to assess the effectiveness of each component of the training session and performance feedback. Lastly, supplemental studies should investigate for whom this intervention is most effective. Research is needed to determine if this intervention may be more effective for new educators who are still developing their classroom management strategies, or for more experienced educators who may have already internalized several classroom management strategies and could find it more feasible to integrate daily classroom management strategies with an SEL curriculum. While most classroom management strategies tend to be simple in nature, the consistent and purposeful implementation of strategies aligned with an SEL curriculum often requires forethought and follow-though.

References

Baughan, C., Correa, V. I., & Muharib, R. (2019). Coaching Head Start teachers on the use of Teaching Pyramid Model practices in the classroom. *HS Dialog: The Research to Practice Journal for the Early Childhood Field, 22*(1).

Beisly, A. (2011). Emotional competence in a pre-kindergarten classroom: Links to social and emotional competence. (*Doctoral dissertation, ProQuest Dissertations and Theses* database, UMI No. 1495027).

Bradshaw, C. P., Bottiani, J. H., Osher, D., & Sugai, G. (2014). The integration of positive behavioral interventions and supports and social and emotional learning. In M. D. Weist, N. A. Lever, C. P. Bradshaw, & J. S. Owens (Eds.), *Handbook of School Mental Health: Research, Training, Practice, and Policy* (pp. 101-118). Springer.

Collaborative for Academic, Social, and Emotional Learning. (2008). *Social and emotional learning (SEL) and student benefits: Implications for the safe schools/healthy students core elements.* http://www.casel.org/downloads/edC_

Collins, L. W., Cook, S. C., Sweigart, C. A., & Evanovich, L. L. (2018). Using performance feedback to increase special education teachers' use of effective practices. *Teaching Exceptional Children, 51*(2), 125-133.

Committee for Children. (1991). *Second Step: A violence prevention curriculum; Preschool-kindergarten.* Seattle, WA: Author.

Committee for Children. (1992a). *Second Step: A violence prevention curriculum; Grades 1–3.* Seattle, WA: Author.

Committee for Children. (1992b). *Second Step: A violence prevention curriculum; Grades 4–5.*Seattle, WA: Author.

Committee for Children. (1997). *Second Step: A violence prevention curriculum; Middle school/junior high.* Seattle, WA: Author.

Committee for Children (2011). *Second Step Early Learning Program.* Seattle, WA: Committee for Children.

Cook, C. R., Frye, M., Slemrod, T., Lyon, A. R., Renshaw, T. L., & Zhang, Y. (2015). An integrated approach to universal prevention: Independent and combined effects of PBIS and SEL on youths' mental health. *School Psychology Quarterly, 30*(2), 166.

Dufrene, B. A., Parker, K., Menousek, K., Zhou, Q., Harpole, L. L., & Olmi, D. J. (2012). Direct behavioral consultation in Head Start to increase teacher use of praise and effective instruction delivery. *Journal of Educational and Psychological Consultation, 22*(3), 159-186.

Durlak, J. A., Weissberg, R. P., Dymnicki, A. B., Taylor, R. D., & Schellinger, K. B. (2011). The impact of enhancing students' social and emotional learning: A meta-analysis of school-based universal interventions. *Child Development, 82*, 405–432.

Elias, M. J., & Haynes, N. M. (2008). Social competence, social support, and academic achievement in minority, low-income, urban elementary school children. *School Psychology Quarterly, 23*(4), 474.

Fallon, L. M., Collier-Meek, M. A., Maggin, D. M., Sanetti, L. M., & Johnson, A. H. (2015). Is performance feedback for educators an evidence-based practice? A systematic review and evaluation based on single-case research. *Exceptional Children, 81*(2), 227-246.

Fox, L., Dunlap, G., Hemmeter, M. L., Joseph, G. E., & Strain, P. S. (2003). The teaching pyramid: A model for supporting social competence and preventing challenging behavior in young children. *Young Children, 58*, 48–52.

Fox, L., Veguilla, M., & Perez Binder, D. (2014). Data decision-making and program-wide implementation of the Pyramid Model. *Roadmap to effective intervention practices #7*. University of South Florida, Technical Assistance Center on Social Emotional Intervention for Young Children.

Greenberg, M.T., & Abenavoli, R. (2017). Universal interventions: Fully exploring their impacts and potential to produce population-level impacts. *Journal of Research on Educational Effectiveness, 10*, 40–67.

Gunter, L., Caldarella, P., Korth, B. B., & Young, K. R. (2012). Promoting social and emotional learning in preschool students: A study of Strong Start Pre-K. *Early Childhood Education Journal, 40*(3), 151-159.

Hemmeter, M. L., Hardy, J. K., Schnitz, A. G., Adams, J. M., & Kinder, K. A. (2015). Effects of training and coaching with performance feedback on teachers' use of Pyramid Model practices. *Topics in Early Childhood Special Education, 35*(3), 144-156.

Hemmeter, M. L., Ostrosky, M., & Fox, L. (2006). Social and emotional foundations for early learning: A conceptual model for intervention. *School Psychology Review, 35*(4), 583.

Hemmeter, M. L., Snyder, P. A., Fox, L., & Algina, J. (2016). Evaluating the implementation of the Pyramid Model for promoting social-emotional competence in early childhood classrooms. *Topics in Early Childhood Special Education, 36*(3), 133-146.

Kessler, R. C., Berglund, P., Demler, O., Jin, R., Merikangas, K. R., & Walters, E. E. (2005). Lifetime prevalence and age-of-onset distributions of DSM-IV disorders in the National Comorbidity Survey Replication. *Archives of General Psychiatry, 62*(6), 593-602.

Kratochwill, T. R., Hitchcock, J., Horner, R. H., Levin, J. R., Odom, S. L., Rindskopf, D. M., & Shadish, W. R. (2010). Single-case designs technical documentation. *What works clearinghouse.*

McCabe, L. A. (2000). Violence prevention in early childhood: Implementing the *Second Step* curriculum in child care and head start classrooms. *ProQuest Dissertations and Theses database*, UMI No. 9941173.

McLeod, B. D., Sutherland, K. S., Martinez, R. G., Conroy, M. A., Snyder, P. A., & Southam-Gerow, M. A. (2017). Identifying common practice elements to improve social, emotional, and behavioral outcomes of young children in early childhood classrooms. *Prevention Science, 18*(2), 204-213.

McMahon, S. D., & Washburn, J. J. (2003). Violence prevention: An evaluation of program effects with urban African American students. *Journal of Primary Prevention,* 24, 43–62.

Moy, G. E., & Hazen, A. (2018). A systematic review of the *Second Step* program. *Journal of School Psychology, 71*, 18-41.

Myers, D., Freeman, J., Simonsen, B., & Sugai, G. (2017). Classroom management with exceptional learners. *Teaching Exceptional Children, 49*(4), 223-230.

Neace, W. P., & Muñoz, M. A. (2012). Pushing the boundaries of education: Evaluating the impact of Second Step®: A violence prevention curriculum with psychosocial and non-cognitive measures. *Child & Youth Services, 33*(1), 46-69.

O'Connell, M. E., Boat, T., & Warner, K. E. (2009). *Preventing mental, emotional, and behavioral disorders among young people: Progress and possibilities* (Vol. 7). National Academies Press.

Reinke, W. M., Herman, K. C., Darney, D., Pitchford, J., Becker, K., Domitrovich, C., & Ialongo, N. (2012). Using the classroom check-up model to support implementation of PATHS to PAX. *Advances in School Mental Health Promotion, 5*(3), 220-232.

Simonsen, B., Myers, D., & DeLuca, C. (2010). Teaching teachers to use prompts, opportunities to respond, and specific praise. *Teacher Education and Special Education, 33*(4), 300-318.

Stormont, M. A., Smith, S. C., & Lewis, T. J. (2007). Teacher implementation of precorrection and praise statements in Head Start classrooms as a component of a program-wide system of positive behavior support. *Journal of Behavioral Education, 16*(3), 280-290.

Sugai, G., & Horner, R. R. (2006). A promising approach for expanding and sustaining school-wide positive behavior support. *School Psychology Review, 35*(2), 245-259.

Uebersax, J. S. (1982). A generalized kappa coefficient. *Educational and Psychological Measurement, 42*(1), 181-183.

Upshur, C. C., Heyman, M., & Wenz-Gross, M. (2017). Efficacy trial of the Second Step Early Learning (SSEL) curriculum: Preliminary outcomes. *Journal of Applied Developmental Psychology, 50*, 15-25.

Upshur, C. C., Wenz-Gross, M., Rhoads, C., Heyman, M., Yoo, Y., & Sawosik, G. (2019). A randomized efficacy trial of the Second Step Early Learning (SSEL) curriculum. *Journal of Applied Developmental Psychology, 62*, 145-159.

Viera, A. J., & Garrett, J. M. (2005). Understanding interobserver agreement: The kappa statistic. *Family Medicine, 37*(5), 360-363.

Wenz-Gross, M., Yoo, Y., Upshur, C. C., & Gambino, A. J. (2018). Pathways to kindergarten readiness: The roles of second step early learning curriculum and social emotional, executive functioning, preschool academic and task behavior skills. *Frontiers in Psychology*, 1886.

Whitcomb, S. A., & Damico, D. M. P. (2016). Merrell's Strong Start—Pre-K.

Appendix

Social Validity Questionnaire

1. This consultation model (professional development session and performance feedback) was an acceptable intervention for aligning classroom management skills with *SSEL* lessons.
   1. Strongly disagree
   2. Disagree
   3. Neither agree nor disagree
   4. Agree
   5. Strongly agree

2. This consultation model made me feel increased efficacy around my classroom management skills.
   1. Strongly disagree
   2. Disagree
   3. Neither agree nor disagree
   4. Agree
   5. Strongly agree

3. Integrating prevention efforts, such as aligning classroom management strategies with *SSEL* lessons, is important.
   1. Strongly disagree
   2. Disagree
   3. Neither agree nor disagree
   4. Agree
   5. Strongly agree

4. I liked the procedures used in the consultation model.
   1. Strongly disagree
   2. Disagree
   3. Neither agree nor disagree
   4. Agree
   5. Strongly agree

5. Aligning classroom management strategies with *Second Step* lessons increases children's generalization of social emotional competencies.
    1. Strongly disagree
    2. Disagree
    3. Neither agree nor disagree
    4. Agree
    5. Strongly agree

6. Aligning classroom management strategies to *SSEL* lessons reduced challenging behaviors in my classroom.
    1. Strongly disagree
    2. Disagree
    3. Neither agree nor disagree
    4. Agree
    5. Strongly agree

7. I believe alignment and increased implementation of classroom management strategies with the *SSEL* lessons will promote more positive child outcomes as compared to implementing *SSEL* lessons alone.
    1. Strongly disagree
    2. Disagree
    3. Neither agree nor disagree
    4. Agree
    5. Strongly agree

8. This invention was meaningful for the children in my classroom.
    1. Strongly disagree
    2. Disagree
    3. Neither agree nor disagree
    4. Agree
    5. Strongly agree

9. I believe these aligned classroom management strategies are sustainable.
   1. Strongly disagree
   2. Disagree
   3. Neither agree nor disagree
   4. Agree
   5. Strongly agree

10. Overall, the consultation model was beneficial.
    1. Strongly disagree
    2. Disagree
    3. Neither agree nor disagree
    4. Agree
    5. Strongly agree

11. What suggestions do you have for improvement for the future?

Avoiding the Summer Slide: Tier One and Two Supports Targeting Early Readers

Sarah W. Harry, Breya L. Whitefield, Kayla E. Bates-Brantley, and Lauren McKinley

Abstract

For more than 100 years, the "summer slide," or the learning losses by students following a long summer break, have been well documented. On average, a typical student loses a little more than one month's worth of skill across each academic area (e.g., language arts and mathematics) throughout the summer months. Research has also demonstrated that the "summer slide" has a particularly harmful impact on reading achievement of students from low-socioeconomic status (SES) backgrounds. The purpose of the present study was to investigate the effectiveness of a tiered system of support for oral reading fluency in early elementary school aged students as part of a summer day camp program, to mitigate some of the academic loss that typically occurs. All students attending the summer day camp completed a survey-level assessment (SLA) process using AIMSweb materials to determine their instructional level in reading. Following the assessment, students were placed in tiered groups where they received intervention up to three times a week for 30 minutes, and progress was monitored weekly. Results were mixed across participants; however, nine of the 11 participants made gains by the end of the summer, and four of 11 participants performed above the predicted summer slide for the grade level they had completed in the spring. Limitations and future directions for research are also discussed for furthering supports in this area.

Keywords: summer reading, summer slide, early elementary, reading intervention

Avoiding the Summer Slide: Tier One and Two Supports Targeting Early Readers

Learning to read is one of the most important skills a child acquires during early elementary school. Oral reading fluency (ORF) often sets the foundation for students' future academic success or failure. ORF is traditionally defined as a student's ability to read with "accuracy and fluency with connected text," when given a one-minute passage (University of Oregon, 2020, p.11). This skill is frequently cited as a predictive factor for a number of long-term academic outcomes (Stevens et al., 2015). Due to its critical importance, it is not surprising that ensuring a child becomes a fluent reader is on the forefront of education literature and a concern for many classroom educators (Hosp & Suchey, 2014).

Reading proficiency, defined as the ability for students to meet state reading standards through readiness, formative, and/or summative assessments, becomes a significant milestone in a student's educational trajectory as proficient reading skills are necessary for subsequent academic success (Liebfreund et al., 2022). Over the past fifteen years, educators have felt increased pressure to ensure that by the end of third grade, all students are proficiently reading as they make the transition from reading to learn instead of learning to read (Toler, 2012). These standards vary by state based upon what assessment is utilized, but reading level can be a means of promotion or retention to the next grade. While great strides have been made across the domain of evidence-based reading interventions (Hatcher et al., 2006; Jones, Conradi, & Amendum 2016; Scammacca et al., 2016), there is a lack of clear remediation strategies when students do not acquire the skills within this developmental window (i.e., first through third grades). Thus, students who are falling behind in reading abilities receive little-to-no support in bolstering reading skills outside of the academic year, especially if they are above third grade.

Reading Exposure, SES, and MTSS

One suggested strategy to mitigate reading deficits is simply to read. Even reading 15 minutes per day has been shown to have marked improvements for early readers (van Bergan et al., 2018). However, across many American households, students are not reading for even this small, suggested amount of time. A 2013 National Endowment for the ARTS (NEA) report indicated that youth are reading on average fewer than 12 minutes per day (Dillon et al., 2017). This deficit is compounded for children in economically disadvantaged areas. For example, low SES students are more likely to live in neighborhoods that are less conducive to education achievement in terms of peer support and role models (Dietrichson et al., 2017). Additionally, it has been found that by the end of second grade, oral language, which is predictive of later oral reading fluency success, differences of up to 4,000 words has been found between same-grade students (Wendling and Mather, 2008). This is largely related to differences in exposure to words during development, which is also largely attributed to SES level (Wendling and Mather, 2008).

The supports offered to students who are falling behind, compared to their same-age peers, are largely limited to within the academic year during classroom time. One problem-solving approach that schools use to support students, both academically and behaviorally, is the multi-tiered system of supports (MTSS; Fuchs & Fuchs, 2006). This provides student-specific support depending on skill level. Tier One supports are universal (i.e., across the whole school and classroom), while Tier Two supports are provided in a smaller group, and Tier Three supports are individualized (Batsche, et al., 2005). By understanding and collecting data at the Tier One level, educators and staff members are able to better understand students who may need more intervention. While MTSS is a beneficial approach during the school year, a student's SES level can still create additional setbacks as students from a lower SES background do not have the same access to resources, support, or materials outside of school and while on breaks. However, as most teachers know, learning should not stop when the academic year is completed. The average school year is 180 days, meaning a child has 185 days during which they are not in school (National Center for Education Statistics, 2020). In addition, very few schools provide an extended school year, meaning that for most students, the days out of school are clumped into a long cluster of time (i.e., summer break). Taken together, when students leave school for extended times, it is not uncommon for them to return to school in the fall with lower academic performance scores than when they left school in the spring (Fälth et al., 2019). This is often referred to as the "summer slide."

The Summer Slide

Notably, the pattern of achievement growth for individual students reflects an upward learning trajectory during the academic year, but a slowing or loss of learning during the summer period. For more than 100 years, the "summer slide," or the learning losses by students following a long summer break, has been well documented (Borman & Dowling, 2006). Specifically, a typical student loses a little more than one month's worth of skill across each academic area (e.g., reading; Cooper et al., 1996).

Research has also demonstrated that the "summer slide" has a particularly harmful impact on reading achievement of students from low SES backgrounds. Specifically, on average, students from low-SES backgrounds fall approximately three months behind their middle-class peers over the summer (Cooper et al., 1996; Slates et al., 2012). These declines in reading are even more pronounced for students from low-SES families in large cities (McDaniel et al., 2017; Fälth et al., 2019; Schmitt et al., 2019; Beach & Philippakos, 2020) due to limited resources and opportunities to practice reading. This difference is equivalent to the amount of learning that takes place during one third of the school year. The negative impact on low-SES students is cumulative and observed every summer following academic instruction.

Alexander and colleagues (2001) sought to explain this phenomenon with the "faucet theory," in that a faucet of resources is available during the school year, but when summer arrives, low SES students are left in a drought of resources (Allington et al., 2010). In contrast, students from high SES backgrounds have more resources year-round (Borman, Benson, & Overman, 2005) and continue to have access to these resources during the summer months. Thus, students from low SES backgrounds may be more vulnerable to the summer slide (Lenhoff et al., 2020; Alexander, Entwisle, &Kabbani, 2001; Alexander, Entwisle & Olson, 2007). This low-SES summer slide trend has been observed repeatedly in the literature (e.g., Burkam et al., 2004; Cooper et al., 1996; McCombes-Tolis & Feinn, 2008; Zvoch & Stevens, 2013). However, students who attended summer school with lengthy and inclusive literacy instruction demonstrated significantly improved oral reading fluency (ORF) rates (Zvoch & Stevens, 2015).

In addition, research has found that students learn best when instruction is continuous. A three-month summer vacation breaks the rhythm of literacy instruction, leads to forgetting of material, and requires that a significant amount of time be spent on review of old material when students return to school in the fall (Cooper et al., 1996).

Summer Slide Remediation

Given that literacy is essential for success in college and in the workplace, several programs have attempted to support students' literacy skills (Beach & Philippakos, 2020). Summer reading programs (SRPs) are one strategy that has been shown to prevent reading loss (Bowers & Schwarz, 2018) when implemented with fidelity.

Summer programs that implement literacy lessons are designed to remediate past reading weaknesses, or to prepare for skills and knowledge that students may encounter in the upcoming year (Garst & Ozier, 2015). Research has shown that providing youth with summer reading opportunities can help them develop a range of reading skills. Most notably, meta-analyses of summer learning programs report positive effects of about .20 to .25 standard deviations when outcomes are collected using ORF measures immediately after participation and at long-term follow-up (Beach & Philippakos, 2020). These summer reading programs are beneficial for students by supplementing school-year learning, closing the achievement gap, and providing beneficial and motivating educational experiences (Schmitt et al., 2019).

The challenge for families, and their respective students, becomes engaging students in summer reading programs. A study conducted by Becnel et al. (2017) found that students who self-identified as readers were more likely to participate in SRPs than those who did not. In addition, those who participated in SRPs cited parental influence and boredom as their primary motivations. In order to engage students in the summer reading process, many community-based resources (e.g., libraries), host reading programs. Public librarians offer a variety of incentives to attract students' attention and motivate them to register for library-sponsored summer reading programs (Small et al., 2017). Summer reading programs in public libraries have been a stalwart of programming for youth for more than a century (Small et al., 2017). These programs are intended to encourage students to continue reading throughout the summer, practice communication skills, and develop a lifelong voluntary reading habit in a safe and friendly learning environment. For example, some libraries frame summer reading programs as a "challenge" in which students earn prizes based on quantitative measures such as number of pages and books read (Small et al., 2017). Students can track progress towards reading goals in order to meet pre-determined expectations, resulting in prizes. Having students work towards quantitative measures of reading increases their reading achievement outcomes (Garst & Ozier, 2015).

Methods of remediating summer reading loss include community-based programming from libraries, providing resources (e.g., instruction, books) to families, and promoting parental encouragement of reading with their children. Through these processes, the summer reading slide can be appropriately addressed so that students transition back into the academic year maintaining their previous level of reading skills. Despite several methodologies to support students' reading skills and ensure they are maintaining their reading level throughout the school year and beyond, scant literature exists on the implications of summer reading programs on ORF for low SES students that target their specific level of support.

Purpose

The purpose of the present study was to help mitigate typical summer loss in oral reading fluency for low SES early elementary aged students in the southeast part of the United States. Researchers divided students based on SLA data into three groups to support their specific ORF needs during the summer reading program. It was hypothesized that students would roughly follow the typical 80%, 15%, and 5% division of MTSS/RTI (Loftus-Rattan et al., 2021) following the SLA process. Researchers then provided tier-specific intervention to help avoid summer reading loss. The following questions were specifically analyzed during this study:

- Will there be gain, loss, or maintenance of ORF skill for students exiting kindergarten through third grade when given a tier-specific intervention?
- Will there be a difference in performance outcome based on how many intervention sessions students were able to attend?
- Will students overall find the interventions to be socially valid?

Method

Participants and Setting

The study included 41 students with written parental consent obtained prior to the start of the summer, which was over half of the total students attending the summer day program. Parents were given the choice when completing initial paperwork for the day camp for their student to receive academic support in lieu of an open gym time. All participants attended a school within the city's public school district, which contains nine schools (i.e., six elementary, two middle, and one high school) with roughly 4,000 students. Although individual demographic data were not available for the 41 students who participated in the program, the following data are shared to provide context for the school district these students attended. The student body of the district consisted primarily of 88% Black, 6% Hispanic, and 3% White individuals. Seventy-seven percent of students were eligible for free and reduced lunch, and 4% of students were English language learners. These statistics are representative of the participant base from this study. District test scores indicated that while in elementary school 40% of students performed at or above their expected grade level for reading; however, by the time these students entered high school this dropped to 27%. The current high school graduation rate is 83%, which is slightly below the national average of 88% (NCES, 2019).

The study was completed at a local elementary school where students attended the summer day camp three times a week. Researchers were present all three days the students were at the school, and the SLA and tiered interventions occurred in individual classrooms within the building. The school building was undergoing some minor construction during the study, but the influence of any background noise or interruption appeared to cause little reactivity, if any.

Materials

Survey Level Assessment

All students were assessed using an SLA process to determine their current grade level performance on Oral Reading Fluency

(ORF) probes using AIMSweb 1.0 printed materials (Shinn & Shinn, 2002). These materials required an administrator to follow along as the student read aloud for one minute and observed for any errors. Following this process, students were divided into one of three tiers for support.

Progress Monitoring

Students' progress was monitored each week using the AIMSweb materials so that comparisons could be made between initial assessment (i.e., the SLA process) and tiered interventions that were provided.

Generalization

Students were administered weekly administered passages from the district's adopted curriculum. These data provided a measure of generalization for student ORF skills based on district curriculum in conjunction with skill development based on random probes (i.e., AIMSweb weekly progress monitoring).

Intervention

Tier One

If a student was placed in Tier One, their intervention materials included access to a wide selection of reading material from the university's library that ranged in reading difficulty. All books were labeled with their corresponding Lexile value, which was determined via the lexile.com tool (Lexile, 2022). For example, an early chapter book like the Junie B. Jones series by Barbara Park, would be a title that ranges 330L-560L depending upon which book is selected. This range of scores means that these books are between an upper kindergarten to early third grade reading level. Kindergarten Lexile ranges are 110L-430L, first grade ranges are 190L-460L, second grade ranges are 380L-580L, and third grade ranges are 510L-700L (MAP, 2021). Lexile takes into consideration the rate, accuracy, readability, and difficulty of a passage when it is calculated (Ardoin et al., 2010). This "mini library" included everything from picture books to chapter books so that students of all reading levels could find appropriate reading material.

Tier Two

If a student was placed in Tier Two, intervention passages from Dynamic Indicators of Basic Early Literacy Skills (DIBELS; University of Oregon, 2018) Eighth Edition were used. Students were also given a timer to implement the intervention and a checklist to ensure that the intervention was being implemented accurately.

Social Validity

The Child Usage Rating Profile (CURP) was used as a measure of social validity for the study (Briesch & Chafouleas 2009). The CURP is a student self-report measure with 21 questions using a four-point Likert scale with a 1 indicating "I totally disagree" and 4 indicating "I totally agree." The scale assesses students' perception across three domains: personal desirability, feasibility and understanding of an intervention with scores closest to 4.0 indicating the highest social acceptability.

Dependent Measures

The primary dependent variable was words read correct per minute (WRCPM) on ORF passages. WRCPM was operationally defined as any word that a student read correctly within 3 seconds during a one-minute read. This was compared against a calculated summer slide value which was dependent upon the grade level at which the student was instructionally performing.

Procedures

The participants in this study were enrolled in a community-based summer day camp that met five days a week. Through a partnership with a local university, and approval through the university's institutional review board, trained undergraduate and graduate students conducted assessment and intervention three times a week (i.e., Monday, Wednesday, and Friday) for a total of 20 days (i.e., three SLA days and 17 intervention sessions). Following the SLA process, students were divided into a tiered group where they received at least 30 minutes of reading intervention each day.

Training

Seven doctoral-level graduate students and six undergraduate psychology and education majors were supervised by one faculty member on the implementation of this project. The doctoral-level graduate students all had prior training with curriculum-based measurement (CBM) administration through didactic course work. Two fourth year students facilitated the day-to-day of the programming and led an initial training for the graduate and undergraduate student volunteers. This was a required one-hour training which briefed everyone on the premise of the study, familiarized them with intervention protocols, and discussed treatment integrity and interobserver agreement forms, which was the primary task of the student volunteers.

Survey-Level Assessment (SLA)

All students with parental consent, either at the beginning of the summer, or when they began attending the camp, were administered AIMSweb probes at the grade level they had just completed the previous spring. Students were typically given three probes to obtain a median score, but some students were only given two if performance was equivalent during both probes. These data were then used as the students' baseline level of ORF performance.

The SLA data also informed the researchers as to which level of support (i.e., tier) each individual student qualified for during the study. Students who were placed in Tier One ($n = 24$; 58.5%) were performing at the instructional or mastery level for the grade level they had just exited that spring. Students who were placed in Tier Two ($n = 11$; 26.8%) performed at the frustrational level for the grade level they had just exited that spring, and were found at an instructional level one grade below their actual grade. Finally, students who were placed in Tier Three ($n = 6$; 14.6%) during the summer reading program were performing at two or more grade levels below their actual grade level.

To draw more fair and accurate conclusions from the data, an inclusionary criterion of student attendance of at least seven intervention sessions was required in order to be evaluated at the end of the summer program. This criterion was set by the primary researchers, as it suggested that students experienced an intervention dose roughly once a week or at least 30% of the time. Additionally, due to the scope of this journal, only students that had just completed grades kindergarten through third grade will be discussed in this article. It is important to note, as seen in Figure 1 that students in upper-grade levels (i.e., fourth through ninth grades), were at least two or more grade levels below their actual level, and for some students, even five grade levels below expected. This further indicates the substantial need for early intervention and support for students with regards to reading, and provides clear data that students, following third grade, fall further behind in their reading abilities if they are not proficient by that point. Therefore, this article will evaluate the outcomes for 11 students, who met the two criteria above. Seven students met criteria for Tier One and four students for Tier Two. The Tier One group consisted of four males (57%) and three females (43%) who averaged 7.6 years of age, and had just exited kindergarten (2 students), first (1 student), second (1 student), or third grades (3 students). The Tier Two group consisted of four females (100%) with an average age of 7.5 years, and had just exited first (2 students), second (1 student), or third grades (1 student).

Tier One

Students in Tier One were identified to be at the instructional level, or performing between the 25th and 75th percentiles for the grade they had just completed using grade level AIMSweb norms via average or median scores. An exception to this was for students (i.e., Henry and Haley) who had just completed kindergarten, since AIMSweb does not target ORF at a kindergarten level. Thus, these students were given first grade level probes against fall norms throughout the study. Tier One students were then administered probes, one grade level at a time, above their most recent grade level to determine where they were instructional and frustrational (i.e., 24th percentile or below). Thus, all students in Tier One were evaluated to determine their performance at their grade, instructional, and frustrational levels.

During the Tier One students' reading session, students read from a book of their choice, from the mini library of books at the camp that were organized by Lexile value. This "classwide" intervention was selected for its similarity to typical local library reading programs that occur in the summer and offer a designated time to expose the student to reading.

Tier Two

Students in Tier Two were identified to be at the instructional level for reading material one grade level below the grade they had just completed. The intervention utilized with the Tier Two group was a 30-minute peer tutoring session, using either repeated reading or continuous reading of passages at students' instructional level. All Tier Two students served as peer tutors and tutees during intervention sessions. Each student received a brief group training on how to provide error correction prior to implementing the intervention.

Figure 1
Summer Benchmark Outcomes by Completed Grade in Spring.

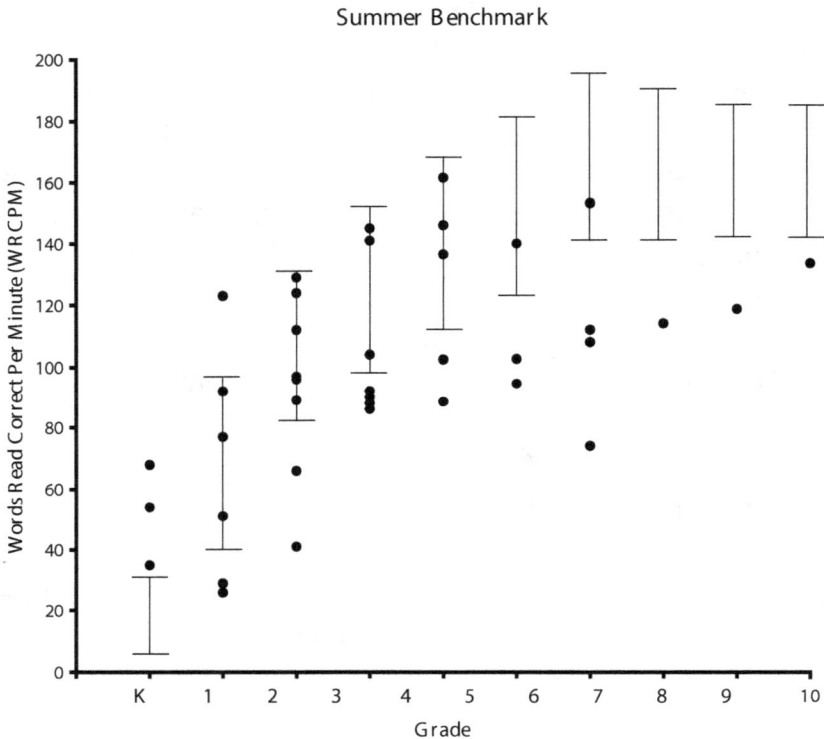

Summer Benchmark

Students in this tier were assigned a partner to form a dyad, and each dyad was randomly placed in one of two conditions (i.e., repeated reading or continuous reading). All students used DIBELS ORF passages during their intervention sessions. For students in the continuous reading condition, they would continue reading where they left off after the one-minute timer elapsed vs. students in the repeated reading condition, in which they read the same passage four times. One student in the dyad functioned as the tutor for 15 minutes and provided error correction as the other student or tutee read aloud the passage. Following 15 minutes, students would switch roles. Trained graduate and undergraduate students monitored the dyads during the intervention to provide praise or feedback to the tutor.

Progress Monitoring

All students, regardless of tier, were progress monitored once a week. Progress monitoring mimicked the procedures of the SLA process, which included a one-minute ORF reading probe at the student's instructional level. Students' data (i.e., WRCPM) were then graphed, comparing their initial grade-level performance with their weekly progress monitoring data.

Generalization

All students were also probed for generalization once a week.

Treatment Integrity

Graduate and undergraduate students completed tier-specific treatment integrity forms during the intervention sessions for each student. Integrity was calculated by dividing the number of completed steps by the total number of steps and multiplying by 100.

Results

Data were analyzed using regression equations to demonstrate a cumulative rate of improvement (ROI) value, a comparison of pre- and post-intervention differences, and visual analysis of the trendlines compared with the summer slide slope. Regression equations were calculated through Microsoft Excel comparing baseline performance to intervention outcomes to determine a ROI for each student (Flinn and McCrea, 2010). For comparison to the typical level of summer reading loss in students at each grade level, a reverse ROI was determined from the AIMSweb norms and multiplied by seven to determine a specific summer loss per grade level. This was based on the number of weeks of progress monitoring following the study intervention, and resulted in 1.5 words/week lost for kindergarten and first grade students, 1.2 words/week lost for second grade students, and 1.1 words/week lost for third grade students.

Pre- and post-intervention data points were calculated by taking the students' final progress monitoring score and subtracting it by the average from their baseline. Visual analysis evaluated whether the slope of the WRCPM was increasing, decreasing, or stable over the intervention period. Overall, the results were mixed across participants and tiers. An individual discussion of each student's performance is discussed below per tier placement.

Tier One Participants
Henry

Henry (Figure 2) was found to be instructional at the second-grade level for reading during the SLA process. Due to his recent completion of kindergarten, and lack of materials at that level, he was assessed and progress monitored at the first-grade level. During the SLA process, Henry averaged 47 WRCPM across three baseline data points.

Henry completed 12 intervention sessions and was administered seven progress monitoring probes during the summer reading program. Using fall norms for first grade, Henry consistently performed in the 80th percentile range (80th-89th), which would be considered mastery during progress monitoring. Treatment integrity was conducted for 11 of the 12 sessions, and was measured at 100%. Henry also completed six generalization probes, and he ranged between 22-38 WRCPM at the kindergarten level. This suggested a lower level of performance with the actual school-based curriculum.

His regression equation indicated a loss of roughly 1.1 words per week, but no overall loss of WRCPM at the end of the program based on a pre- and post-intervention calculation. It is important to note that Henry had an exceptionally high final progress monitoring data point, which is why the pre- and post-intervention calculated resulted in no overall loss. Henry's data indicated a downward slope; however, his performance was still above the predicted summer slide slope for a kindergarten student, which was an expected loss of 1.5 words per week. Thus, because Henry was outperforming (i.e., reading roughly 45 WRCPM) a typical first grade level student (i.e., reading 13 WRCPM), his rate of loss was still above the summer slide slope due to his higher level of performance from the beginning.

Haley

Haley (Figure 2) was also found to be instructional at the second-grade level for reading during the SLA process. Haley began attending the day camp two weeks after it had started and was assessed to average 68 WRCPM across three baseline data points.

She completed 13 intervention sessions and was administered six progress monitoring probes during the summer reading program. Using fall norms for first grade, Haley consistently performed in the 90th percentile range (90th-96th), which would be considered mastery during progress monitoring. Treatment integrity was conducted for 9 of the 13 sessions and was measured at 100% overall. Haley also completed five generalization probes, and she ranged between 47-63 WRCPM at the kindergarten level. This suggested a substantially lower level of performance with the actual school-based curriculum.

Haley's regression equation indicated a gain of roughly 1.7 words per week, and she improved 17 WRCPM at the end of the program based on a pre- and post-intervention calculation. Overall, Haley's data indicated an increasing trendline with visibly steady gains in WRCPM and performance well above the predicted summer slide for a kindergartener.

Figure 2
Kindergarten Participants' Outcome Data

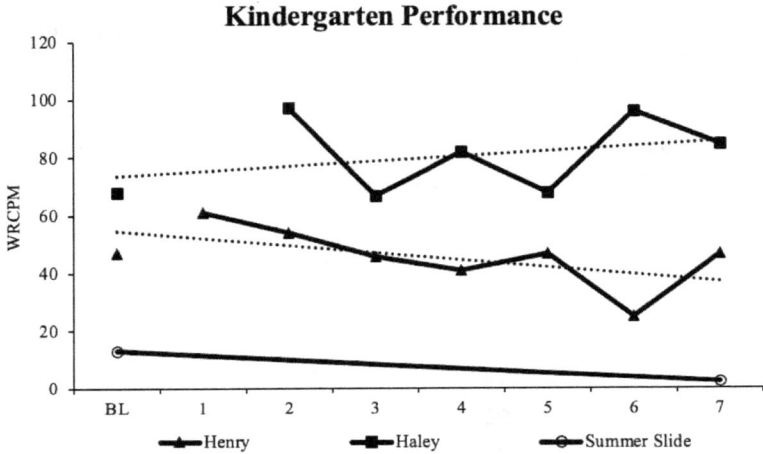

Kindergarten Performance

Katy

Katy (Figure 3) was found to be instructional at the first-grade level for reading during the SLA process, which is also the grade level she had just completed in the spring. Katy was assessed to average 79 WRCPM across three baseline data points. She attended 15 intervention sessions and was administered six progress monitoring probes during the summer reading program. Using spring norms for first grade, Katy consistently performed in the instructional range (43rd – 66th). Treatment integrity was conducted for 13 of the 15 sessions at 99% (range = 89-100%). Katy also completed six generalization probes, and she ranged between 48-80 WRCPM at the first- grade level. This suggested variable performance, and continued evidence of lower scores when compared with the progress monitoring data.

Katy's regression equation indicated a gain of roughly 1.3 words per week, and she improved 5 WRCPM at the end of the program based on a pre- and post-intervention calculation. Overall, these data indicated an increasing trendline and performance well above the predicted summer slide, aside from her initial progress monitoring probe that fell shortly below the summer slide line.

Figure 3
First Grade Participants' Outcome Data

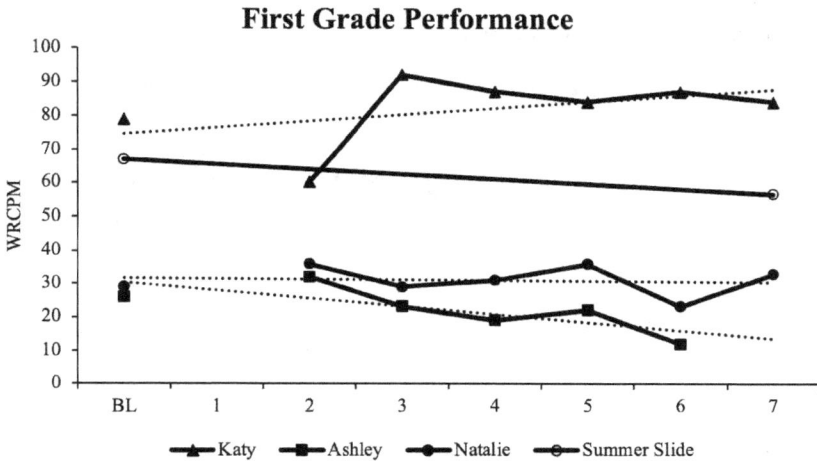

First Grade Performance

Tyler

      Tyler (Figure 3) was found to be instructional at the second-grade level for reading during the SLA process, which was also the grade he had just completed in the spring. Tyler was assessed to average 88 WRCPM across two baseline data points. He attended 15 intervention sessions and was administered six progress monitoring probes during the summer reading program. Using spring norms for second grade, Tyler consistently performed in the instructional range (30th-54th). Treatment integrity was conducted for all 15 sessions at 99% (range = 89 -100%). Tyler also completed six generalization probes, and he ranged between 59-85 WRCPM. This suggested lower scores when compared with the progress monitoring probes.

      Tyler's regression equation indicated a gain of roughly .5 words per week, and he improved 15 WRCPM at the end of the program based on a pre- and post-intervention calculation. Overall, these data indicated a stable trendline across the summer with data that were moderately variable. Tyler's final progress monitoring data point indicated a slight increase of performance relative to the summer slide slope.

Figure 4
Second Grade Participants' Outcome Data

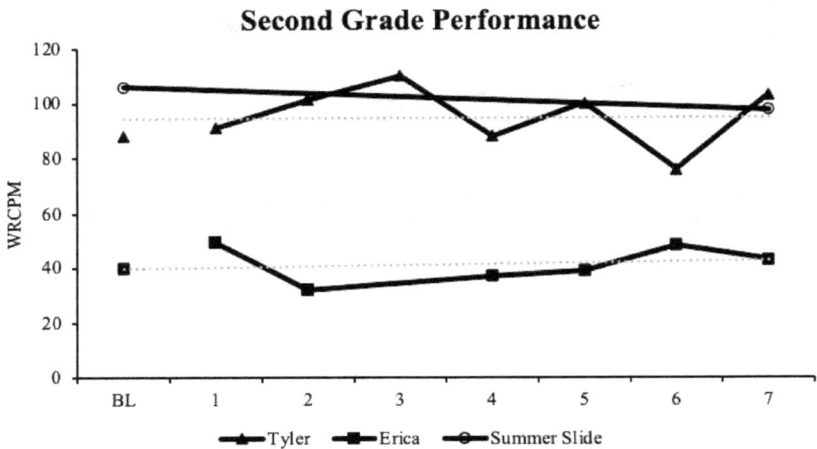

Second Grade Performance

Austin

Austin (Figure 4) had just completed third grade in the spring and was found to be instructional at the fourth-grade level for reading during the SLA process. Austin was assessed to average 140 WRCPM across two baseline data points. He attended 7 intervention sessions and was administered four progress monitoring probes during the summer reading program, and he had one of the highest number of absences for a student who was still included in the study. Using spring norms for third grade, Austin consistently performed in the instructional range (53rd-67th). Treatment integrity was conducted for all 7 sessions he attended at 100%. Austin also completed four generalization probes, and he ranged between 94-127 WRCPM at the third-grade level. This, again, suggested lower scores when compared with the progress monitoring probes.

Austin's regression equation calculated a gain of .25 words per week, and he improved three WRCPM at the end of the program. Austin's trendline was stable, and he was the only third grade student to consistently perform above the summer slide slope throughout intervention, despite his frequent absences.

Chelsea

Chelsea (Figure 4) had just completed third grade in the spring and was found to be instructional at the third-grade level for reading during the SLA process. Chelsea was assessed to average 104 WRCPM across two baseline data points. She attended 10 intervention sessions and was administered seven progress monitoring probes during the summer reading program. Using spring norms for third grade, Chelsea performed variably between the frustrational and instructional ranges (11th-41st). Treatment integrity was conducted for all 9 sessions she attended, and was measured at 100%. Chelsea also completed six generalization probes, and she ranged between 74-106 WRCPM at the third-grade level. This, again, suggested lower scores when compared with the progress monitoring probes. Chelsea's regression equation calculated a gain of 1.6 words of improvement per week with an increasing trendline to match. She showed an overall gain of 13 words at the end of the summer, but was still performing below the predicted summer slide slope. Her last data point was two words away from being consistent with the summer slide slope at week seven.

Robert

Robert (Figure 4) had just completed third grade in the spring and was found to be instructional at the fifth-grade level during the SLA process. Robert was assessed to average 145 WRCPM across three baseline data points. He attended 14 intervention sessions and was administered six progress monitoring probes during the summer reading program. Using spring norms for third grade, Robert performed variably in the frustrational-instructional ranges (11th-87th.). Treatment integrity was conducted for 12 of the 14 sessions at and measured 93.5% (range = 78-100%). Robert also completed seven generalization probes, and he ranged between 53-125 WRCPM at the third-grade level. This, again, suggested lower scores when compared with the progress monitoring probes.

Robert's data were highly variable, with a slight increasing trendline and an overall difference by the end of the summer of 27 improved words. Robert performed below the summer slide slope for a majority of his progress monitoring sessions, but he did outperform the slope during the final two sessions of the summer. Additionally, it is important to note that Robert had a behavior plan implemented part way through the summer, after repeated demonstration of need for more behavioral support to stay on task during the intervention sessions.

Figure 5
Third Grade Participants' Outcome Data

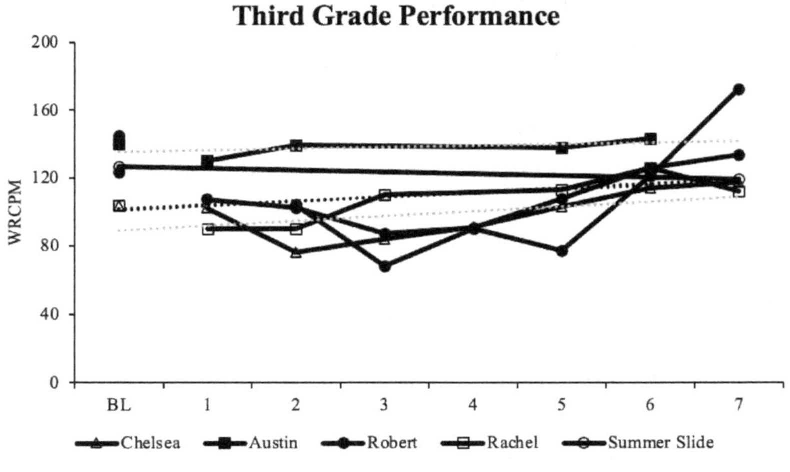

Tier Two Participants
Ashley

Ashley (Figure 2) had just completed first grade in the spring and was found to be instructional at the first-grade level, using fall norms, during the SLA process. Ashley read 26 WRCPM during baseline. She attended 14 intervention sessions and was administered five progress monitoring probes during the summer reading program. Using fall norms for first grade, Ashley consistently performed in the instructional range (46th- 75th) during progress monitoring. This demonstrated she was one grade level behind same-grade peers. Treatment integrity was conducted for 8 of the 14 sessions and measured 100%. Ashley also completed six generalization probes, and she ranged between 9-29 WRCPM at the first-grade level. Her regression equation indicated a loss of 2.9 words per week, and her overall pre- and post-intervention difference indicted a loss of 14 words following the reading program. Ashley's trendline was also visibly decreasing, and she had a particularly low final progress monitoring data point to end the summer.

Natalie

Natalie (Figure 2) had also just completed the first grade in the spring and was found to be instructional at the first-grade level for reading, using fall norms, during the SLA process. Natalie was assessed to average 27 WRCPM across three baseline data points. She attended 11 intervention sessions and was administered six progress monitoring probes during the summer reading program. Using fall norms for first grade, Natalie consistently performed in the mastery range (73rd-78th) during progress monitoring. Treatment integrity was conducted for 9 of the 11 sessions and measured 97% (range = 78-100%). Natalie also completed five generalization probes, and she ranged between 23-30 WRCPM at the first-grade level. Natalie had a loss of .2 words per week as calculated by her regression line and demonstrated a stable trendline during the summer. Her overall difference at the end of the summer was an improvement of four words, compared to the expected loss of 10.5 words as calculated by the reverse ROI of an average first grade student.

Erica

Erica (Figure 3) had just completed second grade in the spring and was found to be instructional for reading at the first-grade level during the SLA process. Erica was assessed to average 50 WRCPM across two baseline data points. She attended 13 intervention sessions and was administered six progress monitoring probes during the summer reading program. Using spring norms for first grade, Erica performed between the frustrational and instructional ranges (13th – 33rd) during progress monitoring. Treatment integrity was conducted for 10 of the 13 sessions and was measured to be 100%. Erica also completed five generalization probes, and she ranged between 23-46 WRCPM at the second-grade level. This, again, suggested lower scores when compared with the progress monitoring probes.

Erica's regression equation suggested a gain of .7 words per week. Her overall difference from baseline was a gain of three words, which was an improvement from the anticipated loss over the seven weeks for second grade at 8.5 words. Erica still performed well below the predicted summer slide as evidenced by Figure 3 with a stable trendline overall.

Rachel

Rachel (Figure 4) had just completed third grade in the spring and was found to be instructional at the second-grade level for reading during the SLA process. Rachel was assessed to average 104 WRCPM across two baseline data points. She attended 16 intervention sessions and was administered six progress monitoring probes during the summer reading program. Using spring norms for second grade, Rachel performed consistently at the instructional range (34th – 50th). Treatment integrity was conducted for 12 of the 16 sessions and measured at 100%. Rachel also completed generalization probes, and she ranged between 37-89 WRCPM at the second-grade level. Rachel's end-of-summer improvement was 8 words, and her regression equation indicated 2.8 words gained each week with a visible increasing trend. This suggests that likely a match with intervention and dosage (i.e., attendance for 16 intervention session) occurred.

Social Validity

Student perceptions of their tier-specific intervention were evaluated through the CURP rating scale, with values closer to 4.0 indicating more agreeability with each factor and the overall intervention. Ten of the eleven students who met inclusion for the study completed the rating scale. Tables 3 and 4 present individual students' social validity ratings, grouped by tier. The average, across all ten participants and also when calculated by tier, was 3.2. The Personal Desirability factor ranged from 1.8-4.0, with an overall average of 3.4, which was the highest rated factor of the three. The Feasibility factor was rated between 1.3-3.6, which suggests the students did not always enjoy the amount of work, time, or frequency required by their intervention. All participants rated the Understanding factor between 3.1-4.0. Overall, these data suggest that the intervention methods utilized in the program were rated favorably by participants.

Table 3
Tier One Participant CURP Scores

	Tyler	Henry	Haley	Chelsea	Robert	Katy
Personal Desirability	3.7	1.8	3.1	3.4	4.0	3.4
Feasibility	3.3	2.3	2.6	1.7	3.7	3.6
Understanding	4.0	3.5	3.8	3.5	4.0	3.0
Overall Average	3.6	2.5	3.1	2.8	3.9	3.3

Table 4
Tier Two Participant CURP Scores

	Ashley	Natalie	Erica	Rachel
Personal Desirability	3.7	3.2	4.0	4.0
Feasibility	3.1	3.2	2.0	1.3
Understanding	3.5	3.1	4.0	4.0
Overall Average	**3.4**	**3.2**	**3.2**	**3.0**

Discussion

The primary goal of the current study was to help reduce typical summer loss, known as the summer slide, in ORF for low-SES elementary aged students with a targeted level of support. When evaluating the first research question, which determined if gains, losses, or maintenance of reading skills would be present, overall mixed results were found across participants. First, when evaluating the students based on performance against the summer slide slope, six of the 11 participants were at or above the expected reading loss for their grade level by the end of the summer program. It is important to note that five of these students were placed in the Tier One group, indicating appropriate grade-level reading abilities from the beginning of the study. Two students from Tier One (i.e., Chelsea and Robert) were slightly below the summer slide slope, and three students from Tier Two (i.e., Ashley, Natalie, and Erica) were visibly below it. Second, when evaluating the students based on pre- and post-intervention values, all students either maintained or improved their reading by the end of summer when compared with the beginning of the summer, except for one student (i.e., Ashley). Henry maintained his baseline level with end-of-summer performance at 47 WRCPM, while the other students ranged from 3-27 WRCPM of improvement across both tiers. Finally, when using visual analysis to determine the trend of each student's growth, eight students had either a stable or increasing trendline, while two students (i.e., Henry and Ashley), had a decreasing trendline. Although it is ultimately unknown without follow up data from the fall, it is likely that reading skills were either maintained or improved through the present study for a majority of the students during the summer break.

The second research question investigated the dosage of intervention based on attendance of each student. This proved to be one of the more challenging aspects of the summer program, as students were inconsistently present throughout intervention. It also required the researchers to sacrifice some progress monitoring to ensure intervention was occurring when the students were present, rather than more assessment. The one student (i.e., Rachel) who attended 16 of 17 sessions did yield some of the strongest outcome data as a Tier Two participant. Rachel improved by 8 WRCPM at the end of the summer, had an increasing trendline, and was the only Tier Two student to be near the predicted summer slide slope. On the reverse end, Austin attended 7 sessions, which was the minimum value to meet the inclusionary criteria for the study, and had only a 3 word improvement at the end of the summer, which was the second lowest for Tier One students. Henry made no improvements, and he attended 12 sessions. Two Tier One students attended 15 interventions and saw improvements of 5 WRCPM (i.e., Katy) and 15 WRCPM (i.e., Tyler); however, Ashley, a Tier Two student attended 14 sessions, and had the only loss of words from the study at 14. Overall, intervention dosage still seems to have some impact on the outcome data, but it was not true for all participants. Certainly, more research and attention are needed to target dosage for the remediation of skill deficits and maintenance of academic skills over the summer to make more definitive conclusions.

Finally, the researchers sought to determine student perceptions of the intervention using the CURP, a social validity rating scale, at the end of the study. Overall, eight of the ten students who completed the CURP indicated scores that suggested favorable acceptability with the intervention they encountered. These scores were all in the 3.0-3.9 range, which included students from both tiers. Unfortunately, the one student who had the least amount of intervention sessions (i.e., Tyler) was not present on the final day, so the extent of acceptability across participants who had a low (40%), moderate (45-79%), and high (80% and above) level of intervention dosage could not be determined. The Personal Desirability factor yielded one low-end score from Henry at 1.8, while the Feasibility factor yielded two low-end scores from Chelsea (1.7) and Rachel (1.3). The Understanding factor suggested high levels of acceptability across all students.

Limitation and Future Research

The present study, while demonstrating stability and growth in WRCPM for most participants, had some limitations that should be considered. One limitation is the small sample size of students that participated in the study. Even though there were 41 students involved with the project, only 11 met the inclusionary criteria. This inevitably makes definitive conclusions difficult. Additionally, attendance was difficult to navigate since this was an elective summer day camp. Many of the students were gone for several weeks on vacation or at other camps, which created large gaps in the data, and this made it more challenging to draw specific conclusions about reading growth without the consistent implementation of the intervention. It also affected intervention dosage and how students were compared. It meant that a student who received approximately 40% of the intervention was compared with a student who received over 80% of the intervention. Warren and colleagues (2007) introduced the idea of different aspects of dosage (e.g., form, frequency, duration, etc.). It would be a valuable contribution to the literature in the future to focus on these different dosage aspects when supporting summer skill loss or remediation. The current study sought to provide a certain dosage to supplement the summer break, but it did not explicitly investigate all the areas of how dosage could be impacting different outcomes at the end of the summer program. As the inclusion criterion of the study was attendance for at least seven intervention sessions (~40% of total opportunity of intervention), it is not ideal to compare students who had differing levels of intervention exposure.

Additionally, the researchers did not compare the efficacy of the differing interventions that students encountered between and across tiers. Without explicit measures taken, such as a brief experimental analysis (BEA) of intervention match with student need, the full effect of these interventions or other potential interventions is unclear. More research is needed to assess these elements of academic interventions as well.

Another limitation is the subjectivity in evaluating the summer slide. Some sources suggest that two to three months of learning occurs during summer, while the researchers for this study utilized AIMSweb norms, which provide explicit guidance on how much is lost from the end of one grade level to the beginning of another. In this study, a reverse ROI was calculated from AIMSweb values, along with a pre- and post-intervention difference; however, there are other alternatives to this method, which might result in a different operational definition of the summer slide.

It also would be beneficial to discriminate, in future studies on the summer slide, between remediating skills and preventing skill regression more specifically. The present study did not discretely analyze the data in that capacity, but it would be a beneficial focus in future studies. More research, especially in post-COVID educational settings, would be helpful.

Additionally, based on the way paperwork was processed for the summer day camp, the specific demographic data were not accessible to the authors. Even though the authors feel confident in sharing the district statistics that mirrored the population in the study, it is still a limiting factor to definitively state findings for low SES and minority individuals who may benefit from such supports, without the availability of explicit data for participants.

Finally, a limiting factor to the study was that the interobserver agreement data were not able to be reported. Although these data were collected, they were not consistently recorded. This limited interpretation of internal validity and reliability.

Conclusions

Overall, the results of this study suggest that even implementing an intervention for 30 minutes, three times a week can help combat against the summer slide. These results are similar to a larger-scale study recently implemented (Lenhoff et al., 2020), and further expand the literature on supporting early elementary aged students with access to academic supports in the summer through targeted measures. This has implications for the field in terms of what types of supports are available to students over the summer, especially with students from low SES backgrounds. It additionally provides data to suggest that skill remediation can occur over the summer months so that early readers do not fall further behind. Despite limitations, such as attendance, intervention dosage, and subjectivity in assessing the summer slide, the results indicate that stability and growth in reading can occur with minimal intervention, and that early elementary aged students overall enjoy a reading structure as described above. Even though summer can be a challenging time to coordinate consistent intervention, it is evident that even some support can help mitigate loss during students' time away from school.

References

Alexander, K. L., Entwisle, D. R., & Kabbani, N. S. (2001). The dropout process in life course perspective: Early risk factors at home and school. *Teachers college record, 103*(5), 760-822.

Alexander, K. L., Entwisle, D. R., & Olson, L. S. (2007). Lasting consequences of the summer learning gap. *American Sociological Review, 72*(2), 167-180.

Allington, R. L., McGill-Franzen, A., Camilli, G., Williams, L., Graff, J., Zeig, J., Zmach, C., & Nowak, R. (2010). Addressing summer reading setback among economically disadvantaged elementary students. *Reading Psychology, 31*(5), 411-427.

Ardoin, S. P., Williams, J. C., Christ, T. J., Klubnik, C., & Wellborn, C. (2010). Examining readability estimates' predictions of students' oral reading rate: Spache, lexile, and forcast. *School Psychology Review, 39*(2), 277-285. https://doi.org/10.1080/02796 015.2010.12087778

Batsche, G., Elliott, J., Graden, J.L., Grimes, J., Kovaleski, J.F., Prasse, D., et al. (2005). *Response to intervention: Policy considerations and implementation.* Alexandria, VA: National Association of State Directors of Special Education.

Beach, K. D., & Philippakos, Z. A. (2020). Effects of a summer reading intervention on the reading performance of elementary grade students from low-income families. *Reading & Writing Quarterly,* 1-21. https://doi.org/10.1080/10573569. 2020.1760154

Becnel, K., Moeller, R. A., & Matzen, N. J. (2017). "Somebody signed me up": North Carolina fourth-graders' perceptions of summer reading programs. *Children & Libraries, 15*(3), 3.

Borman, G. D., Benson, J., & Overman, L. T. (2005). Families, schools, and summer learning. *The Elementary School Journal, 106*(2), 131-150.

Borman, G. D., & Dowling, N. M. (2006). Longitudinal achievement effects of multiyear summer school: Evidence from the Teach Baltimore randomized field trial. *Educational Evaluation and Policy Analysis, 28*(1), 25-48. https://doi. org/10.3102/01623737028001025

Bowers, L. M., & Schwarz, I. (2018). Preventing summer learning loss: Results of a summer literacy program for students from low-SES homes. *Reading & Writing Quarterly, 34*(2), 99-116. https://doi.org/10.1080/10573569.2017.1344943

Briesch, A. M., & Chafouleas, S. M. (2009). Exploring student buy-in: Initial development of an instrument to measure likelihood of children's intervention usage. *Journal of Educational and Psychological Consultation, 19*(4), 321-336.

Burkam, D. T., Ready, D. D., Lee, V. E., & LoGerfo, L. F. (2004). Social-class differences in summer learning between kindergarten and first grade: Model specification and estimation. *Sociology of Education, 77*(1), 1-31.

Cooper, H., Nye, B., Charlton, K., Lindsay, J., & Greathouse, S. (1996). The effects of summer vacation on achievement test scores: A narrative and meta-analytic review. *Review of Educational Research, 66*(3), 227–268. https://doi.org/10.2307/1170523

Dietrichson, J., Bøg, M., Filges, T., & Klint Jørgensen, A. (2017). Academic interventions for elementary and middle school students with low socioeconomic status: A systematic review and meta-analysis. *Review of Educational Research, 87*(2), 243-282. https://doi.org/10.3102/0034654316687036

Dillon, D. R., O'Brien, D. G., & Nichols-Besel, K. (2017). Motivating boys to read: Guys read, a summer library reading program for boys. *Children & Libraries, 15*(2), 3. https://doi.org/10.5860/cal.15n2.03

Fälth, L., Nordström, T., Andersson, U., & Gustafson, S. (2019). An intervention study to prevent 'summer reading loss' in a socioeconomically disadvantaged area with second language learners. *Nordic Journal of Literacy Research, 5*(3), 10-23. https://doi.org/10.23865/njlr.v5.2013

Flinn, C.S., & McCrea, A.E. (2010, March). *Graphing, calculating, and interpreting rate of improvement* [Paper presentation]. National Association of School Psychologists Convention, Chicago, IL.

Fuchs, D., & Fuchs, L. (2006). Introduction to response to intervention: What, why, and how valid is it? *Reading Research Quarterly, 41*(1), 93-99.

Garst, B. A., & Ozier, L. W. (2015). Enhancing youth outcomes and organizational practices through a camp-based reading program. *The Journal of Experiential Education, 38*(4), 324-338. https://doi.org/10.1177/1053825915578914

Hatcher, P. J., Hulme, C., Miles, J. N., Carroll, J. M., Hatcher, J., Gibbs, S., Smith, G., Bowyer-Crane, C., & Snowling, M. J. (2006). Efficacy of small group reading intervention for beginning readers with reading-delay: A randomised controlled trial. *Journal of Child Psychology and Psychiatry, 47*(8), 820-827.

Hosp, J. L., & Suchey, N. (2014). Reading assessment: Reading fluency, reading fluently, and comprehension—Commentary on the special topic. *School Psychology Review, 43*(1), 59-68.

Jones, J. S., Conradi, K., & Amendum, S. J. (2016). Matching interventions to reading needs: A case for differentiation. *The Reading Teacher, 70*(3), 307-316.

Lenhoff, S. W., Somers, C., Tenelshof, B., & Bender, T. (2020). The potential for multi-site literacy interventions to reduce summer slide among low-performing students. *Children and Youth Services Review, 110*, 104806.

Lexile (2022). *Lexile and Quantile Tool.* https://hub.lexile.com/

Liebfreund, M. D., Porter, S. R., Amendum, S. J., & Starcke, M. A. (2022). Using an assessment system for data-driven reform: Effects of mCLASS on third-grade reading test scores and special education placement. *The Elementary School Journal, 122*(3), 341-360. https://doi.org/10.1086/717952

Loftus-Rattan, S. M., Wrightington, M., Furey, J., & Case, J. (2021). Multi-tiered system of supports: An ecological approach to school psychology service delivery. *Teaching of Psychology,* 9862832110242. https://doi.org/10.1177/00986283211024262

MAP. (2021). Using Lexile Measurements https://teach.mapnwea.org/impl/maphelp/Content/ReadFluency/LexileOralReading.htm

McCombes-Tolis, J., & Feinn, R. (2008). Comparing teachers' literacy-related knowledge to their state's standards for reading. *Reading Psychology, 29*(3), 236-265. https://doi.org/10.1080/02702710801982258

McDaniel, S. C., McLeod, R., Carter, C. L., & Robinson, C. (2017). Supplemental summer literacy instruction: Implications for preventing summer reading loss. *Reading Psychology, 38*(7), 673-686. https://doi.org/10.1080/02702711.2017.1333070

National Center for Education Statistics. (2020). *State Education Practices.* https://nces.ed.gov/programs/statereform/tab1_1-2020.asp

National Center for Education Statistics (NCES). High school graduation rates. https://nces.ed.gov/fastfacts/display.asp?id=805

Scammacca, N. K., Roberts, G. J., Cho, E., Williams, K. J., Roberts, G., Vaughn, S. R., & Carroll, M. (2016). A century of progress: Reading interventions for students in grades 4–12, 1914–2014. *Review of Educational Research, 86*(3), 756-800.

Schmitt, A. M., Horner, S. L., & Lavery, M. R. (2019). The impact of summer programs on the English language scores of migrant children. *Literacy Research and Instruction, 59*(1), 78-93. https://doi.org/10.1080/19388071.2019.1687794

Shinn, M. M., & Shinn, M. R. (2002). AIMSweb training workbook: Administration and scoring of reading curriculum-based measurement (R-CBM) for use in general outcome measurement. *Eden Prairie, MN: Edformation.*

Slates, S. L., Alexander, K. L., Entwisle, D. R., & Olson, L. S. (2012). Counteracting summer slide: Social capital resources within socioeconomically disadvantaged families. *Journal of Education for Students Placed at Risk, 17*(3), 165-185. https://doi.org/10.1080/10824669.2012.688171

Small, R. V., Arnone, M. P., & Bennett, E. (2017). A hook and a book: Rewards as motivators in public library summer reading programs. *Children & Libraries, 15*(1), 7. https://doi.org/10.5860/cal.15n1.07

Stevens, R. J., Lu, X., Baker, D. P., Ray, M. N., Eckert, S. A., & Gamson, D. A. (2015). Assessing the cognitive demands of a century of reading curricula: An analysis of reading text and comprehension tasks from 1910 to 2000. *American Educational Research Journal, 52*(3), 582-617. https://doi.org/10.3102/0002831215573531

Toler, A. (2012). IREAD-3 test results: Majority of local students pass, others get exemptions. *The Herald-Times (Bloomington, Ind.).* https://proxy.bsu.edu/login?url=https://search.ebscohost.com/login.aspx?direct=true&db=n5h&AN=2W6832543287&site=ehost-live&scope=site

University of Oregon (2018). *8th Edition of Dynamic Indicators of Basic Early Literacy Skills (DIBELS®): Administration and Scoring Guide.* University of Oregon. https://dibels.uoregon.edu

van Bergen, E., Snowling, M. J., de Zeeuw, E. L., van Beijsterveldt, C. E., Dolan, C. V., & Boomsma, D. I. (2018). Why do children read more? The influence of reading ability on voluntary reading practices. *Journal of Child Psychology and Psychiatry, 59*(11), 1205-1214.

Warren, S. F., Fey, M. E., & Yoder, P. J. (2007). Differential treatment intensity research: A missing link to creating optimally effective communication interventions. *Mental retardation and developmental disabilities research reviews, 13*(1), 70-77.

Wendling, B. J., & Mather, N. (2008). *Essentials of evidence-based academic interventions* (Vol. 57). John Wiley & Sons.

Zvoch, K., & Stevens, J. J. (2015). Identification of summer school effects by comparing the in- and out-of-school growth rates of struggling early readers. *The Elementary School Journal, 115*(3), 433-456. https://doi.org/10.1086/680229

Supporting Intervention Fidelity of Dialogic Reading to Support Preschool Children's Early Literacy Skills

Cara Dillon and Daniel Newman

Abstract

Early literacy skills are key indicators of later reading success, and early literacy instruction in early childhood education can support both positive academic and behavioral child outcomes. Dialogic reading (DR) is an evidence-based intervention that targets early literacy skills like oral language, vocabulary, and print concepts. Although research suggests DR has the potential to impact the early literacy skills of young children, intervention fidelity must be maintained for the intervention to be effective. Two single case design studies were conducted in an early childhood setting that together examined (a) the effects of intervention supports on the intervention fidelity of educators performing interventions, and (b) early child literacy outcomes when educators accessed DR intervention supports. Study 1, an alternating treatment design, focused on intervention scripts and an intervention checklist on intervention fidelity. Findings indicated that both supports equivalently increased educators' (N = 4) intervention fidelity, though the educators preferred using a checklist. Study 2, a multiple baseline design, examined the effects of the intervention supports and subsequent increased intervention fidelity on child early literacy across four children. Findings indicated increased book-based vocabulary for children during the intervention phase when intervention fidelity levels were higher. Taken together, the studies suggest intervention fidelity for DR is best delivered with support from checklists or other methods, and that ensuring that DR is delivered as intended may help bolster children's reading skills.

Keywords: *early literacy, intervention fidelity, dialogic reading*

Dialogic Reading and Supporting Intervention Fidelity

Early literacy skills are key indicators of later reading success. The National Early Literacy Panel (NELP) convened in 2008 to determine key early literacy skills and the implications for teaching reading. Understanding print concepts, letter naming, vocabulary, and phonological awareness are among 18 skills significantly correlated with later reading success (NELP, 2008) and can be targeted through shared reading interventions. Only 35% of children in the fourth grade are proficient in reading, a gap that remains into eighth grade (United States Department of Education, 2019) with low academic achievement identified as a major risk factor for later school dropout (Gubbels et al., 2019). Early intervention in reading is critical to alleviate this problem. Preschools offer an environment for prevention and early intervention efforts that can positively impact the lives of children, including systematically implemented interventions that build early literacy skills (Neuman, 2009). The purposes of this study were to investigate educators' intervention fidelity during a dialogic reading intervention and to consider implications for intervention quality provided to preschool children.

Dialogic reading (DR), a formalized approach to shared reading (i.e., reading story books with children while asking relevant questions), targets early literacy skill development. Whitehurst et al. (1994) developed the intervention to target children's vocabulary and print concepts development and found that 94 children attending Head Start centers who engaged in DR significantly improved in these areas, as compared with a no-intervention control group The intervention included training educators to read with children using a formalized, sequential procedure for extratextual interactions: Prompt, Evaluate, Expand, and Repeat (PEER). Within the Prompt strategy, questions covered any area of the text with these prompts: Completion, Recall, Open-ended, Wh-, and Distancing (CROWD). Given the PEER and CROWD procedures, DR provided a replicable method, as compared with shared reading interventions, which lack a universal approach. DR also included direct instruction with performance feedback for children as well as extratextual questions.

Lonigan and Whitehurst (1998) replicated the DR intervention with preschool children from low SES backgrounds, building on prior DR research with middle-class families, with similarly promising results to those of Whitehurst et al. (1994). More recently, Towson et al. (2016) investigated DR with children with Individualized Education Plans (IEPs) in the special education category of developmental delay and found the method to be effective. Additionally, positive child outcomes related to children's vocabulary development were found across socioeconomic groups (Zevenbergen et al., 2003).

DR research assumes that procedures are consistently implemented as intended, or with intervention fidelity, yet many studies do not fully utilize the PEER and CROWD procedures that are hallmarks of DR (Towson et al., 2017). The original research study by Whitehurst et al. (1994) and the Lonigan and Whitehurst (1998) follow-up both noted that implementer compliance with the intervention was a significant factor limiting the results, and subsequently separated analysis between groups with low and high fidelity. Even when implementers initially implement an intervention as intended, compliance may shift from training. Also, drift may occur that limits the integrity of the intervention, for example Zibulsky et al. (2019) noted that drift occurred in the frequency of CROWD prompts following training.

With low intervention fidelity, child outcomes resulting from an intervention may suffer (Forman et al., 2013). Intervention fidelity can be enhanced through a variety of approaches, including the use of checklists or task lists, and post-training support (Guskey, 1991). Checklists are a form of self-assessment to promote fidelity to evidence-based practices (Barnett et al., 2014), such as shared reading (Pentimonti et al., 2012). Towson et al. (2016) provided interventionists with scripted interactions taped to the books, including fifteen CROWD prompts to target vocabulary words. Fidelity remained high for the intervention. Interventionists were also able to consistently ask questions about target vocabulary words over different readings. In sum, DR may require explicit implementation supports to be implemented with fidelity. Research is needed to understand what supports enhance DR implementation integrity.

Purpose of the Studies

The current project included two interrelated research studies. The first study examined the effects of intervention fidelity supports, including a DR checklist and a full book script, on interventionists' fidelity to a DR protocol. The second study investigated if early child literacy skills were improved with increased implementation fidelity. The utilization of a supporting checklist or script was compared to a no support condition. Research questions were:

1. Does DR, when implemented with a checklist, result in higher fidelity than DR implemented without supports?
2. Does DR, when implemented with a book script, result in higher levels of fidelity than DR implemented with a checklist or DR implemented with no supports?
3. Do children experience more growth in target book vocabulary and print concepts in the best intervention condition compared to DR with no supports?

Method: Study 1

To address the first and second research questions, the researcher manipulated the supports given to interventionists to determine the level of intervention fidelity across conditions.

Participants and Setting

Study 1 participants were four educators from a university-based constructivist preschool in the Midwestern United States. Constructivist schools provide children agency to direct their own learning through exploration. The classrooms in this school included open-ended activity stations and explorative play, with educators following children's lead. All educators at the preschool were emailed about a professional development research opportunity and responding educator pairs who considered shared reading time appropriate for their classroom were included in the study. Rebecca was a Black female in her first year of teaching. Taylor was a White female who had taught at the preschool for three years. Barry was a White male in his eighth-year teaching at the preschool. Kendra was a White female in her first year of teaching. All teachers are identified by pseudonyms. All had master's level training in Early Childhood Education and served between seven and nine children per classroom. Educators worked in pairs within their classrooms (Rebecca with Taylor, and Kendra with Barry). The preschool accepted tuition and Head Start children, with approximately 53% White, 28% Black, and 19% other children of color ($N = 139$ across all classrooms). All classrooms and educators applied some shared reading procedures already, in place during circle time and at a child's request during free exploration periods.

Materials

Books from the classroom were utilized in the study, and two new books (*Caps for Sale* (Slobodkina, 1940) and *No Roses for Harry* (Zion, 1957) were also provided to the educators for the scripted portion of the alternating treatment design as appropriate texts to engage in DR with preschoolers (Zevenbergen & Whitehurst, 2003). These books had limited amounts of text, and large pictures. The researcher developed a training video for educator and data collector training, which included an overview of the PEER and CROWD acronyms associated with DR and examples of each. A checklist bookmark was provided to the educators for a portion of the study. The bookmarks had each portion of the script listed (see Appendix A).

Dependent Variables
Educator Fidelity

Data collectors (i.e., trained school psychology graduate students) used a checklist to collect intervention fidelity data (see Appendix B) wherein DR procedures were converted into a checklist (Hawkins et al., 2008). This checklist included a tally box for eight PEER and CROWD items. To calculate the percent fidelity, the number of areas completed on the checklist was divided by 8 and multiplied by 100. As each letter of the CROWD acronym is a prompt, the "P" in PEER was not counted in the calculation to remove redundancy. Data were collected once a day from an observation booth that viewed the classroom from an adjacent room and two-way mirror. Percent of intervention fidelity was the main variable of interest in the study.

Data Collector Training

Data collectors were trained to recognize DR procedures, and then viewed a pre-coded video and completed a data form to check for appropriate intervention fidelity. The data form and pre-coded form were compared to calculate total count interobserver agreement (IOA) for each area of PEER and CROWD. Observers reached an acceptable level of 85% IOA with the researcher before independent data collection (Kennedy, 2005). IOA was collected for approximately 20% of sessions across all phases (Kennedy, 2005), averaging 91% overall IOA across the study.

Procedure

The researcher met with each educator participant to explain study procedures and gain informed consent. Next, data collection began for the already implemented shared reading procedures. The educators chose to read to children during morning exploratory play and were asked to read at least once during this time period.

Baseline

During this phase, educators read to children as they normally would. Educators were not given special instructions except to read to children at least once during the morning exploratory play period. The educators read classroom books with their children for approximately one week, with baseline data collected using the intervention fidelity checklist.

Educator Training

After initial baseline, the educators viewed a training video and recorded their own book reading to demonstrate the PEER and CROWD sequence. The researcher introduced each acronym, provided explanations, examples and non-examples, and modeled a sample reading. The researcher watched the educator recordings to determine that the educators performed all aspects of the PEER and CROWD sequence before beginning data collection for Phase B. Each area of PEER and CROWD is defined in Appendix C, as well as what was coded in the sample reading to indicate adherence to each portion of the protocol.

Post Video Training

Following training, each educator performed DR with no supports in place, consistent with prior research (e.g., Whitehurst et al., 1994; Lonigan et al., 1999). At the beginning of the condition in this study the researcher prompted: "Please use what you have learned to implement dialogic reading during your reading times." The educators chose books from their classroom to read to their children for approximately one week. Due to a delay in access to the training, Kendra did not complete this phase.

Alternating Treatment Design: Support

When the educators were introduced to the alternating treatment phase (Support), the researcher prompted: "Please use what you have learned to implement dialogic reading during your reading times. This schedule will tell you if you use a scripted book or the bookmark." A schedule was created for each educator with educator pairs being on opposite schedules. One educator's schedule was determined through a coin flip, and the other's was the opposite sequence. Therefore, one educator used the scripted book and the other used the bookmark/checklist. The scripted books, bookmark, and schedule were provided in a folder given to the educator pairs.

DR Checklist. During this portion of the alternating treatment design, the educators were provided a laminated, 11 in x 3 in checklist on a bookmark with the PEER and CROWD acronyms (see Appendix A) and instructed to hold the bookmark during readings.

DR Scripted Prompts. The scripted prompts consisted of a CROWD prompt attached to the top of a page with possible elaborations. At least one of each CROWD prompt was used throughout the scripted books. If the educators utilized each scripted prompt, they would demonstrate fidelity for each prompt as well as the Elaborate portion of PEER (see Appendix C).

Results

Results were analyzed through visual analysis of level, trend, and variability. Effect size was determined through Tau-U calculations to account for overlap in data to determine effect. For the baseline phase of the study, Rebecca's use of DR (Figure 1) ranged from 0-25% intervention fidelity ($M = 10\%$) and following training she ranged from 0-62.5% intervention fidelity ($M = 41.07\%$, $ES = 0.8$). The level of intervention fidelity increased for Rebecca but remained at moderate levels of intervention fidelity with variability. Rebecca completed part of the alternating treatment phase. The two supports do not demonstrate adequate differentiation to determine an effect. As there was not full data collection, the downward trend for the checklist ($M = 75\%$) cannot be confirmed. The script demonstrated high levels of fidelity after the first data point ($M = 87.5\%$), but the overlap between the two demonstrated a small effect size ($ES = .25$). Use of DR ranged from 37.5-87.5% intervention fidelity (*M* = 75%, *ES* = .25) for the final phase of the study. Compared to the training phase, Phase C has a higher level than Phase B; however, there is still overlap.

While the level was low, the data were variable for the baseline phase for Taylor's use of DR (Figure 2) ranging from 25-75% intervention fidelity (*M* = 47.5%). Taylor demonstrated the highest level of intervention fidelity in baseline; however, a descending trend appeared in baseline. Use of DR ranged from 75-100% intervention fidelity (*M* = 87.5%, *ES* = 0.933). While intervention fidelity reached 100%, data for Taylor has a marked descending trend. Taylor completed part of the alternating treatment phase. The two supports do not demonstrate adequate differentiation to determine an effect, and there was complete overlap with Phase B. The checklist (*M* = 87.5%) and script (*M* = 87.5%, *ES* = 0) mirror each other. Overall, in Phase C, use of DR ranged from 75-100% intervention fidelity (*M* = 87.5%, *ES* = 0) with much overlap.

Barry's use of DR (Figure 3) ranged from 0-37.5% intervention fidelity in baseline (*M* = 12.5%). Barry demonstrated low levels of intervention fidelity with some variability in their data, and this educator demonstrated 0% fidelity at the end of the phase. After training, Barry's fidelity raised in level with low variability. Use of DR ranged from 50-87.5% intervention fidelity (*M* = 62.5%, *ES* = 1). Overall, in Phase C, use of DR ranged from 50-100% intervention fidelity (*M* = 76.25 %, *ES* =.56) for the final phase of the study. For Barry, the two supports do not demonstrate adequate differentiation to determine an effect. The checklist (*M* = 80 %) and script (*M* = 72.5 %, *ES* = .06) have significant overlap. Compared to the training phase, Phase C overlaps with Phase B to some degree, but the level of Phase C is higher than Phase B.

Kendra's use of DR (Figure 4) ranged from 0-37.5% intervention fidelity at baseline (*M* = 17.5%). Kendra also demonstrated low levels of fidelity and ended the phase with 0% fidelity. Kendra did not complete Phase 2 due to the study's time constraints. Kendra completed part of the alternating treatment phase. The checklist (*M*

= 84.38%) and the script (*M* = 97.5 %, *ES* = .04) overlap significantly. Overall, in Phase C, use of DR ranged from 62.5-100% intervention fidelity (*M* = 91.67%, *ES* = 1) compared to the baseline phase. Phase C is higher in level than the baseline phase, but, without Phase B, this could be due to training alone.

Social Validity

Educators completed social validity measures for supports (i.e., the checklists and scripts) using the Intervention Usage Rating Profile (URP-I; Briesch et al., 2013) to determine acceptability (see Table 1). The URP-I includes 29 questions concerning treatment efficacy and acceptability with an internal consistency reliability ranging from .88-.98 (Lane et al., 2009). Ratings are from 1 (strongly disagree) to 6 (strongly agree) for statements like: "This intervention is an effective choice for addressing a variety of problems." Neither support (checklist or script) was consistently rated more highly than the other, and differences between them are minimal with all educators endorsing an average rating over 4 ("Slightly Agree"). Educators 1, 3, and 4 did not answer all questions on the survey so their average rankings were only taken from the questions that were completed. The researcher followed up with an informal discussion of the study. When asked which support was preferred, all four educators reported the checklist over the script. One educator noted the inflexibility of the scripts, and another was concerned about the scripts being repetitive.

Method: Study 2

The third research question, concerning child outcomes under the checklist condition, was addressed in Study 2. Improved child outcomes for early literacy skills would provide additional evidence that increasing intervention fidelity is an important consideration for DR. Study 2 was conducted to determine if the intervention was more effective with increased fidelity, and therefore meaningful to address in real-world intervention implementation.

Table 1
URP-Intervention ratings

		Rebecca	Taylor	Barry	Kendra
Checklist	Total Score	91	120	111	96
	Average Rating	4.33	4.29	4.83	4.17
Script	Total Score	93	114	110	99
	Average Rating	4.23	4.07	4.78	4.30

Table 2
Book Target Vocabulary List

Book	1	2	3	4	5	6	7	8	9	10
Do Like Kyla	Mirror	Footsteps	Page	Jar	Store	Braid	Oatmeal	Snow boots	Window	Apron
I Took My Frog to the Library	Frog	Desk	Hen	Pelican	Python	Giraffe	Hyena	Elephant	Librarian	Home
A Pocket for Corduroy	Laundromat	Soap	Chair	Towels	Beret	Bear	Overalls	Sketch pad	Cage	Card
Sheep in a Shop	Sheep	Pockets	Clock	Box	Stack	Piggy Bank	Rackets	Ribbon	Pennies	Wool

Figure 1
Percent Intervention Fidelity: Rebecca

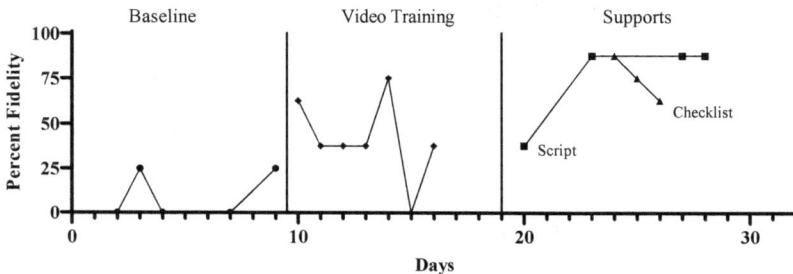

Figure 2
Percent Intervention Fidelity: Taylor

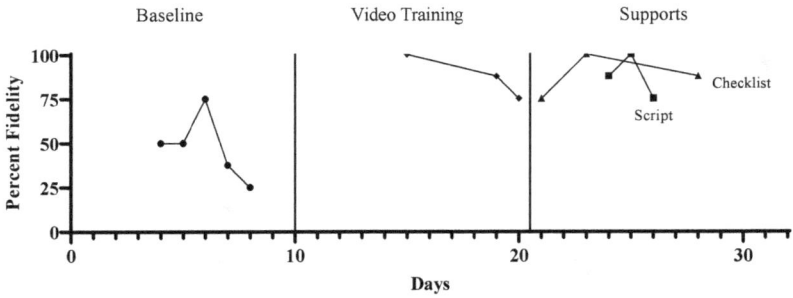

Figure 3
Percent Intervention Fidelity: Barry

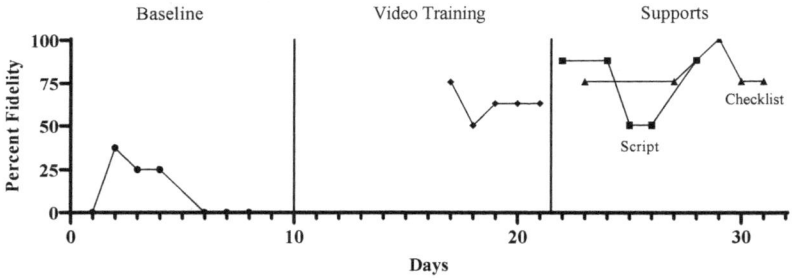

Figure 4
Percent Intervention Fidelity: Kendra

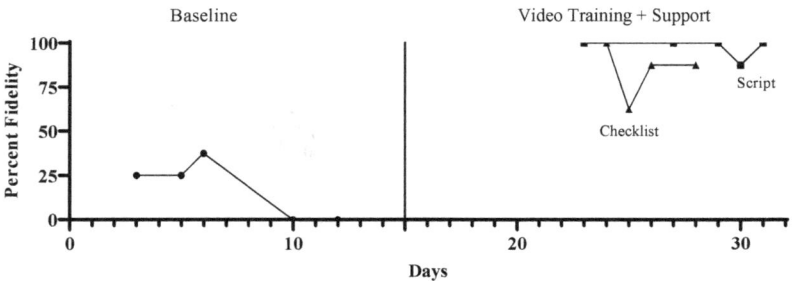

Figure 5
Vocabulary Mastery and Print Concepts

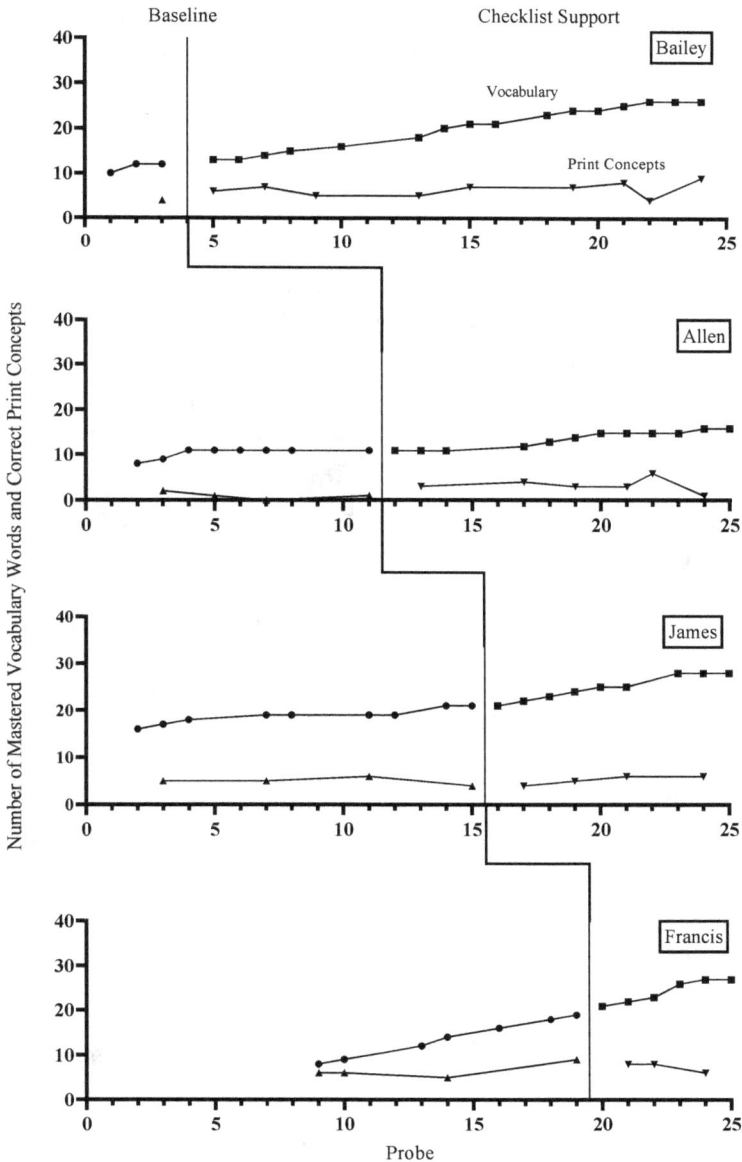

Participants and Setting

Four children from the same preschool center used in the first study were selected by the same educator participants from Study 1, who agree to continue serving as interventionists. The children's parents were informed of the opportunity for additional book reading time for their child, and children whose parents consented to their participation were screened. Children identifying 25% or less of pictures of target book vocabulary were eligible for the study (Coogle et al., 2018). Each educator ($N = 4$) was paired with a target child for the second study. Bailey was a four-year-old, White female who had not previously attended preschool. Allen was a three-year-old, Korean male who had not previously attended preschool. His home language was Korean and he was learning English during his time in preschool. James was a three-year-old, biracial male who had not previously attended preschool. Francis was a four-year-old, White male who had attended the preschool the previous year. All child participants are identified with pseudonyms.

Materials

A new set of books indicated as appropriate texts to engage in DR with preschoolers (Zevenbergen & Whitehurst, 2003) were provided to the educators. These books had limited amounts of text and large pictures including *Do Like Kyla* (Johnson, 1990), *Sheep in a Shop* (Shaw, 1991), *A Pocket for Corduroy* (Freeman, 1978), and *I Took My Frog to the Library* (Kimmel, 1990).

Dependent Variables
Target Vocabulary

The researcher selected ten target vocabulary words from each book (Table 2). Vocabulary words were both mentioned in the text and represented by a picture in the book. Children's knowledge of vocabulary words was assessed bi-weekly. Each participant was assessed individually by being asked, "What's this called?" as the researcher pointed to the picture representing the vocabulary word from the book on a PowerPoint slide. If the participant correctly labeled the picture within 5 seconds of the prompt, the word was considered "known," and if labeled correctly in three concurrent data collection sessions, it was considered "mastered." Once a participant mastered a vocabulary word, the word was removed from the assessment. This variable was the main decision-making variable for the study.

Print Concepts

Participants' print concepts knowledge was assessed weekly with the Concepts of Print Assessment (CPA; Lovelace & Stewart, 2007), a 20-question measure adapted from Clay's Concepts About Print for use with non-reading children for accessibility and equity reasons. The CPA asks questions like "Show me the title of the book" and "Show me where the book begins."

Inter-Observer Agreement

For target vocabulary words and print concepts, graduate students in a school psychology program were trained in the data collection procedures through a script and training video. Initial IOA was collected from a training video, and if they reached 85% agreement with the researcher on the training video, they could begin collecting data for the study (Kennedy, 2005). IOA was collected virtually through an online meeting program for approximately 48% of data collection sessions across phases. All data collectors remained above 85% IOA with an average of 95.6% for the vocabulary measure and 92.2% for the print concepts measure.

Procedure

After identifying children, gaining parental consent, and pre-assessing vocabulary, educators were given a set of the four books to read to child participants, with one book read daily. Implementation of DR with no supports began (Baseline). Once the first participant demonstrated steady responding over at least three data collections, the next phase began (i.e., checklist support), and their educator was given the checklist to read with the child during every session. The same group of books were read in this condition. The second, third, and fourth participants followed a similar trajectory within the multiple baseline design.

Results

Vocabulary Mastery

Again, results were analyzed through level and trend with Tau-U calculated for effect size from baseline to intervention. While level, trend, and variability are the three major areas of visual analysis, variability is not discussed in this section as variability in vocabulary mastery, as defined in the study, should not be present. Bailey demonstrated a low level of mastered vocabulary and a slightly increasing trend during baseline ($M = 12$) for vocabulary mastery as seen in Figure 5. During the intervention phase, the trend increased in slope ($M = 21.36, ES = 1$) with an overall higher level. Allen showed an initially increasing trend during baseline that leveled off towards no increase ($M = 10.38$) and had a low level for vocabulary mastery. During the intervention phase, the trend increased in slope after initial no increase with an overall higher level of vocabulary mastery ($M = 13.67, ES = .81$). James showed an initially increasing trend during baseline that leveled off towards no increase ($M = 18.78$) for vocabulary mastery with a higher level of initial mastery than the other participants. During the intervention phase, the trend increased in slope with an overall higher level of mastery ($M = 24.89, ES = .97$). Finally, Francis demonstrated a steadily increasing trend in baseline with a low level of initial vocabulary mastery ($M = 13.71$) which continued in the intervention phase ($M = 24.33, ES = 1$). A higher level of mastery was noted in the intervention phase.

Print Concepts

Print Concepts is a measure of participants' knowledge of books and features of books. Bailey's level of knowledge slightly increased in print concepts from baseline ($M = 5$) to intervention ($M = 6.5$, $ES = .56$) with a moderate effect size, though data are variable and only one baseline point was collected. Allen increased in print concept knowledge from baseline ($M = 1$) to intervention ($M = 3.4$, $ES = .8$) with a large effect size. Figure 5 shows an increasing trend in the data; however, this change is, overall, small. James demonstrated negligible progress from baseline to ($M = 5$) to intervention ($M = 5.25$, $ES = .19$) as seen in the level and trend of the data. Francis increased in print concept knowledge during the baseline period ($M = 6.5$) and remained stable in the intervention with no increase ($M = 7.33$, $ES = .33$).

Intervention Fidelity

Intervention fidelity was measured throughout the study with the same checklist as Study 1 (Appendix B) by a graduate student trained on the protocol in Study 1. Intervention fidelity was collected weekly for each educator for approximately 19% of baseline intervention days and 21% of supported intervention days. Mean intervention fidelity was low during the baseline phase for each educator. Mean intervention fidelity increased for each educator during the checklist support phase of the intervention, converging with findings from Study 1.

Discussion

Study 1

In Study 1, the researchers examined the effects of intervention supports (i.e., a checklist and scripted prompts), on educators' intervention fidelity while implementing DR. Data indicated that both the checklist and scripted prompts supported increased intervention fidelity, and both were endorsed as socially valid. These findings support the study's first hypothesis, that DR bolstered by a checklist would encourage higher levels of intervention fidelity than an unsupported condition. Findings partially support the second hypothesis, that the script would encourage higher fidelity than no supports. However, the hypothesis that scripted prompts would be superior to a checklist was not supported even though following the scripted prompts would have led to teachers completing at least seven of nine fidelity steps. Although DR research has examined the effects of scripts on intervention fidelity (Towson et al., 2016), no prior research has examined the effects of a checklist support or compared intervention scripts to other supports. This study expands the DR literature and opens additional avenues of research to support intervention fidelity, as is discussed in the Future Research section.

Social Validity

Educators endorsed positive ratings of both intervention supports, but the checklist was preferred by all four educators due to its flexibility. One educator expressed preference for the checklist over the repetitive nature of the scripted prompts, and their potential negative impact on children's interest levels during reading. This was reflected in the scripts not being fully followed (there was lower than 78% fidelity in some observations). It is possible that this perception is indicative of a mismatch between the direct intervention supports and the constructivist instructional framework of the preschool, which is associated with the educators' interest in engaging children in a way that speaks to each child's interests. A set script may not allow the flexibility for the educators to reference the child's interests and engage each child in a differentiated way.

The checklist preference may also reflect a disconnect between researcher prompts and educator prompts. The researcher developed prompts to mitigate time constraints on the educators and to simply examine the effects of the supports on intervention fidelity. Hawkins et al. (2008) recommended consulting with educators concerning procedures of interventions to build agency of the educators in the process, and this process would include development of intervention scripts. If the scripts were developed in collaboration with the educators, the educators might have had a greater sense of ownership of the intervention script, perhaps increasing their preference for scripts. However, such procedures would incur an additional time commitment to the intervention, which could ultimately decrease acceptability.

Study 2

With neither support demonstrating superior comparative benefits, educators were asked to choose a support for Study 2. The checklist support was preferred by all educators, and subsequently applied during Study 2 to examine the effects of child outcomes under a no support baseline DR condition and a DR checklist condition. Both the checklist condition and the script condition promoted high intervention fidelity, and therefore the application of a checklist was deemed appropriate for Study 2. Selecting intervention components should include considerations of what is most likely to work and preference-consideration for interventionists, which can influence implementation fidelity (Dart et al., 2012).

Data partially supported the hypothesis that DR, when implemented with checklist supports, would increase child vocabulary. An increase in trend was noted for book vocabulary from baseline to intervention, but not for print concepts. The increase in child vocabulary growth when the support was implemented is consistent with previous studies such as Whitehurst et al. (1994), which demonstrated less growth when interventionists implemented DR with low levels of fidelity. Intervention fidelity was low in the baseline period of the present study even though the educators had experience with DR from Study 1. However, the educators' levels of intervention fidelity in baseline is higher than the baseline in Study 1, showing a possible practice effect. This still suggested that the supports were helpful in boosting intervention fidelity higher than in baseline, although an optimal level of intervention fidelity (85% or higher) was not reached. Moreover, these findings support the idea that intervention fidelity can be maintained over time instead of drifting (Zibulsky et al., 2019).

Although DR is considered effective for increasing child print concepts (Whitehurst et al., 1994), Study 2 did not result in a notable change in print concepts across the four participants. One reason for the lack of change may be a difference in the measure used in this study versus prior research. Whitehurst et al. (1994) utilized the Developing Skills Checklist as a pre- and post- test measure, whereas the present study included a measure derived from Clay's Concepts of Print to probe the skill weekly. These measures may differ to the extent that they measure different aspects of print concepts and were utilized in different ways. However, the NELP (2008) considers oral language, vocabulary included, as one of the best predictors of reading success later in a child's schooling. Therefore, although the study does not show growth in print concepts, this skill is also less predictive of later success.

Taken together, the results of these two studies provide further evidence that DR is an effective intervention, and that high intervention fidelity results in improved growth for child outcomes. Without the DR supports provided in this study, children may not receive the intervention as intended. The studies support the overall need for intervention fidelity supports for high quality interventions (Sanetti & Collier-Meek, 2019).

Implications

The study has implications for practitioners providing DR interventions, or consulting with educators and other staff on early reading interventions. To close the literacy gap (NELP, 2008), empirically-supported interventions that are implemented with fidelity are needed. Early childhood educators and those providing consultative supports must choose appropriate interventions such as DR to respond to children's literacy gaps. Beyond selecting a strong intervention such as DR, ensuring implementation fidelity is critical. There is limited time in the school day for children to develop skills, and the most time-efficient and effective form of an intervention should be implemented. Supports like a checklist require little time to develop and implement but support higher levels of implementation fidelity and, in turn, increased child learning. The present study offers a practical example of a checklist and script which can be used by practitioners to support DR implementation.

Limitations

Although the study adds to the literature on DR, it is not without limitations. Educators informally expressed a preference for checklists, though social validity scores did not indicate this preference, perhaps due to the researcher's connection to the educators and school. While the researcher limited discussion of the study with the educators, the researcher had worked with the educator participants in prior projects which may have influenced social validity ratings. This limits the social validity measure utilized, and the choice of the checklist over the script when interviewed may reflect the true social validity of the supports.

Given school closures from COVID-19, a limited number of data points could be collected in each phase, and not all phases for all participants have five data points for both studies. Each phase has at least three data points, which is acceptable in single-case design research, though not ideal as additional data points would help further indicate intervention effects (Kennedy, 2005). The second study is also limited in that the fourth participant did not have a steady baseline trend established before the checklist was implemented, making it difficult to determine how the checklist condition impacted that participant. Additionally, data like vocabulary mastery does not have variability and may not be as well represented by a single case design. Also due to COVID-19, the preschool setting had smaller than normal class sizes of six to nine children, and it is not clear if this intervention is as feasible with larger classes. The setting was a specialized, constructivist preschool with time allotted for one-on-one child and educator interaction, which is not available in every setting where DR might be performed. Finally, the sample of educator and children does not match every child's experience, limiting the generalizability of the findings.

Future Research

To further develop this research, additional studies should examine intervention supports for DR in other contexts. This study focused on DR in the constructivist preschool context; however, DR interventions could be delivered in the home, in clinics, or in traditional school settings. Although educators in this setting preferred the checklist, parents with less expertise in early literacy may prefer having a scripted intervention. Additionally, supports like checklists or prompts could provide valuable additions to intervention fidelity for other school-based interventions beyond DR; exploring their potential applicability would be fruitful.

References

Barnett, D., Hawkins, R., McCoy, D., Wahl, E., Shier, A., Denune, H., & Kimener, L. (2014). Methods used to document procedural fidelity in school-based intervention research. *Journal of Behavioral Education, 23*(1), 89-107. https://doi.org/10.1007/s10864-013-9188-y

Briesch, A. M., Chafouleas, S. M., Neugebauer, S. R., & Riley-Tillman, T. C. (2013). Assessing influences on intervention implementation: Revision of the Usage Rating Profile-Intervention. *Journal of School Psychology, 51*(1), 81-96. https://doi.org/10.1016/j.jsp.2012.08.006

Coogle, C., Floyd, K. K., & Rahn, N. L. (2018). Dialogic reading and adapted dialogic reading with preschoolers with autism spectrum disorder. *Journal of Early Intervention, 40*(4), 363-379. doi/10.1177/1053815118797887

Dart, E. H., Cook, C. R., Collins, T. A., Gresham, F. M., & Chenier, J. S. (2012). Test driving interventions to increase treatment integrity and student outcomes. *School*

Psychology Review, 41(4), 467-481. https://doi.org/10.1080/02796015.2012.12
087500

Forman, S. G., Shapiro, E. S., Codding, R. S., Gonzales, J. E., Reddy, L. A., Rosenfield,
S. A., Sanetti, L. M, & Stoiber, K. C. (2013). Implementation science and school
psychology. *School Psychology Quarterly, 28*(2), 77. http://dx.doi.org/10.1037/
spq0000019

Freeman, D. (1978). *A Pocket for Corduroy.* Viking Press.

Gubbels, J., van der Put, C. E., & Assink, M. (2019). Risk factors for school absenteeism
and dropout: A meta-analytic review. *Journal of Youth and Adolescence, 48*(9),
1637-1667. https://doi.org/10.1007/s10964-019-01072-5

Guskey, T. R. (1991). Enhancing the effectiveness of professional development
programs. *Journal of Educational and Psychological Consultation, 2*(3), 239-247.
https://doi-org.uc.idm.oclc.org/10.1207/s1532768xjepc0203_3

Hawkins, R. O., Morrison, J. Q., Musti-Rao, S., & Hawkins, J. A. (2008). Treatment integrity
for academic interventions in real-world settings. *School Psychology Forum, 2* (3).

Johnson, A. (1990). *Do Like Kyla.* (J. Ransome, Illus.). Scholastic Inc.

Kennedy, C. H. (2005). *Single-case designs for educational research.* Pearson/A & B.

Kimmel, E. (1990) *I Took My Frog to the Library* (B. Sims, Illus.) Penguin Random House

Lane, K. L., Kalberg, J. R., Bruhn, A. L., Driscoll, S. A., Wehby, J. H., & Elliott, S. N.
(2009). Assessing social validity of school-wide positive behavior support plans:
Evidence for the reliability and structure of the Primary Intervention Rating
Scale. *School Psychology Review, 38*(1), 135-144. https://doi.org/10.1080/027960
15.2009.12087854

Lonigan, C. J., Anthony, J. L., Bloomfield, B. G., Dyer, S. M., & Samwel, C. S. (1999).
Effects of two shared-reading interventions on emergent literacy skills of
at-risk preschoolers. *Journal of Early Intervention, 22*(4), 306-322. https://doi.
org/10.1177/105381519902200406

Lonigan, C. J., & Whitehurst, G. J. (1998). Relative efficacy of parent and educator
involvement in a shared-reading intervention for preschool children from low-
income backgrounds. *Early Childhood Research Quarterly, 13*(2), 263-290. https://
doi.org/10.1016/S0885-2006(99)80038-6

Lovelace, S., & Stewart, S. R. (2007). Increasing print awareness in preschoolers with language
impairment using non-evocative print referencing. *Language, Speech, and Hearing
Services in Schools. 38(1),* 16-30. https://doi.org/10.1044/0161-1461(2007/003)

National Early Literacy Panel (2008). *Developing early literacy: Report of the National Early
Literacy Panel: A scientific synthesis of early literacy development and implications
for intervention.* National Institute for Literacy. https://lincs.ed.gov/publications/
pdf/NELPReport09.pdf

Neuman, S. B. (2009). *Changing the odds for children at risk: Seven essential principles of educational programs that break the cycle of poverty.* Educators College Press.

Pentimonti, J. M., Zucker, T. A., Justice, L. M., Petscher, Y., Piasta, S. B., & Kaderavek, J. N. (2012). A standardized tool for assessing the quality of classroom-based shared reading: Systematic Assessment of Book Reading (SABR). *Early Childhood Research Quarterly, 27*(3), 512-528. https://doi.org/10.1016/j.ecresq.2011.12.007

Sanetti, L. M. H., & Collier-Meek, M. A. (2019). Increasing implementation science literacy to address the research-to-practice gap in school psychology. *Journal of School Psychology, 76,* 33-47. https://doi.org/10.1016/j.jsp.2019.07.008

Shaw, N. (1991). *Sheep in a Shop.* (M. Apple, Illus.). Scholastic Inc.

Slobodkina, E. (1940). *Caps for Sale.* Scholastic Inc.

Towson, J. A., Fettig, A., Fleury, V. P., & Abarca, D. L. (2017). Dialogic reading in early childhood settings: A summary of the evidence base. *Topics in Early Childhood Special Education, 37*(3), 132-146. https://doi.org/10.1177/0271121417724875

Towson, J. A., Gallagher, P. A., & Bingham, G. E. (2016). Dialogic reading: Language and preliteracy outcomes for young children with disabilities. *Journal of Early Intervention, 38*(4), 230-246. https://doi.org/10.1177/1053815116668643

United States Department of Education (2019). National achievement-level results. *NAEP Report Card: Reading.* https://www.nationsreportcard.gov/reading/nation/achievement/?grade=4

Whitehurst, G. J., Epstein, J. N., Angell, A. L., Payne, A. C., Crone, D. A., & Fischel, J. E. (1994). Outcomes of an emergent literacy intervention in Head Start. *Journal of Educational Psychology, 86*(4), 542. https://doi.org/10.1037/0022-0663.91.2.261

Zevenbergen, A. A. & Whitehurst, G. J. (2003). Dialogic reading: A shared picture book reading intervention for preschoolers. In A. van Kleeck & S. Stahl (Eds.). *On reading books to children: Parents and educators* (170-191). Routledge.

Zevenbergen, A. A., Whitehurst, G. J., & Zevenbergen, J. A. (2003). Effects of a shared-reading intervention on the inclusion of evaluative devices in narratives of children from low-income families. *Journal of Applied Developmental Psychology, 24*(1), 1-15. https://doi.org/10.1016/S0193-3973(03)00021-2

Zibulsky, J., Casbar, C., Blanchard, T., & Morgan, C. (2019). Parent question use during shared reading time: How does training affect question type and frequency? *Psychology in the Schools, 56*(2), 206-219. https://doi.org/10.1002/pits.22219

Zion, G. (1957). *No Roses for Harry.* (M.B. Graham, Illus.). Harper Collins.

Appendix A
Checklist Bookmark

Prompt

Evaluate

Elaborate

Repetition

Completion

Recall

Open-ended

Wh-

Distancing

Appendix B
Fidelity Data Sheet

Tally occurrences of PEER and CROWD by the educator during the reading. Record beginning and end time of reading and educator reading.

Begin: ____ : ____ End: ____ : ____ Date: _____

Educator: _____

<u>Prompt (see below)</u>

> <u>Completion (I see a ____ looking at me)</u>

> <u>Recall (How big was Clifford when Emily got him?)</u>

> <u>Open-ended (Tell me how the people feel.)</u>

> <u>Wh- (Who took the keys?)</u>

> <u>Distancing (When was a time that you shared like Rainbow Fish?)</u>

<u>Evaluate</u>

<u>Elaborate</u>

<u>Distance</u>

Appendix C
PEER and CROWD procedures adapted from Whitehurst & Zevenbergen, (2003)

	Definition	Examples
Prompt	A question or statement that directs children to label objects in the story.	"Tell me about this picture." "What will he do?" "When did you feel like Corduroy?"
Evaluate	A statement that provides performance feedback for a prompted statement.	"That's right, the bear is in the child's arm." "Let's look again, what color is this?"
Elaborate	Any word addition to a child's original statement.	Child: "They are in a laundry." Reader: "They are in a *busy* laundry."
Repeat	A prompt for children to repeat a corrected or elaborated sentence.	"Say it with me: He is a stuffed bear." "Look, he wears *green* pants. What color pants?"
Completion	Any prompt where part of the statement is omitted.	"She wants to be like____." "Harry got a _____." "The sheep are in a ____."
Recall	Any prompt that requires the children to respond with information from a previous page.	"Who took the caps?" "Where was Corduroy left?"
Open-ended	Statements that prompt the children to respond to the pictures or story in their own words.	"Tell me what you see." "Tell me about the page." "Tell me how Harry feels."
Wh-	What, Where and, Why questions that do not fall under the other CROWD definitions.	"What does Harry think about the sweater?" "Where is Corduroy?"
Distancing	Prompts that require children to relate book content to the real world.	"When did you feel like Corduroy?" "Have you ever copied someone like Kyla and her sister?"

Interdisciplinary Collaborative Practice in Early Childhood

Sara Kupzyk, Brenda Bassingthwaite, Adam D. Weaver, and Philip D. Nordness

Abstract

Young children often present with challenging behaviors such as tantrums, aggression, and noncompliance. Rates of expulsion for behavior concerns in early childhood are alarming and can have long-term negative implications for children and their families (Early Childhood Learning and Knowledge Center, 2022). Implementation of a systematic multi-tiered system of supports framework can improve behavioral outcomes of young children. To effectively meet child and family needs within these frameworks, it is integral for members of the team to collaborate. Interdisciplinary teams within early childhood might include families, teachers, school psychologists, behavior analysts, speech language pathologists, physical therapists, occupational therapists and other related mental health and medical providers. The Interprofessional Education Collaborative outlined competencies for interdisciplinary collaborative practice that are organized within four domains: values and ethics, roles/responsibilities, interdisciplinary communication, and teams/teamwork. To facilitate interdisciplinary collaboration (IC) in practice, it is important to provide opportunities for collaboration across disciplines within coursework and field experiences. In this paper, we provide an example of an interdisciplinary training program to support behavioral and mental health needs of children. The training includes graduate students in applied behavior analysis, school psychology, and special education. Scholars participating in the program complete coursework for their specific programs in addition to joint coursework, seminars, and practicum activities in school settings. Throughout the program, scholars gain knowledge and skills in eight competencies identified for the program. Based on the literature and our training experience, we also outline insights and actions for training at the university-level and practitioner-level to implement interdisciplinary teaming.

Keywords: *Interdisciplinary, collaboration, challenging behavior, pre-service training, early childhood*

Interdisciplinary Collaborative Practice in Early Childhood

The use of effective multi-tiered interventions in schools can have profound positive effects on child and teacher success. A Multi-Tiered Systems of Support (MTSS) framework can be defined as "an educational framework for continuous improvement, problem-solving, and decision-making" (Nebraska Department of Education, 2022). The successful implementation of an MTSS framework should include universal screening, differentiation of goals and objectives, tiered social and academic interventions, and ongoing progress monitoring. MTSS within an early childhood framework addresses the mental health and behavioral needs of every child, regardless of their ability, eligibility, or cultural background, and can be addressed by integrating assessment and intervention (Council for Exceptional Children Division for Early Childhood [CEC], 2021). When implementing an MTSS framework, the goal is to identify the needs of the children and to match them with appropriate supports across the tiers (i.e., universal, targeted, intensive). The supports are often provided by interdisciplinary teams of professionals with expertise in child development and behavior which can be integrated in inclusive settings to meet the diverse needs of all children (Grisham-Brown & Hemmeter, 2017). The key to effectively implementing an MTSS framework is to make certain that it is a data driven decision-making process (CEC, 2021). This approach emphasizes preventative and responsive approaches to children's behavioral needs (Marsh & Mathur, 2020).

The Pyramid Model has been promoted as an early childhood MTSS framework which augments the three tiers mentioned above with the foundation of an effective workforce (National Center for Pyramid Model Innovations, n.d.). This foundation includes training, policies, and systems to ensure that early childhood professionals are skilled in delivering evidence-based practices to the children they serve. Previous research on the application of the Pyramid Model in early childhood settings has demonstrated that when teachers receive proper training and coaching on the implementation of tiered supports, children with or at-risk of disabilities can improve their social skills and reduce problem behavior (Hemmeter et al., 2014).

Despite calls for use of a more positive, preventative approach to respond to common behavior challenges (e.g., aggression, tantrums, and noncompliance), negative discipline strategies such as expulsion continue to be used in early childhood. In fact, within state-funded programs, each year approximately 8,710 three- and four-year old children are expelled or excluded from attending a school for disciplinary reasons (National Association for the Education of Young Child, 2017). These rates are 3.2 times higher than those found in kindergarten through twelfth grade and discrepancies exist between student enrollment demographics and expulsions (Gilliam, 2005). Boys are more likely to be expelled than girls and students who are Black and those with disabilities are expelled at rates that are more than twice their enrollment (Black students account for 18.2% of enrollment, but 38.2% of expulsions; students with disabilities account for 22.7% of enrollment, but 56.9% of expulsions) (U.S. Education Department, Office of Civil Rights, 2021). Overall, rates of expulsion in early childhood are alarming and can have long-term negative repercussions for children and their families. For example, children who are expelled have fewer opportunities for learning and socializing, may develop negative views of themselves and school, and continue to show behavior concerns that impact their functioning and future school success

(Early Childhood Learning and Knowledge Center [ECLKC], 2022). Behavior concerns are also linked to high student dropout rates, later unemployment, incarceration, and homelessness (Kataoka et al., 2002). Expulsion also places a burden on families and is associated with increased stress, job loss, and harsher parenting practices (ECLKC, 2022). Furthermore, without effective services delivered within school systems, children are unlikely to receive necessary intervention (Whitney & Peterson, 2019). Unfortunately, limited coordination across disciplines can result in fragmented and less effective intervention (Holmes et al., 2021). Coordinating efforts across disciplines is important to enhancing outcomes and decreasing stress placed on families to be case managers between school, medical, and community providers (Kervick et al., 2021).

A systems approach to meet children's needs will often involve several individuals including families, early childhood special education teachers, school psychologists, behavior analysts, developmental pediatricians, and mental health providers (see Table 1 for an overview of individuals commonly involved in early childhood). For example, special education teachers provide instruction, accommodations, and modifications to curriculum to meet the unique needs of the child. They are part of the multi-disciplinary team for determining eligibility for special education services and will often serve on school teams for implementing school-wide supports for learning and behavior. They are also responsible for individualized education programs (IEP) or individualized family service plans (IFSP) that detail the services, accommodations, and modifications necessary to support the child's development and inclusion in the general education setting. Furthermore, they collaborate with families and professionals across disciplines to coordinate services to ensure children have access to a free appropriate education in the least restrictive environment (Individuals with Disabilities Education Improvement Act, 2004, 2012). School psychologists provide comprehensive services to children with disabilities, supporting their academic, social-emotional, and behavioral success. This is accomplished both through direct educational and mental health services to children, as well as by indirect and consultative service to parents, teachers, and other educational professionals. For children with severe and high-intensity needs, school psychologists are instrumental in the identification and evaluation of disability, and the development and progress monitoring of services and supports. Board Certified Behavior Analysts (BCBA) have extensive understanding of behavior within the environmental context. In school settings, applied behavior analysts are well positioned to assess the function or reasons for challenging behaviors and develop focused behavior intervention plans in coordination with other providers to prevent, intervene, and teach more adaptive skills.

Although each of these individuals aim to support children and families, coordination of their efforts may be limited as most school mental health professionals indicate that they do not receive training in how to engage in interdisciplinary collaboration (IC) (Arora et al., 2016). When individuals receive training related to IC in coursework and field experiences, they report feeling more prepared and are more likely to engage in IC in their work (Arora et al., 2019). To facilitate training and supports for children, families, and teachers, there is a need within pre-service programs to develop interdisciplinary leaders that are able to effectively team and collaborate with professionals across disciplines (Bradley-Klug et al., 2013). The purpose of this paper is to describe: (a) the value of IC and teaming within these frameworks, (b) an example of an interdisciplinary graduate training program focused on developing leaders to support behavioral needs of children, and (c) insights and actionable steps for training at the university and practitioner level to encourage IC.

Value of Interprofessional Teaming and Education

In clinical settings, interprofessional teaming is defined as "The levels of cooperation, coordination and collaboration characterizing the relationships between professions in delivering patient-centered care" (Interprofessional Education Collaborative, 2016). In educational settings, this same type of teaming among professionals and families is imperative for creating successful educational environments for all children but especially for those with severe emotional or behavioral health needs. For children whose needs represent an educational disability, the Individuals with Disabilities Education Improvement Act requires that special education services be planned and provided through an interdisciplinary team (IDEA 2004, 2012).

The principles of interprofessional teaming apply to IC in school settings. Common barriers also exist, such as differences in policies/standards, lack of understanding roles and responsibilities, lack of common language, and logistical barriers (Manor-Binyamini, 2007; O'Keeffe & McDowell, 2004). These challenges have likely been exacerbated in interdisciplinary educational teams because team members often received their pre-service training from separate programs with little overlap in coursework and little exposure to the roles, competencies, and strengths of other education professionals (Dobbes-Oates & Morris, 2016).

Interprofessional education (IPE) is a means of addressing the siloed approach in pre-service training environments to promote the development of interdisciplinary teaming skills. IPE occurs when two or more professionals learn with each other and are equipped to develop a collaborative relationship across their professions that improves the quality of care provided (World Health Organization (WHO), 2010). IPE was first implemented within healthcare in the 1960s to help create a collaborative-ready workforce equipped with the understanding of various professionals and the skills to team with them to address health care needs. The WHO conducted a survey with 396 respondents from 42 countries to better understand the impact of IPE programs. Respondents reported benefits in educational experiences for trainees (e.g., real world experiences, guidance from different professionals, learning about other professions) and in benefits to the healthcare systems (e.g., improved outcomes, staff morale; WHO, 2010). There is significant potential for positive effects on educational systems, educational policy, and child outcomes when IPE is adopted in pre-service educational programs.

Education professionals are well-suited for IPE given the various fields and backgrounds that come together to support children. There have been numerous demonstrations of IPE training experiences for disciplines within education including programs for school psychologists and speech and language pathologists (DeVeny & Mckevitt, 2021); special educators and school counselors (Dobbs-Oates & Morris, 2016); early childhood educators and social workers (Anderson, 2013); and special educators and physical therapists (George & Oriel, 2009). Engaging pre-service trainees from different disciplines in IPE has resulted in positive benefits that should result in stronger interdisciplinary teams when they enter the workforce. Trainees reported an improvement in their perceptions of their own profession and training and their perceptions of the other professionals included in the interprofessional program (DeVeney & McKevitt, 2021). Trainees also reported being better able to understand the roles and responsibilities that each discipline contributes to a collaborative, teaming relationship (Anderson, 2013). Trainees' perceptions of the importance of collaboration and teaming is higher after participating in IPE (Dobbs-Oates & Morris, 2016; DeVeney & McKevitt, 2021). Finally, language barriers based in professional jargon decreased as pre-services trainees worked together on projects and spent time questioning each other's jargon (Anderson, 2013).

The Interprofessional Education Collaborative (2016) developed specific competencies for best practices across disciplines to provide a foundation for interprofessional development. The competencies are organized into four domains: (a) values and ethics, (b) roles/responsibilities, (c) interdisciplinary communication, (d) and teams/teamwork. Direct training in these competencies across special education and specialty service may address deficits in interdisciplinary training and practice. These competencies served as a basis for interdisciplinary training for our personnel preparation program.

Table 1

Individuals Commonly Involved in Early Childhood Programs and Related Care

Profession/Field	Description	Professional Association
Applied Behavior Analysts	Conduct behavioral assessments, design interventions to improve adaptive behaviors and decrease maladaptive behaviors, provide training and coaching support	Behavior Analyst Certification Board https://www.bacb.com/about-behavior-analysis/
Developmental-Behavioral Pediatricians	Pediatricians that have specialized training and expertise to evaluate and provide treatment for developmental, learning and behavioral difficulties	American Pediatric Association https://www.academicpeds.org/sig/developmental-behavioral-pediatrics/ https://www.aap.org/en/community/aap-sections/developmental-and-behavioral-pediatrics/
Families	Provide insight into their children and are critical when making decisions about intervention	Center for Parent Information and Resources https://www.parentcenterhub.org/
Mental Health Professional (Psychologist, Licensed Mental Health Practitioners, Clinical Social Worker, or Counselor)	Psychologists conduct evaluations and provide evidence-based treatment for mental health concerns Licensed mental health practitioners, clinical social workers, and counselors provide treatment to address identified mental health concerns.	American Psychological Association https://www.apa.org/ American Board of Clinical Social Work https://www.abcsw.org/what-is-clinical-social-work American Counseling Association https://www.counseling.org/
Occupational Therapists	Use therapeutic techniques to rehabilitate, improve, or maintain a persons' ability to perform everyday activities	American Occupational Therapy Association https://www.aota.org
Paraeducators	Provide daily behavioral and instructional support to students with disabilities	National Resource Center for Paraeducators https://nrcpara.org/
Physical Therapists	Provide intervention and strategies to improve movement, reduce or manage pain, and prevent disability	American Physical Therapy Association https://www.apta.org/
School Administrator	Manages the organization and climate (safety, well-being) of the school, serves as an instructional leader, supports program accountability	The School Superintendents Association https://www.aasa.org/home/
School Counselor	Provide social-emotional classroom lessons, short-term counseling to individual students, and referrals for long-term supports	American School Counselor Association https://www.schoolcounselor.org
School Psychologists	Consult with teachers, families, and other support staff; conduct assessments to inform programs; provide direct support and interventions for mental health, learning and behavior	National Association of School Psychologists https://www.nasponline.org
Special Education Teacher	Ensure students with disabilities' needs are being met and that accommodations are being implemented	Council for Exceptional Children https://exceptionalchildren.org/

Table 1 continued
Individuals Commonly Involved in Early Childhood Programs and Related Care

Profession/Field	Description	Professional Association
Speech-Language Pathologists	Provide intervention and strategies to improve students' speech sounds, language, literacy, social communication, voice, fluency, cognitive-communication, and feeding and swallowing	American Speech-Language-Hearing Association https://www.asha.org

Interdisciplinary Program Development and Evaluation

Prior to developing our interdisciplinary training program, faculty from Applied Behavior Analysis (ABA), Special Education, and School Psychology had an extensive history of collaboration. These collaborations included development of a specialized ABA program track in school psychology and special education. In addition, faculty in all three programs had a history of partnering in student and faculty research. Each of these experiences reinforced a shared interest among faculty in supporting our students' professional growth in the knowledge and skills of their respective fields, but also in the ability to successfully collaborate across disciplines. Because effective school teams are so critical to the success of young children who demonstrate behavioral challenges, we determined that IC was a necessary skill for students in our programs. We realized that students who are not provided with experiences and coaching in collaboration across disciplines may struggle to effectively team with these professionals after graduation.

Moreover, without sufficient exposure to the role and function of each profession, graduates may not be aware of the training and expertise that other professionals have and may even see other team members as competition rather than as partners (see Table 1). For these reasons, the Interdisciplinary Behavioral Consultation (IBC) Scholars project was developed. We received grant funding through the personnel development program through the Office of Special Education and Rehabilitative Services, Department of Education.

Table 2

Actionable Steps for Preservice Programs and Individuals in Practice

Pre-Service Education Program Actions

Values/Ethics
1. Identify programs working with similar population group/who have shared goals for children and families
2. Keep focus on the needs and goals of children and families
3. Show respect for diversity and individual differences
4. Develop trusting relationships

Roles/Responsibilities
1. Share roles and responsibilities of your discipline with faculty and staff in other programs
2. Explore complementary roles across professions

Interprofessional Communication
1. Establish effective and reciprocal methods of communication across program faculty and students
2. Avoid use of discipline-specific terminology in conversations with other disciplines
3. Listen and encourage ideas and provide instructive feedback in a respectful manner

Teams and Teamwork
1. Examine each discipline's program of study to determine potential for joint course work
2. Establish joint seminars and professional learning opportunities
3. Create simulations/group experiences across programs (e.g., case-based scenario discussions, mock Individualized Family Service Plan meeting)
4. Establish partnerships with local schools and organizations for field experience opportunities

Practitioner/Educator Actions

Values/Ethics
1. Establish administrative support for interdisciplinary communication and teaming
2. Demonstrate respect for other disciplines and team members
3. Collaborate with team to identify shared goals
4. Show respect for diversity and individual differences and recognize the need for culturally and linguistically appropriate services

Roles/Responsibilities
1. Explore the roles and responsibilities of other providers within and outside of the early childhood education setting
2. Meet with individuals from other disciplines to learn more about their role and responsibilities on the team

Interprofessional Communication
1. Include administrators in establishing routine team meetings and communication related to care coordination
2. Actively participate in routine team meetings
3. Determine who needs to be on the team

Teams and Teamwork
1. Build rapport and trust
2. Use effective and efficient meeting procedures
3. Examine how each team member can facilitate goals

Note. Action based on IPEC (2026) Core Domains for Interprofessional Collaborative Practice

Within the program, scholars from the three disciplines participate in the following training activities: (a) unique coursework for their individual program; (b) joint coursework; (c) weekly professional seminars that include clinical topics, leadership and skill-building opportunities, speakers from the community, and case discussions; and (d) interdisciplinary practicum in high-needs schools (e.g., early childhood, elementary, middle, high school and transition programs) providing behavioral consultation and supporting systems change efforts. Scholars receive supervision and mentoring from on-site supervisors and university faculty teams. Across these activities, scholars develop knowledge and skills in competencies we outlined as essential to all disciplines in meeting the needs of children with and at-risk for challenging behavior.

Identified Competencies

In addition to IC as described above, we selected core competencies for participating scholars to achieve within the program. The competencies were selected based on a review of overlapping content for each field aimed at meeting the needs of children with or at-risk for emotional and behavior disorders (e.g., National Association of School Psychologists Blueprint for Training and Practice, Council for Exceptional Children Professional Preparation Standards, Behavior Analyst Certification Board Task List) and based on review of the knowledge and skills related to MTSS/Pyramid. The eight competencies identified included: (1) child and adolescent development, (2) applied behavior analysis, (3) family-centered services, (4) intensive instruction, (5) identification of behavioral health needs, (6) functional behavioral assessment, (7) data-based decision making, and (8) systems-change and leadership. Each is seen as foundational to effective leadership in collaborative and coordinated interdisciplinary services to children receiving behavioral intervention services.

Child and Adolescent Development

An understanding of typical childhood development is essential to the design and delivery of effective early childhood education and intervention practices. This is particularly important when determining whether a child's challenging behaviors (e.g., tantrums or defiance) represent age-appropriate behavior or a more serious concern (Tzuo, 2007). This is also a necessary consideration when conducting developmental and behavioral screeners and diagnostic or needs-based assessments. Knowledge of developmental milestones, including typical and atypical development, is promoted in our project through coursework and supervised experiences in school settings. For example, during case discussions, we prompt scholars to describe developmental considerations that contributed to selection of assessments and interventions.

Applied Behavior Analysis

ABA involves assessing behavior in relation to environmental contexts (e.g., setting events, antecedents, consequences) and using principles of learning to develop, implement, and evaluate socially significant behavior change procedures. ABA is an evidence-based practice (Slocum et al., 2014) that is applicable to all children in special and general educational contexts and applicable across a range of presenting problems (i.e., behavior, academic, social, cognitive, emotional). An understanding of learning, function, motivation, and reinforcement is foundational to understanding a child's behavior in the context of environmental variables, and this understanding is essential to the development of effective interventions (Kazdin, 2013). In addition to providing a framework for case conceptualization, ABA is the foundational science for specific evidence-based practices such as: behavioral consultation (Bergen & Kratochwill, 1990); Pyramid model (National Center for Pyramid Model Innovations, n.d.); classroom management strategies such as use of behavior-specific praise (LaBrot et al., 2022) the Good Behavior Game (Donaldson et al., 2018), and Preschool Life Skills program (Fahmie & Luczynski, 2018); and individualized behavior and educational interventions for children across the continuum of developmental and functional capabilities (e.g., Moran & Malott, 2004; Walker, et al., 2004).

IBC Scholars develop knowledge and skills in ABA that permeate assessment techniques and the design of appropriate behavioral interventions. For example, in practicum, scholars receive guidance from site supervisors in using data (e.g., function, present levels of the target and desired behavior), literature, and ABA principles to develop interventions and evaluate the effectiveness of the interventions for individual children.

Family-Centered Services

Because of the specific focus in early childhood of meeting both the child's needs and those of the family (e.g., supports, training, resources), effective teaming must include strategies to engage and partner with families. While some families may take initiative in collaborating with school teams to support their children, often it is necessary for school personnel to actively invite, encourage, and reinforce participation (Epstein, 2011). School personnel should be skilled in communicating the importance of families in the problem-solving process (Christenson & Sheridan, 2001). This will frequently require school personnel to examine their own beliefs, experiences, and culture, so that potential bias or structural obstacles can be addressed (Beaulieu & Gomez, 2022; Goldenberg 2014). Within the seminar, we integrate several activities for scholars to deepen their understanding and the value of including parents as equal partners in the special education process. Specifically, scholars attend a panel discussion with parents of children with disabilities, complete paired in-depth discussions with a parent of a child with a disability, and engage in conversation around problem-based scenarios that aim to challenge implicit biases and encourage proactive strategies to engage diverse families in all aspects of the special education process (e.g., assessment, selection of goals, decision-making, etc.). Following these activities, the scholars complete brief reflections about the highlights of the experience and actions they can use in their future work. For example, in the past, scholars have described increased appreciation of families, ways to better engage families, consideration of additional challenges families may be facing that might impact feasibility of interventions, actions to help the families know they are an important part of the team, ways to connect families to community resources, and methods to establish open communication.

Intensive Instruction

Children with behavioral and learning challenges often require intensive direct skills instruction (Blewitt et al., 2021). Direct instructional methods might include discrete trial training (Rabideau et al., 2018), pivotal response training (Brock et al., 2018), and errorless learning (Mueller et al., 2007) to teach pre-academic or social skills. School personnel need the ability to assess when such methods are needed, the understanding of how such techniques work, and skill in implementing various instructional procedures with integrity. All of the scholars in our program obtain experience in delivering intensive skill-acquisition programs for academic, developmental, or behavioral skills. For example, scholars have implemented functional communication training and taught social skills included in the Preschool Life Skills curriculum. Scholars in the special education program receive additional training in intensive instruction within unique coursework for their program.

Identification of Behavioral Health Needs

School professionals supporting behavioral health needs should be familiar with best practices in assessment. This requires knowledge of both Diagnostic and Statistical Manual of Mental Disorders (DSM) and IDEA diagnostic frameworks and eligibility criteria for special education services (Mattison, 2014). A thorough understanding of assessment within an MTSS framework is also important so that the child's needs can be identified early, and appropriate supports can be implemented. This competency includes assessment practices in screening for developmental concerns, behavioral health needs, diagnostic and eligibility evaluations, and progress monitoring of social-emotional-behavioral goals (Martens & Ardoin, 2010). Within the disciplines represented in the IBC Scholars project, it is common for special educators and school psychologists to be trained in IDEA eligibility criteria and MTSS models, whereas behavior analysts are often less familiar with this content because it is not included within the Task List that informs coursework for university programs. Because all content is relevant for educational professionals serving children with and at-risk for behavioral concerns, we have supplemented the coursework found in IBC Scholars' respective programs with additional experiences and seminars in behavioral assessment (e.g., applied case scenario discussions, records review to inform questions, family interviews, use of behavior rating scales, common mental health disorders during childhood and adolescence, criteria for IDEA disability categories).

Functional Behavioral Assessment

The functional behavioral assessment (FBA) and behavior intervention plans (BIP) mandated in IDEA were largely derived from the science and practice of ABA (Gresham et al., 2001). In conducting an FBA, direct measures, including systematic direct observation and antecedent, behavior, and consequence (A-B-C) data, as well as indirect measures such as interviews and questionnaires, are used to examine potential functional relationships between child behavior and environmental variables (Steege et al., 2019). A determination of the function of problem behavior is then used to develop an appropriate function-based BIP. A great deal of research exists to support the use of FBAs to develop BIPs in early childhood and school-age populations (e.g., Cumming & O'Neill, 2019; Wood et al., 2014); however, there is also evidence that school teams frequently struggle to implement best practices in this area (Benazzi et al., 2006; Van Acker et al., 2005).

This may be due in part to the fact that while IDEA mandates FBAs in certain situations, the procedures involved are not defined explicitly (Zirkel, 2011). This gives the school professional a great deal of flexibility in choosing the methods best matched to the presenting concerns and environment of the child. If the school professional lacks training and experience in conducting FBAs, the quality of their work will suffer and ineffective BIPs may be prescribed.

The responsibility for conducting and interpreting FBAs often varies from school to school, so scholars from each field are given opportunities to conduct FBAs, use the information to develop BIPs, and evaluate the effectiveness of BIPs. Scholars' practicum placements vary from preschool to high school settings, and they complete at least one FBA per semester that include indirect assessment (e.g., record reviews, interviews) and direct assessment measures (e.g., ABC observations, antecedent and functional analyses). Scholars gradually increase their independence with the evaluations as they progress through the program. They also learn how to select appropriate methods for progress monitoring (e.g., definition, dimension of behavior, type of data collection, frequency of data collection, specification of data collector). Feedback is provided by the site supervisor and through discussions in supervision with university faculty. Scholars present one case study each semester in seminar so that similarities and differences in FBA and intervention practices across the various school placements can be discussed.

Data-Based Decision Making

To adequately and efficiently meet the behavioral needs of children, school teams need to be fluent in assessment practices and in the use of data to make educational decisions. These skills are foundational to an effective MTSS approach (Stoiber, 2014). Within an MTSS framework, school personnel should be fluent in assessment methods for identifying children's strengths and needs, measuring the success of core instruction, and progress monitoring to determine when additional supports and interventions are necessary (Gresham, 2014). In addition to appropriate assessment practices, it is also essential that the data they yield are used to make decisions that benefit children. This requires school teams to understand how to interpret data and use single case designs for decision-making (Gould et al., 2018). For example, within practicum, scholars have provided training and coaching support to staff on how to implement and use data from the Behavior Incident Reporting System (National Center for Pyramid Model Innovations, 2020) to inform intervention selection.

Systems-Change and Leadership

Finally, effective leadership in the schools requires an understanding of implementation science. School personnel must understand how to facilitate the scale-up processes, build capacity, and address barriers to implementation. Effective leaders involved in educational change need skill in developing a shared vision among stakeholders, building relational trust with staff, using multiple sources to solve problems, and maintaining focus on teaching and learning (Holmes et al., 2013). School administrators are often the identified leaders in school systems, but all professionals interested in systemic change and supports for evidence-based practices should have some understanding of the leadership skills required to make change come about and to sustain effective practices. Within the professional seminar, we incorporate trainings from the National Implementation Research Network (NIRN) that focus on systems change process in school settings. To enhance skills in practice, we gave scholars opportunities to participate in teams at the school-level and state-level. For example, third-year scholars in school psychology helped develop and refine training materials for MTSS teams throughout the state focused on social-emotional-behavioral learning.

Program Evaluation

In coordination with an external evaluator, we outlined methods to evaluate the effectiveness of our interdisciplinary program. The evaluation involves a multi-method approach that includes quantitative and qualitative data to inform progress toward program goals, modifications needed, and summative program outcomes. For example, to assess scholar progress toward competencies several methods are used including (a) pre- and post-surveys of scholar's perception of skills and knowledge across the competencies, (b) focus group and individualized interviews, (c) site supervisor's ratings of independence, and (d) faculty review of scholar portfolio of works related to the competencies. To determine the effectiveness of the professional seminar and coursework, an external evaluator reviewed and provided feedback for improvements. In addition, the scholars complete course evaluations each semester. Complete data from the program are not yet available.

Actions for Improving Interdisciplinary Teaming in Practice

Through our experiences developing and implementing interdisciplinary training, we can share insights and recommendations for enhancing collaborative practices. Table 2 provides an outline of actions that can be taken at the university and individual practitioner-level based on four domains of IC: values, roles and responsibilities, interprofessional communication, and teamwork.

University Program/Pre-Service Training Actions

In the area of values, faculty and instructors can begin by identifying other programs on campus or across campuses that have similar goals to promote children's behavioral outcomes. For example, in early childhood settings, it is common for professionals from early childhood special education, school psychology, speech-language pathology, social work, developmental pediatrics, and behavior analysis to collaborate to assess and intervene to meet child and family needs (see Table 1). In our case, we identified three programs that had a common goal and similar conceptual approach to meeting behavioral needs. When contacting personnel in the identified programs, it is important to communicate respect for the disciplines' contributions in addressing the needs and goals of children and families. As partners are invited to collaborate, time should be dedicated to establishing trusting relationships.

Each discipline can share common roles and responsibilities for practitioners/educators in the field. We found roles that overlapped across the disciplines such as FBA, intervention development, and data-based decision-making that allowed for a strong foundation. We also outlined the unique contributions of each discipline for meeting children's needs. For example, special educators have unique knowledge and skills related to academic instruction and curriculum, school psychologists have skills in evaluation and consultation, and behavior analysts have extensive training in behavioral assessment and intervention.

Effective communication is essential to collaborative teams. Establishing regular meetings and a framework for communication is critical to making progress toward goals. Active listening and related communication skills should be outlined and applied. Within meetings, we encourage individuals (e.g., faculty, scholars, professionals) to avoid using discipline-specific terminology. When these terms are needed, team members should provide definitions and examples that are accessible and understandable to others on the team. At times, jargon might unintentionally be used and team members can respectfully notice and ask for clarification.

Specific goals for the interdisciplinary team might include: (a) examining each discipline's program of study to determine potential for joint coursework, (b) establishing joint seminars and professional learning opportunities, (c) creating simulations/group experiences across programs (e.g., case-based scenario discussions, mock Individualized Family Service Plan meetings), and (d) establishing partnerships with local schools and organizations for field experience opportunities. Interdisciplinary activities, such as simulations, are associated with increased relationship building, open communication, positive attitudes toward other professions, and enhanced learning experiences that are more similar to those encountered in practice (Bullard et al., 2019).

Practitioner-Level Actions

Similarly, practitioners and educators in the field can also strive to establish ICs by taking actions within each domain. Administrative support is key to prioritizing time and resources needed for effective teaming (Sista & Robledo, 2021). Strong leadership is critical for teams to be able to engage in collaborative processes and can also be supported through interdisciplinary coaching (Page & Eadie, 2019). It is important to recognize the family as an essential member of the team as families bring valuable background and information about behavior to the team. In addition, they often serve as a case manager between home, school, and community providers (Kervick et al., 2021) and are most likely to be the constant across time and teams for their child. When learning about the family, a care map can be created to visualize the web of services that a child and family receive (Antonelli & Lind, 2012). A practitioner can then gather information about the roles and responsibilities of each person or group listed and the goals they are supporting. Although it may not be possible for all parties across disciplines or agencies to meet on a routine basis, establishing methods for periodic communication is beneficial to best accomplish goals and support the family. Within early childhood team meetings, updates from other service providers can be shared.

Although teams often collaborate at the beginning of services (i.e., assessment and goal development), they are less likely to continue to collaborate in the provision of services (Sista & Robledo, 2021). A collaborative team-approach to working on goals means that strategies to facilitate goals are embedded in instruction/intervention by each person on the team when possible.

For example, a goal might be developed to improve expressive language skills that might also be associated with frustration and tantrum behavior. Across the child's day, naturalistic teaching strategies can be embedded to provide opportunities to support language development. Similarly, the strategies outlined on a behavior intervention plan (e.g., how to prevent tantrums, how to respond when the behavior happens, how to teach more adaptive skills) can be used across team members to increase consistency and predictability.

Overall, IC is integral to providing high quality early intervention programs, reducing the rate of expulsion, and improving behavioral outcomes of young children. To increase use of IC in practice, universities can to provide coordinated and collaborative interdisciplinary coursework and experiences to pre-service educators and related practitioners that serve young children. It is also important to continue to address system barriers (e.g., time and resources) to encourage IC and thereby enhance child and family outcomes.

References

Anderson, E.M. (2013) Preparing the next generation of early childhood teachers: The emerging role of interprofessional education and collaboration in teacher education, *Journal of Early Childhood Teacher Education, 34*, 23-35. https://doi.org/10.1080/10901027.2013.758535

Antonelli, R. & Lind, C. (October, 2012). *Care Mapping: An Innovative Tool and Process to Support Family-Centered, Comprehensive Care Coordination.* Poster session presented at the annual Primary Care Innovation Conference of the Harvard Medical School Primary Care Center, Boston, MA. https://www.childrenshospital.org/integrated-care/care-mapping

Arora, P. G., Connors, E. H., Biscardi, K. A., & Hill, A. M. (2016). School mental health professionals' training, comfort, and attitudes toward interprofessional collaboration with pediatric primary care providers. *Advances in School Mental Health Promotion, 9*(3-4), 169–187. https://doi.org/10.1080/1754730X.2016.1181526

Arora, Levine, J. L., & Goldstein, T. R. (2019). School psychologists' interprofessional collaboration with medical providers: An initial examination of training, preparedness, and current practices. *Psychology in the Schools, 56*(4), 554–568. https://doi.org/10.1002/pits.22208

Beaulieu, L., & Jimenez-Gomez, C. (2022). Cultural responsiveness in applied behavior analysis: Self-assessment. *Journal of Applied Behavior Analysis, 55*(2), 337–356. https://doi.org/10.1002/jaba.907

Benazzi, L., Horner, R. H., & Good, R. H. (2006). Effects of behavior support team composition on the technical adequacy and contextual fit of behavior support plans. *The Journal of Special Education, 40*(3), 160-170.

Bergan, J. R., & Kratochwill, T. R. (1990). *Behavioral consultation and therapy.* Plenum Press.

Blewitt, C., O'Connor, A., May, T., Morris, H., Mousa, A., Bergmeier, H., Jackson, K., Barrett, H., & Skouteris, H. (2021). Strengthening the social and emotional skills of pre-schoolers with mental health and developmental challenges in inclusive early childhood education and care settings: a narrative review of educator-led interventions. *Early Child Development & Care, 191*(15), 2311–2332.

Bradley-Klug, K.L., Jeffries-DeLoatche, A., St. John Walsh, L.P. Bateman, N.J., Powers D.J., and Cunningham, J. (2013). School psychologists' perceptions of primary care partnerships: Implications for building the collaborative bridge. *Advances in School Mental Health Promotion 6*(1), 51–67. https://doi.org/10.1080/17547 30X2012.760921.

Brock, M. E., Dueker, S. A., & Barczak, M. A. (2018). Brief report: Improving social outcomes for students with Autism at recess through peer-mediated pivotal response training. *Journal of Autism & Developmental Disorders, 48*(6), 2224–2230.

Bullard, M.J., Fox, S.M., Wares, C.M., Heffner, A.C., Stephens, C., & Rossi, L. (2019). Simulation-based interdisciplinary education improves intern attitudes and outlook toward colleagues in other disciplines. *BMC Med Educ* 19, 276. https://doi.org/10.1186/s12909-019-1700-1

Christenson, S.L. & Sheridan, S.M. (2001). *Schools and families: Creating essential connections for learning.* Guilford Press.

Council for Exceptional Children Division for Early Childhood (2021). *Position statement on multitiered system of support framework in early childhood.* https://www.dec-sped.org/single-post/new-position-statement-multitiered-system-of-support-framework-in-early-childhood

Cumming, T. M., & O'Neill, S. C. (2019). Using data-based individualization to intensify behavioral interventions. *Intervention in School and Clinic, 54*(5), 280-285.

DeVeney, S.L. & McKevitt, B. (2021) Interprofessional experience for future education professionals: School psychology and speech-language pathology students. Teaching and Learning in Communication Services & Disorders, 5(1). https://doi.org/10.30707/TLCSD5.1.1624982519.476871

Dobbs-Oates, J. & Morris, C.W. (2016) The case for interprofessional education in teacher education and beyond, *Journal of Education for Teaching, 42*(1), 50-65. https://www.doi.org/10.1080/02607476.2015.1131363

Donaldson, Matter, A. L., & Wiskow, K. M. (2018). Feasibility of and teacher preference for student-led implementation of the good behavior game in early elementary classrooms. *Journal of Applied Behavior Analysis, 51*(1), 118–129. https://doi.org/10.1002/jaba.432

Early Childhood Learning and Knowledge Center (ECLKC). (2022). *Understanding and eliminating expulsion in early childhood programs.* https://eclkc.ohs.acf.hhs.gov/publication/understanding-eliminating-expulsion-early-childhood-programs

Epstein, J.L. (2011). *School, family, and community partnerships* (2nd ed.). Westview Press.

Fahmie, T. & Luczynski, K. C. (2018). Preschool life skills: Recent advancements and future directions: *Journal of Applied Behavior Analysis, 51*(1), 183–188. https://doi.org/10.1002/jaba.434

George, C. & Oriel, K. (2009). Interdisciplinary learning experience: Two years of experience with an interdisciplinary learning engagement for physical therapy and special education students. *Journal of Allied Health, 38*(1), 22E-28E.

Gilliam, W.S. (2005). *Prekindergarteners left behind: Expulsion rates in state prekindergarten systems.* Policy Brief series no. 3. New York, NY: Foundation for Child Development. https://www.fcd-us.org/prekindergartners-left-behind-expulsion-rates-in-state-prekindergarten-programs/

Goldenberg, B.M. (2014). White teachers in urban classrooms: Embracing non-White students' cultural capital for better teaching and learning. *Urban Education, 49(1),* 111 - 144. https://doi.org/10.1177%2F0042085912472510

Gould, K., Gaither, J., Dart, E., & Weaver, A. D. (2018). Research-based practice: A practical guide to single case design graphing. *NASP Communique, 47*(1).

Gresham, F.M. (2014). Best practices in diagnosis of mental health and academic difficulties in a multitiered problem-solving approach. In P. Harrison & A. Thomas (Eds.), *Best practices in school psychology: Data-based and collaborative decision making* (pp. 147-158). National Association of School Psychologists.

Gresham, F.M., Watson, T.S., Skinner, C.H. (2001). Functional behavioral assessment: Principles, procedures, and future directions. *School Psychology Review, 30,* 156-172.

Grisham-Brown, J. & Hemmeter, M. L. (2017) *Blended practices for teaching young children in inclusive settings* (2nd ed.). Paul H. Brookes

Hemmeter, M. L., Fox, L., Snyder, P., & Algina, J. (2014). A classroom wide model for promoting social emotional development & addressing challenging behavior in preschool children. The National Center for Pyramid Model Innovations. https://challengingbehavior.cbcs.usf.edu/Pyramid/overview/research.html

Holmes, K., Clement, J., & Albright, J. (2013). The complex task of leading educational change in schools. *School Leadership & Management, 33,* 270-283.

Holmes, S. R., Reinke, W. M., Herman, K. C., & David, K. (2021). An examination of teacher engagement in intervention training and sustained intervention implementation. *School Mental Health: A Multidisciplinary Research and Practice Journal.* https://doi.org/ /10.1007/s12310-021-09457-3

Individuals with Disabilities Education Improvement Act of 2004. 2012. 20 U.S.C.§§1400–1444.

Interprofessional Education Collaborative (2016). *Interprofessional Education Collaborative releases revised set of core competencies.* https://www.ipecollaborative.org/news-releases.html

Kame'enui, E.J., Fien, H., & Korgesaar, J. (2013). Direct instruction as eo nomine and contronym: Why the right words and details matter. In Swanson, H.L., Harris, K.R., & Graham, S. (Eds). *Handbook of learning disabilities* (2nd ed.). Guilford Press.

Kataoka, S., Zhang, L., & Wells, K. (2002). Unmet need for mental health care among U.S. children: Variation by ethnicity and insurance status. *The American Journal of Psychiatry, 159,* 1548-55.

Kazdin, A. (2013). Evidence-based treatment and usual care: Cautions and qualifications. *JAMA Psychiatry,70,* 666-667.

Kervick, Haines, S. J., Green, A. E., Reyes, C. C., Shepherd, K. G., Moore, M., Healy, E. A., & Gordon, M. E. (2021). Engaging interdisciplinary service providers to enhance collaboration to support refugee families whose children have special health care needs. *Educational Action Research, ahead-of-print*(ahead-of-print), 1–23. https://doi.org/10.1080/09650792.2021.1877165

LaBrot, Dufrene, B. A., Whipple, H., McCargo, M., & Pasqua, J. L. (2019). Targeted and intensive consultation for increasing Head Start and elementary teachers' behavior-specific praise. *Journal of Behavioral Education, 29*(4), 717–740. https://doi.org/10.1007/s10864-019-09342-9

Manor-Binyamini, I. (2007). Meaning of language differences between doctors and educators in collaborative discourse. *Journal of Interprofessional Care, 21*(1), 31-43. https://doi.org/10.1080/13561820601049468.

Marsh, R. J., & Mathur, S. R. (2020). Mental health in schools: An overview of multitiered systems of support. *Intervention in School and Clinic, 56*(2), 67–73.

Martens, B.K. & Ardoin, S.P. (2010). Assessing disruptive behavior within a problem-solving model. In G. Gimpel Peacock, R.A. Ervin, E.J. Daly III, & K.W. Merrell (Eds.), *Practical handbook of school psychology* (pp. 157-174). Guilford Press.

Mattison, R.E. (2014). The interface between child psychiatry and special education in the treatment of students with emotional/behavioral disorders in school settings. In H.M. Walker & F.M. Gresham (Eds.), *Handbook of evidence-based practices for emotional and behavioral disorders* (pp. 104-126). Guilford Press.

Moran, D.J., & Malott, R.W. (2004). *Evidence-based educational methods*. Elsevier Academic Press.

Mueller, M. M., Palkovic, C. M., & Maynard, C. S. (2007). Errorless learning: Review and practical application for teaching children with pervasive developmental disorders. *Psychology in the Schools, 44*(7), 691–700.

National Association for the Education of Young Child. (2017). *Standing together against suspension & expulsion in early childhood-joint statement*. National Association for the Education of Young Children, Washington, D.C. https://www.naeyc.org/resources/blog/suspension-and-expulsion-early-childhood

National Center for Pyramid Model Innovations (n.d.). *The pyramid model for promoting social emotional competence in infants and young children*. Retrieved May 3, 2022, from https://challengingbehavior.cbcs.usf.edu/Pyramid/overview/index.html

National Center for Pyramid Model Innovations, (2020). *Behavior Incident Reporting System*. Retrieved July 11, 2022 from https://challengingbehavior.cbcs.usf.edu/Implementation/data/birs.html

Nebraska Department of Education. (2022). *About NeMTSS*. https://nemtss.unl.edu/about/

O'Keeffe, M. J., & McDowell, M. (2004). Bridging the gap between health and education: Words are not enough. *Journal of Paediatrics and Child Health, 40*(5-6), 252–257. https://doi.org/10.1111/j.1440-1754.2004.00359.x

Page, J., & Eadie, P. (2019). Coaching for continuous improvement in collaborative, interdisciplinary early childhood teams. *Australasian Journal of Early Childhood, 44*(3), 270–284. https://doi.org/10.1177/1836939119855542

Rabideau, L. K., Stanton-Chapman, T. L., & Brown, T. S. (2018). Discrete trial training to teach alternative communication: A step-by-step guide. *Young Exceptional Children, 21*(1), 34–47. https://doi-org.leo.lib.unomaha.edu/10.1177/1096250615621357

Sista, M.K., & Robledo, J.A. (2021). Interdisciplinary collaboration practice between education specialists and related service providers. *Journal of Special Education Apprenticeship, 10*(1), 1-19.

Skiba, R. J., Horner, R. H., Chung, C.-G., Rausch, M. K., May, S. L., & Tobin, T. (2011). Race is not neutral: A national investigation of African American and Latino disproportionality in school discipline. *School Psychology Review, 40*(1): 85–107.

Slocum, T., Detrich, A., Wilczynski, R., Spencer, S., Lewis, M., & Wolfe, T. (2014). The evidence-based practice of Applied Behavior Analysis. *The Behavior Analyst, 37*, 41-56.

Soares, D.A., Harrison, J.R., Vannest, K.J., & McClelland, S.S. (2016). Effect size for token economy use in contemporary classroom settings: A meta-analysis of single-case research. *School Psychology Review, 45*, 379-399.

Steege, M.W., Pratt, J.L., Wickerd, G., Guare, R., & Watson, T.S. (2019). *Conducting school-based Functional Behavioral Assessments: A practitioner's guide* (3rd ed). Guilford Press.

Stoiber, K.C. (2014). A comprehensive framework for multitiered systems of support in school psychology. In P. Harrison & A. Thomas (Eds.), *Best practices in school psychology: Data-based and collaborative decision making* (pp. 41-70). National Association of School Psychologists.

Sugai, G. (2015). Positive behavioral interventions and supports: Application of a behavior analytic theory of action. www.winginstitute.org

Tzuo, P. (2007). The tension between teacher control and children's freedom in a child-centered classroom: Resolving the practical dilemma through closer look at the related theories. *Early Childhood Educational Journal, 35*, 33–39.

U.S. Department of Education, Office for Civil Rights (2021). Civil Rights Data Collection, 2017-18 State and National Estimations. https://ocrdata.ed.gov/estimations/2017-2018.

Van Acker, R., Boreson, L., Gable, R. A., & Potterton, T. (2005). Are we on the right course? Lessons learned about current FBA/BIP practices in schools. *Journal of Behavioral Education, 14* (1), 35-56.

Walker, H.M., Ramsay, E., & Gresham, F.M. (2004). *Antisocial behavior in school: Evidence-based practices* (2nd ed.). Belmont, CA: Wadsworth/Thomson Learning.

Whitney, D.G. & Peterson, M.D. (2019). US national and state-level prevalence of mental health disorders and disparities of mental health care use in children. *JAMA Pediatrics, 173(4)*, 389 – 391.

Wood, B. K., Drogan, R. R., & Janney, D. M. (2014). Early childhood practitioner involvement in functional behavioral assessment and function-based interventions: A literature review. *Topics in Early Childhood Special Education, 34*(1), 16–26. https://doi.org/10.1177/0271121413489736

World Health Organization. (2010). *Framework for action on interprofessional education and collaborative practice* (No. WHO/HRH/HPN/10.3). World Health Organization.

Zirkel, P. A. (2011). State special education laws for functional behavioral assessments and behavior intervention plans. *Behavioral Disorders, 36*, 262–278.

Building Future Capacity of School Psychologists to Address the Demand for Inclusive Evidence-Based Consultation: Moving Beyond K-12 to Include School Readiness Frameworks

Chloe Beacham, Catherine Perkins, Andrew T. Roach, Brian Barger, Claire Donehower, and Kathleen M. Baggett

Abstract

There is high demand for future school psychologists to address the need for continuous evidence-based consultation that moves beyond K-12 settings, and includes evidence-based consultation to promote school readiness for infants and toddlers with and at risk for developmental disabilities. While there exists a demand for school psychologists in infant and toddler settings, the primary focus of training programs is preparing graduates to work in school-based settings. Currently, a gap exists in graduate training opportunities in evidence-based consultation practices that support school readiness for infants and toddlers with and at risk for disabilities served through Part C services. While school psychologists typically are trained on evidence-based consultation mechanisms that have largely been utilized in K-12 contexts, they rarely receive consultation training with families of infants and toddlers. Therefore, expansion of training is necessary to support infants and toddlers through evidence-based consultation models. To underscore the importance of continuity in application of evidence-based consultation models, the current manuscript compares an evidence-based consultation model validated in K-12 settings and a consultation model for promoting infant and toddler developmental competencies. An illustration of the application of evidence-based consultation frameworks within multi-tiered systems of support and recommendations for graduate training, to better prepare school psychologists for work in birth-to-three settings, is provided.

keywords: *early childhood consultation, toddler consultation frameworks, infant consultation frameworks, early childhood graduate training.*

Building Future Capacity of School Psychologists to Address the Demand for Inclusive Evidence-Based Consultation: Moving Beyond K-12 to Include School Readiness Frameworks

The National Association of School Psychologists (NASP) indicates that school psychologists are well-positioned to provide services to infants, toddlers, and their families in early intervention settings (NASP, 2015). Although it is well-established that the earliest years of development are a critical time for promoting developmental competencies that are foundational for school readiness (Horm et al., 2016), school psychologists report infrequent engagement in service delivery for infants and toddlers in Part C of the Individuals with Disabilities Education Act (IDEA; Albritton et al., 2019). In addition, when school psychologists provide services to infants and toddlers, activities rarely include consultation (Albritton et al., 2019), although collaboration with educators and families is a core principle of early childhood services (NASP, 2015). Therefore, there is a clear need for future school psychologists to understand and build competence in implementing inclusive, evidence-based consultation that promotes healthy development. This is foundational for school readiness for infants and toddlers with and at risk for developmental disabilities in very early childhood settings.

History and Background

Over the past few decades, there have been calls for a shift in school psychologists' roles beyond typical educational settings (e.g., K-12) to reach young children and their families in home-based and community settings (Bagnato, 2006; Bagnato et al., 1987; NASP, 2003; 2015; Widerstrom et al., 1989). This movement toward expansion of school psychology services to early intervention contexts coincides with federal educational legislation. With the passing of the Education for All Handicapped Children Act, an amendment known as Public Law 99-457 in 1986 (Smith, 2005), which included the provision of multidisciplinary early intervention services to infants and toddlers aged 0 to 3 who have identified disabilities, the role of school psychologists expanded to providing services in early childhood settings as a part of multidisciplinary teams (Short et al., 1990; Widerstrom et al., 1989). In 1990, this law merged into IDEA, which was reauthorized in 2004.

IDEA (2004) includes two sections relevant to early childhood services and settings: (1) providing early intervention services to infants and toddlers with disabilities and their families through Part C services, and (2) services for young children and preschoolers aged three to five through Part B services. While Part B of IDEA clearly outlines the roles and responsibilities of school psychologists, these services are not fully extended to Part C. Under Part C services of IDEA, federal law requires states to identify, screen, assess, evaluate, and implement interventions for children needing early intervention services through a multidisciplinary approach (IDEA, 2004). However, school psychologists are not explicitly named or mandated as service providers on these multidisciplinary teams (Albritton et al., 2021), resulting in a lack of funding for school psychologists to engage in infant and toddler program spaces. Further, states vary in the agencies responsible for overseeing and implementing these procedures (Bricker et al., 2013). Most states' leading agencies align with educationally or developmentally related services, such as the Department of Education or the Department of Health and Social Services (Early Childhood Learning and Knowledge Center [ECLKC], 2018). However, some states' leading agencies are not clearly connected to child development or education. For example, oversight for Part C services in Arizona is provided by the Economic Security Agency, and by the Public Welfare Office in Pennsylvania (ECLKC, 2018). Unlike Part B services provided in educational settings, Part C services are often provided within a family's home to foster intervention that serves the family unit. This service delivery system differs from the traditional educational-based setting (i.e., school, district office) where school psychologists are typically housed. These widely varying agencies and roles within early intervention settings, coupled with the absence of explicit federal policy and funding, may partly explain the lack of consistent involvement of school psychologists in these non-traditional settings.

Beyond legislation that warrants involvement of school psychologists in early intervention, the National Association of School Psychologists (NASP) has long recommended involvement of school psychologists in these early intervention contexts to provide services to families and to support early childhood providers in implementing evidence-based interventions (NASP, 2003). In 2003, NASP first recommended the provision of empirically-based mental health and educational services by school psychologists in early intervention settings. NASP reiterated these recommendations in a 2015 position statement (NASP, 2015). In addition, this paper added to NASP's previous guidance by including recommendations regarding school psychologists' engagement in multi-tiered systems of support (MTSS) in early childhood contexts. Expanding the role of school psychologists in providing services to infants and toddlers with disabilities is also consistent with the *Professional Standards of the National Association of School Psychologists* (NASP, 2020). One of the guiding ethical principles of school psychologists is to "promote school, family, and community environments that are safe and healthy for children and youth" (NASP, 2020, p. 53). In their 2015 position statement, NASP indicated that school psychologists should provide services to children with and without identified disabilities and risk factors from birth to age 8 (NASP, 2015). NASP further recommended that school psychologists engage in early childhood services by collaborating with community partners and families, providing evidence-based interventions, and consulting with educators or early interventionists on effective instructional strategies. In addition, throughout NASP's Policy Playbook (2019), which describes NASP advocacy initiatives, the prevention of academic and social-behavioral problems through early identification and early intervention are consistently noted, although services for infants and toddlers are not specifically mentioned. Given this guidance, expansion of the traditional role of the school psychologist is necessary to support infants and toddlers in early childhood settings.

The Role of the School Psychologist

School psychologists are generally more involved in Part B services than Part C services, likely due to differences in funding and federal legislation as described above. However, these services remain limited in scope. In a study by Hosp and Reschly (2002), a sample of participating school psychologists from a specific geographic location reported administering approximately seven preschool assessments monthly. However, in the same study, participating school psychologists nationwide reported administering two preschool assessments on average every month. In addition to the limited time spent providing services to address the needs of infants and toddlers, school psychologists' roles in very early intervention are restricted as well. A recent survey revealed that school psychologists' contributions generally are limited to assessment and evaluation for special education services through Part B (Albritton et al., 2019). Further, this survey revealed that less than half of school psychologists practicing in early childhood settings spend time consulting with families and teachers regarding individual children's learning or behavior.

Despite accrediting body recommendations for providing services through Part C, school psychologists' involvement in early intervention settings has traditionally been limited (Albritton et al., 2019). Given the growing demands to provide very early intervention services (Office of Special Education Programs, 2020), school psychologists must shift from diagnosis-centered to prevention-focused services in early childhood settings (Albritton et al., 2019). This shift can be accomplished by the reconceptualization of school psychologists' role as health service providers through greater engagement in consultation, and supporting implementation of universal screening, evidence-based intervention, and mental health services in early childhood settings (Albritton et al., 2019). There is a need to better understand how school psychologists may increase and enhance collaboration with families in early intervention settings to positively impact children's school success.

Unfortunately, there is limited information regarding training for school psychologists to provide comprehensive, evidence-based services in Part C settings, despite the documented call to prepare more school psychologists to engage in these contexts (NASP, 2015; Widerstrom et al., 1989). While there exists an increased opportunity for school psychologists to engage in work with infants and toddlers, graduate programs generally remain focused on preparing practitioners to work in K-12 educational settings. In a recent study by Stein and Albritton (2022), the authors examined school psychology graduate training syllabi for inclusion of content related to early childhood. Results revealed that when early childhood training is included, it primarily occurs in courses focused on assessment strategies or lifespan development. In addition, school psychologists working in early childhood settings reported minimal training in early childhood service provision in their graduate program (Albritton et al., 2019). These respondents also indicated that they received most of their training in early childhood practices through on-the-job experience, reading journal articles, professional conferences, and district workshops. Ultimately, when school psychologists are underprepared to provide services in early childhood settings, vulnerable families and children are negatively impacted by practitioners' limited knowledge, competency, and efficacy (Albritton et al., 2019). Thus, it is imperative that school psychology graduate programs adequately prepare graduates to provide the same array of services to infants and toddlers as those provided to children in K-12 settings.

When the field focuses its efforts solely on K-12 contexts, thus deemphasizing a lifespan development perspective (inclusive of birth to five), practitioners are limited to the degree to which they can provide effective consultative services that optimize developmental outcomes foundational for school readiness. Therefore, the purpose of this paper is to advocate for the expansion of the traditional role of the school psychologist to include services for infants and toddlers. To accomplish this goal, the following extensions to graduate training are presented: (a) an example of an evidence-based consultation model for promoting infant and toddler developmental competencies foundational for school success, which is congruent with a K-12 model, and (b) examples of needed didactic training, opportunities for field training, and assessment coursework in professional preparation programs.

Evidence-Based Consultation Models

Despite the inclusion of early childhood consultation models in the field's professional standards and evidence of positive outcomes, a recent survey of school psychology graduate training programs revealed that no participating programs provided training in this area (Stein & Albritton, 2022). While school psychologists typically are trained in evidence-based consultation frameworks widely implemented in K-12 contexts, they rarely receive consultation training with early childhood interventionists or families with infants and toddlers (Albritton et al., 2019). Although the literature is limited, evidence suggests that the implementation of evidence-based infant and toddler consultation frameworks is associated with reduction in challenging behaviors (Gilliam et al., 2016; Poole et al., 2012) and improved social skills (Perry et al., 2008), decreased activity levels (Sheridan et al., 2014), decreased expulsion and suspension from early childhood programs (Gilliam, 2005), and teachers' increased use of praise (Dufrene et al., 2012). Moreover, multiple studies have demonstrated that school psychologists and school psychology graduate students can be effective consultants in early childhood settings beyond Part C, such as in Head Start classrooms (Dufrene et al., 2012; Poole et al., 2012) and preschool classrooms (Sheridan et al., 2006).

Mechanisms by which greater consultation by school psychologists may be achieved exist in infant and toddler settings. Parallel to Multi-Tiered System of Support (MTSS) in K-12 contexts, the Pyramid Model has an extensive and expanding research base establishing this framework's effectiveness in supporting infants, toddlers, and preschoolers (Fox et al., 2003; Hemmeter et al., 2016; NASP, 2015). The Pyramid Model is an evidence-based multi-tiered approach to addressing social and emotional development of infants and toddlers (Hemmeter et al., 2016). This model is intended to guide the efforts of early childhood educators, early interventionists, families, and other professionals (e.g., school psychologists) in providing increasingly intense and specialized supports to infants and toddlers, to promote healthy development and prevent later social-emotional and behavioral challenges (Fox et al., 2003; Hemmeter et al., 2016). Evidence for the effectiveness of employing consultation within the Pyramid Model to support infant and toddler social-emotional development and school readiness has been accumulating over the past decade (Baggett et al., 2010a, 2010b, 2010d, 2011). A visual depiction of the Pyramid Model is shown in Figure 1.

The Pyramid Model and MTSS serve as conceptual models for providing consultation from birth to young adulthood. Several frameworks for consultation that could be implemented through MTSS in early intervention settings exist that align with commonly taught consultation models validated in K-12 settings. For example, Conjoint-Behavioral Consultation (Sheridan, 1997) is based on Bergan and Kratochwill's (1990) behavioral consultation model; the Getting Ready intervention was developed based on principles of both Conjoint-Behavioral Consultation (Sheridan, 1997) and triadic consultation (Marvin et al., 2020; McCollum & Yates, 1994); and Early Childhood Mental Health Consultation (ECMHC; Cohen and Kaufman, 2005) is derived from Caplan's Mental Health

Figure 1
The Pyramid Model

Note. Figure from National Center for Pyramid Model Innovations (2020).

Consultation model (Caplan et al., 1994). Knowledge of K-12 and infant and toddler consultation models, including their commonalities and differences, is critical to preparing school psychologists to implement evidence-based consultative services to support young children and their caregivers. The following evidence-based consultation model provides a framework by which school psychologists can conceptualize consultation work in early intervention settings.

Example Infant and Toddler Consultation Framework

One possible reason for the gap in training in infant and toddler consultation models is that K-12 school-based consultation models have a longer history and more extensive evidence base, relative to the more recent and emerging consultation approaches used in birth to three contexts. Despite the currently limited training on early childhood consultation models, school psychologists are positioned with the foundational knowledge of school-based consultation models to inform their early childhood consultative practices. To demonstrate how these consultation frameworks overlap, a K-12 consultation model frequently taught in school psychology graduate programs, Teachers and Parents as Partners (TAPP; Sheridan, 2014), and an evidence-based consultation approach to support parents in fostering infant and toddler social-emotional and communication developmental competencies, Baby Net (Baggett et al., 2010c, 2020, 2021b), are presented below. Further, an illustration is provided of how school psychologists can draw upon the TAPP model to provide services in early childhood contexts by highlighting the intersections between TAPP guiding principles and Baby Net intervention components.

TAPP was developed as an extension of the traditional conjoint-behavioral-consultation model (CBC; Sheridan, 1997). TAPP focuses on consulting and collaborating with stakeholders in a child's life to address academic, behavioral, and social challenges (Sheridan, 2014a). It is well-established that effective collaboration between families and educators is crucial for promoting optimal academic and social-emotional outcomes (Smith et al., 2020). Prior research indicates that TAPP effectively addresses behavioral, academic, and social-emotional challenges in students enrolled in pre-kindergarten and kindergarten (Sheridan et al., 2006). The TAPP model has primarily been examined in K-12 settings, and its utility and effectiveness have not yet been explored in Part C contexts. However, as mentioned previously, school psychologists may draw on common K-12 frameworks to apply and extend their understanding of these consultative approaches to early childhood contexts.

Baby Net is a version of the Infant-Net Program (Baggett et al., 2010c), which is an adaptation of the Play and Learning Strategies program (PALS; Landry et al., 2008). The PALS program is an evidence-based intervention implemented with infants, toddlers, and preschoolers to promote social-emotional, communication, and cognitive competencies foundational to school readiness (Landry et al., 2008). Using the PALS strategies, the Baby Net Program includes parent coaching that focuses on enhancing sensitive parenting skills (e.g., identifying and responding to baby's signals, maintaining the interest of the child, promoting early literacy skills), and incorporating these skills into daily routines (Baggett et al., 2010b, 2021b; Feil et al., 2020). Parents engage in learning new content on the program-specific phone app, upload a 5-minute video of a typical interaction with their baby, and then participate in a video call with their coach to reinforce learning, co-view the interaction video for coach feedback, and co-create an action plan for the mother to practice strategies before the next call (Baggett et al., 2021b). To date, there is mounting evidence of the efficacy of Baby Net for promoting infant social-emotional and social communication competencies (Baggett et al., 2010c, 2010d; Feil et al., 2020), as well as strong support for the program's ability to engage families who often struggle to engage in home visiting supports (Baggett et al., 2020, 2021a). The similarities between the models and explicit examples of how the TAPP principles are enacted in the Baby Net Program are presented in Table 1.

The similarities between the TAPP and Baby Net components and principles allow future school psychologists to see how their existing skills may be leveraged to provide consultation to support the development and well-being of infants and toddlers, which are foundational to school readiness. Prior to school entry, services through Part C are typically implemented either in the family's home or a clinic setting. The remote-delivery option of Baby Net illustrates how school psychologists, who are primarily based in educational settings, may be effective consultants within the context of home-based services.

Higher Education Training for School Psychologists

Field Training

In order to implement and receive supervision on the above practices, graduate students should be provided with practicum and placement experiences in infant and toddler settings. These experiences could include involvement in Head Start programs, partnering with the leading agency of Part C for their state, and/ or collaborations with community networks that serve children and families prior to school entry. Such applied experiences have been shown to enhance key consultation skills in participating graduate students (Donovan et al., 2015).

It should be noted that while most school psychology graduates will continue to serve primarily in K-12 contexts, it is important that those interested in working in early intervention settings be provided with the opportunity to hone their skills while still receiving supervision as graduate students (Donovan et al., 2015)Students should also be provided with field training and supervision within infant and toddler settings in order to grow the school psychology workforce to address the growing demands for intervention with very young children and their families.

Didactic Training

Prior to field training, school psychology graduate students should engage in classroom-based learning on infant and toddler development and contexts. School psychology graduate training programs should provide instruction on the legal mandates and professional standards that warrant practitioners' involvement in infant and toddler services. Instruction should include current discrepancies between the policies of Part C leading agencies, the referral process to Part C services, the differences between Individualized Family Service Plans (IFSPs) and Individual Education Programs (IEPs), ways school psychologists can support transition from Part C to Part B services, early childhood development of social-emotional and pre-academic skills, and the preventative and social justice nature of involvement in early intervention.

Assessment Sequence

Graduate programs should include coursework that allows students to learn and practice assessment tools and techniques for working with infants and toddlers. Students should learn to identify screening measures that are appropriate for caregiver concerns, such as the Ages and Stages Questionnaires, Third Edition, (Squires & Bricker, 2009) and the Devereux Early Childhood Assessment (LeBuffe & Naglieri, 1999). Further, students should have the opportunity to practice and receive feedback on developmental and play-based assessments.

Table 1
TAPP Central Components and Potential Enactment in the Baby Net Program

TAPP Components & Principles	Baby Net Examples of Enactment
TAPP Principles	
Principle 1: Communicate frequently and clearly. • Options for mode of communication • Regular check-ins with caregivers to describe expectations • Child-focused	The Baby Net Program was designed to be a remote-delivery option that addresses many barriers often experienced by parents (Baggett et al., 2020; Beacham et al., 2019; Feil et al., 2020). Coaches communicate with families often regarding reported challenges, help with the application of skills, and frequently let the mother know that the coach is thinking about her and her baby.
Principle 2: Ask open-ended questions and listen. • Ask the parent for help • Engage parents in conversation besides providing advice • Active listening	There is an emphasis on open-ended questions regarding knowledge acquisition and practice of skills. The coach asks the mother her thoughts about what she did well and what things she would like to try differently next time. The mother is regarded and valued as the expert on her child.
Principle 3: Express the importance of working together. • Collaborate with parents to identify ways to address the child's behavioral challenges • Acknowledge parents' effort and express appreciation	Coaches actively work to build relationships with parents and their babies. The concept of collaboration is a central tenet of the Baby Net program. Coaches frequently request the mother's input on the program, such as how skills align with her daily routines, what skills are not working, and how the coach can help. The mother's successes, however small, are celebrated on each call.

Table 1 - continued
TAPP Central Components and Potential Enactment in the Baby Net Program

TAPP Components & Principles	Baby Net Examples of Enactment
Principle 4: Focus on the positives. • Describe behaviors of the child and not inherent characteristics • Affirm the parent's role in changing their child's behavior	When co-viewing parent-recorded interaction videos, coaches select time points that showcase the mother using the skill correctly. The mother's role in the infant's positive response (e.g., smile, laugh, eye contact) is directly attributed to the mother's change in behavior.
TAPP Rules	
Rule 1: Make positive contacts with parents.	Coaches frequently make positive remarks about the parent's participation in the program, use of a new skill, and the positive impact the mother's behavior has on the baby. For example, a coach may send a screenshot from an interaction video of the mother and baby smiling at one another to reinforce use of parenting skills.
Rule 2: Act sooner rather than later.	Each concept presented in the Baby Net Program follows a progression of skill building. Therefore, if the mother has not yet mastered a foundational skill, the coach will spend time practicing the skill with the mother. The coach can also identify a mother's challenge with a skill through the parent-uploaded interaction videos. Challenges are discussed with the mother, and an action plan is co-created to outline specific situations (e.g., practice the skill when you are dressing your baby) for the mother to practice.
Rule 3: Conduct collaborative parent-teacher conferences.	Coaches conduct weekly video calls with participants to review newly learned concepts, address challenges and celebrate successes, emphasize progress towards goals, actively listen to the mother, and co-create action items for the mother to practice before the next call with her coach.
Rule 4: Use a home-school note system to communicate frequently.	The ePALS Baby Net app includes a secure messaging system called "Coach Talk." Coaches and mothers frequently converse through Coach Talk about the baby's progress, developmental milestones, and positive remarks about the mother's use of the skills.

The Neonatal Behavioral Assessment Scale-Fourth Edition (Brazelton & Nugent, 2011), the Mullen Scales of Early Learning (Mullen, 1995), the Bayley Scales of Infant and Toddler Development-4 (Bayley & Aylward, 2019), and the Battelle Developmental Inventory-3rd Edition (Newborg, 2020) are common measures used for developmental evaluations and are normed for children from birth into early childhood.

An example of a course that focuses on providing services to infants, toddlers, and preschoolers and their caregivers is the University of Nebraska Omaha's school psychology program's assessment course called "Early Childhood Assessment." Students in this course learn about early academic and play assessment and how to address mental health needs in early childhood. Further, they must engage in an immersive consultation experience with a local Head Start program to provide consultation regarding children's social-emotional development. This course emphasizes the incorporation of coursework and field experiences as an important way for graduate training programs to effectively prepare future school psychologists with the critical tools needed to provide high-quality services in early childhood settings.

Conclusions

In summary, school psychologists are encouraged to reconceptualize their role as health service providers across multiple development stages (i.e., early childhood, elementary, secondary, and postsecondary education). Despite growing interest in the field and NASP guidance, systemic barriers that include lack of federal funding, clear policy for school psychologists in early childhood settings, and limited communication and collaboration among agencies may hinder school psychologists' engagement in infant and toddler settings. However, to adhere to NASP's (2020) guidance and broad legislative requirements, it is necessary that school psychologists use their knowledge of screening, evidence-based consultation frameworks, and effective intervention practices to support children in (or soon to enter) early childhood settings. Specifically, school psychologists may provide consultation with all stakeholders in infant and toddler care through their understanding of tiered frameworks of support and applicable consultation models. Ultimately, by providing such services, school psychologists may prevent later academic and behavioral challenges while promoting school readiness for infants and toddlers.

References

Albritton, K., Chen, C. I., Bauer, S. G., Johnson, A., & Mathews, R. E. (2021). Collaborating with school psychologists: Moving beyond traditional assessment practices. *Young Exceptional Children, 24*(1), 28-38.

Albritton, K., Mathews, R. E., & Boyle, S. G. (2019). Is the role of the school psychologist in early childhood truly expanding? A national survey examining school psychologists' practices and training experiences. *Journal of Applied School Psychology, 35*(1), 1-19. https://doi.org/10.1080/15377903.2018.1462280

Baggett, K. M., & Broyles, L. (2011, April). *Applying the Pyramid Model within birth - three programs to support social-emotional development* [Conference session]. National Head Start Conference, Kansas City, MO, United States.

Baggett, K. M., Carta, J. J., & Broyles, L. (2010a, October). *Social-emotional development of infants and toddlers with and at risk for disabilities: The Pyramid Model* [Conference session]. Birth to Three National Conference, Washington, DC, United States.

Baggett, K. M., Carta, J. J., Broyles, L., & Perry, D. F (2010b, March). *The Pyramid framework within early intervention programs: Promoting social-emotional development of infants and toddlers* [Conference session]. Technical Assistance Center on Social Emotional Intervention's National Training Institute on Challenging Behavior, Clearwater, FL, United States.

Baggett, K. M., Davis, B., Feil, E. G., Sheeber, L. B., Landry, S. H., Carta, J. J., & Leve, C. (2010c). Technologies for expanding the reach of evidence-based interventions: Preliminary results for promoting social-emotional development in early childhood. *Topics in Early Childhood Special Education, 29*(4), 226–238. https://doi.org/10.1177/0271121409354782

Baggett, K. M., Davis, B., Landry, S. H., Feil, E. G., Whaley, A., Schnitz, A., & Leve, C. (2020). Understanding the steps toward mobile early intervention for mothers and their infants exiting the Neonatal Intensive Care Unit: Descriptive examination. *Journal of Medical Internet Research, 22*(9), e18519. https://doi.org/10.2196/18519

Baggett, K. M., Davis, B., Mosley, E. A., Miller, K., Leve, C., & Feil, E. G. (2021a). Depressed and socioeconomically disadvantaged mothers' progression into a randomized controlled mobile mental health and parenting intervention: A descriptive examination prior to and during COVID-19. *Frontiers in Psychology, 12*, 1-8. https://doi.org/10.3389/fpsyg.2021.719149

Baggett, K. M., Davis, B., Sheeber, L., Miller, K., Leve, C., Mosley, E. A., Landry, S., & Feil, E. G. (2021b). Optimizing social-emotional-communication development in infants of mothers with depression: Protocol for a randomized controlled trial of a mobile intervention targeting depression and responsive parenting. *JMIR Research Protocols, 10*(8). https://doi.org/10.2196/31072

Baggett, K.M., Hemmeter, M. L., Squires, J., Schertz, H., & Odom, S. L. (2010d, October). *Interventions for promoting social-emotional competency in young children: Monitoring progress* [Roundtable presentation]. Division of Early Childhood at the International Conference on Young Children with Special Needs, Kansas City, MO, United States.

Bagnato, S. J. (2006). Of helping and measuring for early childhood. *School Psychology Review, 35*(4), 615–620.

Bagnato, S. J., Neisworth, J. T., Paget, K. D., & Kovaleski, J. (1987). The developmental school psychologist professional profile of an emerging early childhood specialist. *Topics in Early Childhood Special Education, 7*(3), 75–89.

Bayley, N. & Aylward, G.P. (2019). *Bayley Scales of Infant and Toddler Development, 4th edition: Administration Manual.* Pearson.

Beacham, C., Baggett, K. M., & Patterson, A. (2019). *Increasing access to effective intervention for improving postpartum parenting mood and practices: A case examination of maternal engagement in a mobile health intervention* [Poster presentation]. Southeastern Pediatric Research Conference, Atlanta, GA, United States.

Bergan, J. R., & Kratochwill, T. R. (1990). *Behavioral consultation and therapy.* Plenum Press.

Brazelton, T. B., Nugent, J .K. (2011). *The Neonatal Behavioral Assessment Scale. 4th edition.* McKeith/Blackwell Press.

Bricker, D., Macy, M., Squires, J., & Marks, K. (2013). *Developmental screening in your community.* Paul H. Brookes.

Caplan, G., Caplan, R. B., & Erchul, W. P. (1994). Caplanian mental health consultation: Historical background and current status. *Consulting Psychology Journal: Practice and Research, 46*(4), 2.

Cohen, E. & Kaufmann, R. (2005). *Early childhood mental health consultation.* Washington, DC: Center for Mental Health Services of the Substance Abuse and Mental Health Services Administration and the Georgetown University Child Development Center.

Donovan, L., McCoy, D., Denune, H., Barnett, D. W., Graden, J. L., & Carr, V. (2015). Preparing doctoral-level consultants for systems change: Implementing and supervising multitiered practices in early childhood education. *Journal of Educational & Psychological Consultation, 25*(2/3), 252–275. https://doi.org/10.1080/104744 12.2014.929957

Dufrene, B. A., Parker, K., Menousek, K., Zhou, Q., Harpole, L. L., & Olmi, D. J. (2012). Direct behavioral consultation in head start to increase teacher use of praise and effective instruction delivery. *Journal of Educational and Psychological Consultation, 22*(3), 159-186.

Early Childhood Learning and Knowledge Center. (2018, July 16). *ECTA list of part C lead agencies*. https://eclkc.ohs.acf.hhs.gov/children-disabilities/article/ecta-list-part-c-lead-agencies

Feil, E. G., Baggett, K. M., Davis, B., Landry, S., Sheeber, L., Leve, C., & Johnson, U. (2020). Randomized control trial of an internet-based parenting intervention for mothers of infants. *Early Childhood Research Quarterly, 50*, 36-44. https://doi.org/10.1016/j.ecresq.2018.11.003

Fox, L., Dunlap, G., Hemmeter, M. L., Joseph, G. E., & Strain, P. S. (2003). The teaching pyramid: A model for supporting social competence and preventing challenging behavior in young children. *Young Children, 58*, 48–52.

Gilliam, W. S. (2005). *Prekindergarteners left behind: Expulsion rates in state prekindergarten systems*. New York, NY: Foundation for Child Development.

Gilliam, W. S., Maupin, A. N., & Reyes, C. R. (2016). Early childhood mental health consultation: Results of a statewide random-controlled evaluation. *Journal of the American Academy of Child & Adolescent Psychiatry, 55*(9), 754-761.

Hemmeter, M. L., Snyder, P. A., Fox, L., & Algina, J. (2016). Evaluating the implementation of the Pyramid Model for promoting social emotional competence in early childhood classrooms. *Topics in Early Childhood Special Education, 36*, 133-146.

Horm, D., Norris, D., Perry, D., Chazan-Cohen, R., & Halle, T. (2016). *Developmental foundations of school readiness for infants and toddlers: A research to practice report* (OPRE Report # 2016-07). Washington, DC: Office of Planning, Research and Evaluation, Administration for Children and Families, U.S. Department of Health and Human Services.

Hosp, J. L., & Reschly, D. J. (2002). Regional differences in school psychology practice. *School Psychology Review, 31*(1), 11-29. https://doi.org/10.1080/02796015.2002.12086139

Landry, S. H., Smith, K. E., Swank, P. R., & Guttentag, C. (2008). A responsive parenting intervention: The optimal timing across early childhood for impacting maternal behaviors and child outcomes. *Developmental Psychology, 44*(5), 1335–1353. https://doi.org/10.1037/a0013030

LeBuffe, P. A., & Naglieri, J. A. (1999). *The Devereux Early Childhood Assessment*. Kaplan Press.

Marvin, C. A., Moen, A. L., Knoche, L. L., & Sheridan, S. M. (2020). Getting Ready strategies for promoting parent–professional relationships and parent–child interactions. *Young Exceptional Children, 23*(1), 36-51.

McCollum, J. A., & Yates, T. J. (1994). Technical assistance for meeting early intervention personnel standards: Statewide processes based on peer review. *Topics in Early Childhood Special Education, 14*(3), 295-310.

Mullen, E. M. (1995). *Mullen Scales of Early Learning*. American Guidance Service Inc.

National Association of School Psychologists. (2003). *NASP Position Statement on Early Intervention Services*. https://casponline.org/pdfs/pdfs/nasp01.pdf

National Association of School Psychologists. (2019). *NASP Policy Playbook. https://www. nasponline.org/resources-and-publications/resources-and-podcasts/early-childhood/ policy-training-and-practice*

National Association of School Psychologists. (2020). *The Professional Standards of the National Association of School Psychologists*. https://www.nasponline.org/ x55315.xml

National Association of School Psychologists. (2015). *Early Childhood Services: Promoting Positive Outcomes for Young Children*. https://www.nasponline.org/x32403.xml

National Center for Pyramid Model Innovations. (2020). *Pyramid model overview*. Pyramid Model Tiers Levels, Framework, Promotion Prevention Intervention. https://challengingbehavior.cbcs.usf.edu/Pyramid/overview/tiers.html.

Newborg, J. (2020). *Battelle Developmental Inventory, Third Edition (BDI-3)*. Riverside Insights.

Office of Special Education Programs. (2020, June 24). OSEP fast facts: Infants and toddlers with disabilities. United States Department of Education. https://sites. ed.gov/idea/osep-fast-facts-infants-and-toddlers-with-disabilities-20/

Perry, D. F., Dunne, M. C., McFadden, L., & Campbell, D. (2008). Reducing the risk for preschool expulsion: Mental health consultation for young children with challenging behaviors. *Journal of Child and Family Studies, 17*(1), 44-54.

Poole, V. Y., Dufrene, B. A., Sterling, H. E., Tingstrom, D. H., & Hardy, C. M. (2012). Classwide functional analysis and treatment of preschoolers' disruptive behavior. *Journal of Applied School Psychology, 28*(2), 155-174.

Sheridan, S. M. (2014). *The tough kid: Teachers and parents as partners (TAPP)*. Pacific Northwest Publishers.

Sheridan, S. M. (1997). Conceptual and empirical bases of conjoint behavioral consultation. *School Psychology Quarterly, 12*(2), 119-133.

Sheridan, S. M., Knoche, L. L., Edwards, C. P., Kupzyk, K. A., Clarke, B. L., & Kim, E. M. (2014). Efficacy of the Getting Ready Intervention and the role of parental depression. *Early Education and Development, 25*(5), 746–769. https://doi.org/1 0.1080/10409289.2014.862146

Sheridan, S. M., Clarke, B. L., & Knoche, L., & Pope Edwards, C. (2006). The effects of conjoint behavioral consultation in early childhood settings. *Early Education and Development, 17,* 593-617. https://doi.org/10.1207/s15566935eed1704_5

Short, R. J., Simeonsson, R. J., & Huntington, G. S. (1990). Early intervention: Implications of Public Law 99–457 for professional child psychology. *Professional Psychology: Research and Practice, 21*(2), 88–93.

Smith, T. E. (2005). IDEA 2004: Another round in the reauthorization process. *Remedialand Special Education, 26,* 314-319

Smith, T. E., Sheridan, S. M., Kim, E. M., Park, S., & Beretvas, S. N. (2020). The effects of family-school partnership interventions on academic and social-emotional functioning: A meta-analysis exploring what works for whom. *Educational Psychology Review, 32*(2), 511-544.

Squires, J., & Bricker, D. (2009). *Ages & Stages Questionnaires®, Third Edition (ASQ®-3): A Parent-Completed Child Monitoring System.* Paul H. Brookes Publishing Co., Inc.

Stein, R., & Albritton, K. (2022). Early childhood-focused training in school psychology. *Training and Education in Professional Psychology, 16*(1), 36-43. http://dx.doi.org/10.1037/tep0000350

Widerstrom, A. H., Mowder, B. A., & Willis, W. G. (1989). The school psychologist's role in the early childhood special education program. *Journal of Early Intervention, 13*(3), 239–248. https://doi.org/10.1177/105381518901300305

Perspectives for the Delivery of Early Intervention Services via Telemedicine in Rural States: Outcomes from the COVID-19 Pandemic

Christopher M. Furlow, Laura K. Barker, Robyn R. Brewer, Mary N. Thomason, Alexandra G. Brunner, and Frances K. Huff

Abstract

The current study describes outcomes for seven families who participated in telehealth services from an early intervention clinic in a rural state during the COVID-19 pandemic. Families received different levels of care from a Board-Certified Behavior Analyst (BCBA®) over three months, ranging from one hour to 20 hours per week. The telemedicine sessions primarily focused on teaching caregivers to implement protocols that focused on rapport-building (i.e., Time-In [TI]), increasing child compliance with instructions (i.e., Effective Instruction Delivery [EID]), and language acquisition programs selected from the Promoting Emergence of Advanced Knowledge (PEAK) Comprehensive Assessment and Curriculum. At the conclusion of the telemedicine sessions, parents implemented the protocols with high degrees of treatment integrity, and improvements in skill acquisition on a standardized language assessment were observed for children with autism spectrum disorder (ASD). Implications for providing telemedicine services to rural and underserved communities without access to early intervention services and future directions for research are discussed.

Keywords: Telehealth, Applied Behavior Analysis (ABA), Autism Spectrum Disorder (ASD), Effective Instruction Delivery (EID), Time-In (TI), Parent Training, Skill Acquisition, Rural Communities, Underserved Communities, Early Intervention Services

Perspectives for the Delivery of Early Intervention Services via Telemedicine in Rural States: Outcomes from the COVID-19 Pandemic

Autism spectrum disorder (ASD) is estimated to affect 1 in 44 children in the United States (Maenner et al., 2021). Empirically supported early intensive behavioral intervention (EIBI) programs that utilize methods from Applied Behavior Analysis (ABA) for the treatment of ASD (Roane et al., 2016) can be difficult to access, especially in rural states. For example, in Mississippi, access to care can be limited due to long waiting lists and the lack of practitioners. Mississippi is a state that is affected by a shortage of ABA practitioners in rural or underserved communities (Belfer & Saxena, 2006). There are an estimated 13,337 children with ASD in Mississippi alone (Mississippi Autism Advisory Committee, 2020). Currently, there are approximately 100 Board Certified Behavior Analysts (BCBAs) with active certification in the state (Behavior Analyst Certification Board, 2021), and approximately 16 agencies providing some level of ABA services in the state (Mississippi Autism Board, 2021). EIBI interventions offer many young children with an ASD diagnosis an opportunity to expand their verbal repertoires and skillsets more rapidly than comparable interventions (Dai et al., 2020). Thus, it is imperative for these children to have access to ABA services (Aishworiya & Kang, 2020). However, with a severe shortage of practitioners to provide medically necessary ABA treatment to children with ASD, many families have little or no access to care.

In addition, many families in these areas must manage expensive travel or equipment costs to obtain timely intervention (Wacker et al., 2013). According to Cidav et al. (2017), costs for children receiving ABA services with the Early Start Denver Model were estimated to be approximately $14,000 more than those receiving community-based ABA services annually. Rodgers et al. (2020) published a systematic review of 20 studies with participants receiving approximately 20-50 hours of individualized, one-on-one

ABA services per week within the United Kingdom. Of the 20 studies reviewed, 15 included individual participant data and estimated that the usual EIBI treatment for a client per lifetime was approximately the equivalent of £189,122 per quality-adjusted life-year.

EIBI is typically described as evidence-based, one-on-one ABA programs for young children. These interventions are individualized under the supervision of a BCBA and include an emphasis on language acquisition, reducing problem behaviors, daily living skills, and parent-training (Mounzer & Stenhoff, 2022). Discrete Trial Training (DTT), Naturalistic Environment Teaching (NET), and token economies are interventions that are often used in EIBI programs (Thomson et al., 2009; Klintwall & Eikeseth, 2014; Gillis & Pence, 2015). Assessments that are commonly used within EIBI programs may include the Brigance Diagnostic Comprehensive Inventory of Behavior Skills-Revised (CIBS-R; Brigance, 1999), Brigance Inventory of Early Development (IED)-II (Brigance, 2004), Verbal Behavior-Milestones Assessment and Placement Program (VB-MAPP; Sundberg, 2014), and Vineland Adaptive Behavior Scale (VABS)-III (Sparrow, Cicchetti, & Saulnier, 2016). Of these assessments, Gould et al. (2011) determined that none alone could be used as the basis of a comprehensive EIBI curriculum because they did not encompass a multitude of skills across multiple domains. The Promoting the Emergence of Advanced Knowledge Relational Training System (PEAK; Dixon et al., 2014) is both a standardized assessment and a curriculum guide that can be used in EIBI programs. Though EIBI programs that utilize such assessments and interventions are typically delivered by staff (e.g., Registered Behavior Technicians) supervised by a BCBA in the clinic, home, and community settings, telemedicine provides an alternative treatment delivery model for families in rural communities.

Telehealth is a treatment modality that has been used to increase accessibility across healthcare fields. Also referred to as telemedicine, telehealth allows providers to deliver interventions remotely using communication technology (Bearss et al., 2018a).

There is a rising body of literature supporting parent training via telehealth as an option to help parents act as the primary change agent in their children's individualized treatment plans (Barretto et al., 2006; Gerow et al., 2021; Tsami et al., 2019; Vismara et al., 2013; Wacker et al., 2013). Specifically, the onset of the COVID-19 pandemic has resulted in an emerging literature base on the use of telehealth for treating individuals with ASD through direct therapy and parent-mediated therapy (Roberts et al., 2019; Hao et al., 2021). Interventions via telehealth have been shown to be an effective method for teaching interventions and assessments to caregivers (Ingersoll et al., 2017), but also one that is largely effective in improving several outcomes in early childhood — namely, reducing challenging behavior (e.g., Lindgren et al., 2020) and improving communication skills (e.g., Baharav & Reiser, 2010; Vismara et al., 2013). Based on the current literature base, The Council of Autism Service Providers (CASP; 2021) released suggested guidelines for direct telehealth services provided to children in EIBI programs (ranging from ages 18 months to 5 years old), including minimum prerequisite skills (e.g., basic joint attention skills, basic discrimination skills, ability to follow 1-step instructions, etc.) and advanced prerequisite skills (e.g., tolerating delayed reinforcement, staying in view of the camera, independently joining a telehealth session, etc.). Another key element the CASP discussed in their suggestions for telehealth practices was parental involvement, specifically noting that parental involvement is paramount to successful client outcomes. The CASP guidelines also note the importance of telehealth services in rural and underserved communities, cost-effectiveness for treatment, and the importance of continuity of care for clients in situations such as global pandemics or other unprecedented events.

Parents are often involved in the care their child receives from an EIBI program by practicing many of the same clinic-based protocols with their child at home. Previous studies have utilized behavioral skills training (BST) either in-person or via telehealth to train parents to implement ABA protocols. In many telemedicine programs, parents essentially serve in the role of the therapist, providing direct treatment to their children, while the BCBA's are responsible for developing protocols, training the parents, monitoring treatment integrity, and progress monitoring target skills (Boisvert et al., 2010). Some evidence suggests that virtual training programs are successful in establishing the skills necessary to implement ABA protocols. In Fisher et al. (2014), researchers provided preliminary findings of a virtual training program for ABA technicians. The 40-hour virtual training program provided participants with complete e-learning modules for behavior reduction and skill acquisition protocols in discrete-trial and play-based formats. The training program's goal was for the technicians to become proficient in their understanding of ABA principles and procedures used in EIBI so that they could implement them with clients. Participants in this study showed improvements through the reduction of problem behavior as well as improvements in skill acquisition, showing potential for this study to extend access to ABA services to families in rural or underserved areas and populations. Rios et al. (2020) presented results indicating that using BST to conduct functional analyses through telehealth was not only a viable option but one that could be a possible solution for those in rural or underserved areas, a feat LeBlanc and colleagues (2021) described as both important and challenging. Boutain et al. (2020) used BST to train three sets of parents that who demonstrated high levels of fidelity in implementing graduated guidance and then individual completion of self-care skills. Parent training programs provided through telehealth have become increasingly necessary, so much so that researchers such as Yi & Dixon (2021) have developed and evaluated a model for parent training via telehealth that incorporates Acceptance and Commitment Therapy (ACT).

In some cases, telemedicine parent training programs focus on specific assessment methods or skill acquisition treatment protocols, without paying specific attention to rapport building and increasing child compliance. For example, the Research Units in Behavioral

Intervention (RUBI) structured parent training manual (Bearss et al., 2018b) was developed specifically for children with ASD and disruptive behaviors. Some evidence-based antecedent strategies used with children to increase compliance in the presence of a demand are Time-In (TI; Speights Roberts et al., 2008) and Effective Instruction Delivery (EID; Radley & Dart, 2016). Ford et al. (2001) describe TI as social reinforcement that can be either an antecedent or consequence in a child's natural environment. TI uses praise, reflection, imitation, description, and enthusiasm to provide social reinforcement to children as an antecedent strategy, before a child is expected to engage in a certain behavior. The components of EID described by Ford et al. (2001) included making eye contact, being specific and direct, providing only one demand at a time, and allowing a 5-second response time. TI and EID have been used in clinical settings as tools to increase a child's compliance using only positive procedures (Speights-Roberts et al., 2008; Bellipanni et al., 2013; O'Handley et al., 2021). Mandal and colleagues (2000) studied the generalization of TI and EID for achieving child compliance with parents. In this study, using TI and EID alone showed increases in child compliance among participants, but additional increases in compliance were noted when TI and EID were used in conjunction. LaBrot et al. (2022) described the results of a caregiver training using BST to teach TI and EID as being maintained and generalizable to the home setting.

In the present study, a clinic providing EIBI in an ABA clinic to children with ASD in rural areas temporarily suspended in-person services due to the COVID-19 pandemic. Some families receiving services opted to participate in telehealth services while the clinic was closed. Families that continued services via telehealth participated in parent training that specifically focused on protocols for TI, EID, DTT, and NET that were previously used by Registered Behavior Technicians (RBTs) in the clinic setting. BST was used to teach caregivers TI and EID procedures, in order for caregivers to build rapport and achieve higher rates of child compliance before completing individualized language acquisition protocols. The levels of service were provided depending upon the caregiver's availability to participate in telemedicine sessions. While there have been improved outcomes for parenting skills and communication skills for children with ASD when telemedicine services are provided for as little as 1 hour per week for 12 weeks (Vismara et al., 2009), to our knowledge, no current literature has assessed outcomes for families that participate in more intensive telemedicine programs. The purpose of this study was to explore the effects of caregiver-led telemedicine sessions on the acquisition of language skills as measured by a standardized language assessment for children with ASD in rural, underserved areas. In addition, this study aimed to investigate the average treatment integrity for each protocol the caregiver implemented over 12 weeks of telemedicine sessions.

Method

Experimental Design

A pre-test, post-test quasi-experimental design was employed to evaluate the improvement in language skills before and after telehealth services, using the PEAK Comprehensive Assessment (PCA). The primary dependent variable was the score achieved by each participant on the PCA. The secondary dependent variable was the average treatment integrity score for each protocol implemented by the participant's caregiver. Since each caregiver met the mastery criterion for the implementation of each protocol, single case design graphs are not included but are available from the primary author upon request.

Materials

PEAK Comprehensive Assessment

The PEAK Comprehensive Assessment (PCA) is an empirically supported assessment system designed to evaluate the existence of, and deficits in, a wide variety of functional, cognitive, and language abilities. As part of a comprehensive ABA assessment of the participant's skill and language functioning, the PCA was conducted prior to clinic closure and upon return to the clinic setting. A direct and indirect assessment of the Direct Training (PEAK-DT), Generalization (PEAK-G), Equivalence (PEAK-E), and Transformation (PEAK-T) modules were included. Each module of the PCA contains 184 specific skills in the participant's language repertoire, providing a maximum PEAK score for the entire assessment of 736. PEAK PCA assessments were conducted by Board Certified Behavior Analysts (BCBAs) in the Early Intervention Clinic.

The PCA includes two norm-referenced modules, the PEAK-DT and PEAK-G modules. Participant performance for the PEAK-DT module can be compared to the performance of same-age, typically developing peers that range from one to ten years old. The PEAK-DT module focuses on one of the learning processes called contingency-based (or directly trained) learning. Contingency-based learning occurs when responses to questions or instructions are increased by feedback following the participant's response, such as error correction procedures or socially mediated reinforcers. The PEAK-G module compares participant performance to the performance of same-age, typically developing peers that range from one to sixteen years old. The PEAK-G module focuses on the basic principle of behavior that occurs when an individual emits a learned response under different or novel conditions. The PEAK-G module can help identify deficits in generalized skills and provide explicit curriculum programming designed to assist with the development of generalized, flexible, and adaptive language skills.

At present, there are no comparative, normative data by age for the PEAK-E or PEAK-T modules. Instead, participant scores are compared to the overall number of skills that are targeted within each respective module. The primary goal of the PEAK-E module is not only to teach clients to emit directly trained responses but to derive novel responses that have never been directly taught in a variety of different and novel conditions. Stimulus equivalence occurs when a learner provides a correct response to untrained stimuli. In other words, the learner begins to form relationships among stimuli, formulate response classes, and to generalize information that was previously trained in new, untrained conditions. The PEAK-E module evaluates a learner's current ability to derive stimulus relations across four different patterns of responding: *reflexivity, symmetry, transitivity,* and *equivalence.* The most basic of the derived stimulus relations, the process of making a reflexive relation among stimuli, is simply relating a stimulus to itself. In other words, stimulus A is directly trained with stimulus A, resulting in an (A-A) relation. Within the PEAK-E module, the next derived stimulus relation targeted for treatment is symmetry. Generally speaking, this is the process of making a derived relation in the opposite direction of a trained relation. For example, if one were to directly train stimulus A with stimulus B (i.e., A-B relation), the derivation occurs between the B-A relation. Once deriving symmetrical relations is established in a participant's repertoire, clinicians focus on establishing derived stimulus relations known as transitivity. This occurs when a participant must make a derivation across stimuli such that the two items being related were never paired together during the training history. The final, most complex relation targeted for treatment within the PEAK-E module is equivalence relations. This occurs when stimulus A is directly trained with stimulus B (i.e., A-B relation) and stimulus C (i.e., A-C relation). Then, a derivation occurs between the B-C and C-B relations.

Transformation of stimulus function occurs when relating events in terms of other events transforms the meaning of those events in a relatively permanent way. The PEAK-T module establishes a learner's ability to expressively and receptively relate events in the following relational contexts: coordination, comparison, opposition, distinction, hierarchical, and deictic (perspective-taking). The first and most basic relational context is coordination, which describes various ways in which stimuli may relate as same or equal to each other. Once participants learn this relational context, they can begin to make relations among stimuli when all but one item are the same. This relational context is known as distinction. The concept of opposition requires that participants acquire skills in the relational contexts of coordination and distinction. For the opposition context, the stimuli must be opposite one another, and at least one aspect of the paired stimuli needs to be distinct. Once the previous relations are mastered, the participant may progress to considerably more abstract hierarchical relations. Hierarchical relations are often stated as "A is an attribute of B" or "A is contained by B" and denotes belongingness between a group of stimuli and a common categorical relation. The relations contained within the deictic relational context family are those that specify a relation in terms of the perspective of the participant. Each of these relational contexts is targeted within each subsection of the PEAK-T module with increasing complexity: Non-arbitrary, Cultural, Arbitrary, and Complex. The non-arbitrary relational contexts are constructed by the utilization of the physical features of the stimuli and the relations among them. In contrast, culturally established relational contexts are not constructed by the physical or formal features of the stimuli but are established by cultural or social conventions that specify the relation between words and the objects they represent. The third level of complexity, arbitrary applicable relational frames, is constructed by utilizing arbitrary words or images and incorporating them into the relations between actual words or stimuli. The final, most complex level that is perhaps the most meaningful of the relational contexts within PEAK-T is the complex transformation of function within relational contexts. This is constructed utilizing arbitrary stimuli and requiring the participant to transform the function of relational skills when presented with a novel verbal problem.

Participants and Setting

Seven clients with a diagnosis of Autism Spectrum Disorder (ASD) and their caregivers served as participants in this study. The participants had received Early Intensive Behavioral Intervention services (EIBI) services from an early intervention clinic in a rural state prior to the COVID-19 pandemic. However, participants' involvement in the early intervention clinic shifted to telemedicine during the COVID-19 pandemic, due to the stay-at-home order issued by the state's governor. Caregivers met with their child's Board Certified Behavior Analyst (BCBA) for parent training sessions conducted in their homes via telemedicine for the duration of time that the clinic was closed, for approximately 12 weeks. At the time the clinic closed, each of the BCBAs had been certified by the Behavior Analyst Certification Board (BACB) and licensed to practice within the state for between two and three years. BCBAs had varying levels of experience with conducting therapy in an early intervention setting prior to becoming a BCBA. One BCBA had been an RBT for two years, one BCBA had been an RBT for three years, and another BCBA had been an RBT for ten years. BCBAs who were responsible for the supervision of each participant's case collected data prior to clinic closure, over the course of caregiver-led telemedicine sessions, and upon returning to the clinic. Since the BCBAs were responsible for the telemedicine sessions and additional staff were not available to collect data while the clinic was closed, IOA data were not collected.

Participant Details

At the time of the clinic closure, Sadie was four years and five months old. She communicated with others by using the Picture Exchange Communication System (PECS)®. Her PEAK score in the PEAK-DT module was 24, which was 43 points lower than the average score of her typically developing 4-year-old peer group. Sadie's PEAK-G score was not applicable, as a minimum score of 30 in the PEAK-DT module is required before conducting the PEAK-G assessment. Though Sadie's score in PEAK-DT was not high enough to include PEAK-G in the assessment, typically developing four-year-olds score 39 in the PEAK-G module. Sadie did not demonstrate mastery of skills in either PEAK-E or PEAK-T module prior to the clinic shutdown. Prior to the clinic closure,

Sadie's parents mastered the implementation of TI and EID. The parents began working with the behavior analyst on implementing NET protocols and a behavior reduction protocol designed to decrease visual and motor stereotypy. Before the onset of COVID-19, Sadie received 31 hours per week of intensive, 1:1 ABA therapy at an early intervention clinic. She did not receive any additional forms of therapy and was not enrolled in school. Sadie's mother had a high school diploma and was not employed prior to the pandemic. During the clinic closure, Sadie's family participated in 10 hours per week of telemedicine with the BCBA.

Claire was seven years and three months old at the time of the clinic closure. Claire used vocal speech as her method of communication. Claire's most recent assessment prior to clinic closure had been completed while she was six years old. Thus, her performance was compared to her typically developing six-year-old peers. Her PEAK skill set in the DT Module was 146, exceeding her typically developing 6-year-old peer group by 1. Claire's PEAK-G skill set was 78, which exceeded the score of her typically developing peers by three. Although her scores exceeded the expectations of her typically developing peer group in the PEAK-DT and PEAK-G modules, her derived relational responding skills were limited and warranted additional treatment. Claire's skill set in the PEAK- E module was 24, and in the PEAK-T module, it was 23. Prior to the clinic closure, Claire's mother mastered the implementation of TI and EID and began working on NET programs. Claire's mother participated in two hours per week of telemedicine therapy during the clinic closure. Prior to the pandemic, Claire received 8 hours of intensive, 1:1 ABA therapy and 8 hours of group ABA therapy at the early intervention clinic. She did not receive additional forms of therapy but received school instruction via distance learning during the shelter-in-place orders. Claire's mother had a college degree and worked full-time before the pandemic.

Cora was five years and two months old at the time of the clinic closure. Cora used vocal speech as her method of communication.

Her PEAK-DT module skill set was 48, which was 97 points lower than the average score of her typically developing 5-year-old peer group. Cora's PEAK-G score was 8, which was 51 points lower than the average score of her typically developing 5-year-old peer group. Cora scored a three in the PEAK-E and PEAK-T module. Prior to the clinic closure, Cora's mother mastered the implementation of TI and EID and began working on NET implementation. Cora's mother participated in 10 hours per week of telemedicine therapy while the clinic was closed. Prior to the pandemic, Cora received 29 hours of intensive, 1:1 ABA therapy at the early intervention clinic. She was not enrolled in school and did not receive additional forms of therapy during the study. Cora's mother had a college degree but was unemployed during the onset of COVID-19.

At the time of clinic closure, Kayla was three years and seven months old. She used vocal speech as her method of communication. Her PEAK-DT score was 65, which was two points lower than the average score of her typically developing 3-year-old peer group. Kayla's Generalization score was 24, which was nine points lower than the average score of her typically developing 3-year-old peer group. Kayla's PEAK-E and PEAK-T score was four. Prior to the clinic closure, Kayla's mother mastered the implementation of TI and EID and began working on implementing NET protocols. Kayla's mother participated in 10 hours per week of telemedicine therapy over the 12 weeks the clinic was closed. Prior to the pandemic, Kayla received 29 hours of intensive, 1:1 ABA therapy at the early intervention clinic. She was not enrolled in school and did not receive any additional forms of therapy over the course of the study. Kayla's mother had a college degree and worked full-time from home during the clinic closure.

At the time of clinic closure, Nash was six years and one month old. He used vocal approximations as his primary way of communicating with others. His PEAK-DT score was 32, which was 113 points lower than the average score of his typically developing 6-year-old peer group. His PEAK-G score was seven, which was 51 points lower than the average score of his typically developing 6-year-old peer group. Nash's PEAK-E score was three, and his PEAK-T score was two. Prior to the clinic closure, Nash's mother mastered the implementation of TI and EID and began working on implementing NET protocols. Nash's mother participated in 10 hours per week of telemedicine therapy during the clinic closure. Prior to the pandemic, Nash received 29 hours of intensive, 1:1 ABA therapy. He was not enrolled in school and did not receive any additional forms of therapy. Nash's mother had a college degree but was unemployed at the onset of the pandemic.

Jack was three years and ten months old at the time of the clinic closure. Jack used PECS® and a limited number of vocal approximations for highly preferred items (e.g., chips). Jack's PEAK-DT score was 9, which was 58 points lower than the average score of his typically developing 3-year-old peer group. For the PEAK-G module, Jack scored 0, which was 39 points lower than the average score of his typically developing 3-year-old peer group. Jack's score for the PEAK-E module was two and for the PEAK-T module was one. Prior to the clinic closure, Jack's mother was working on establishing TI skills and EID. Jack's mother participated in one hour per week of telemedicine therapy. Prior to the pandemic, Jack received 23 hours per week of intensive, 1:1 ABA therapy, and he was not enrolled in school. He did not receive any additional forms of therapy over the course of this study. Jack's mother had an associate's degree and was unemployed at the onset of the COVID-19 pandemic.

Anna was four years and seven months old at the time of the clinic closure. Anna used PECS® for preferred items and American Sign Language (ASL) (e.g., help, more, play). Anna's PEAK-DT score was 27, which was 13 points lower than the average score of her typically developing 4-year-old peer group. Anna's PEAK-G score was zero, which was 39 points lower than the average score of her typically developing peers. For PEAK-E, Anna scored three, and for PEAK-T, her score was two. Prior to the clinic closure, Anna's mother mastered the implementation of TI and EID and began working on

NET implementation, specifically demands (i.e., requests), as well as discrete trials training (PEAK protocol implementation). Anna's mother participated in 20 hours per week of telemedicine therapy over the course of 12 weeks. Before the pandemic, Anna received 29 hours per week of intensive, 1:1 ABA therapy and was not enrolled in school. She did not receive any additional forms of therapy over the course of this study. Anna's mother had a high school diploma and was unemployed at the onset of the COVID-19 pandemic.

Procedures
Behavioral Skills Training

Behavioral Skills Training (BST; Koegel, Russo, & Rincover, 1977) is an empirically supported training method that consists of a didactic presentation, modeling, rehearsal, and corrective feedback on the targeted skill. Each BCBA verbally reviewed each targeted skill with the participant's caregiver. Then, the BCBA provided a video model demonstrating the correct implementation of the skill and role-played the skill with the caregiver. Finally, the BCBA observed the parent implement the targeted skill with the participant. Contingent on incorrect delivery of or missed opportunity to engage in the targeted skills, the BCBA would deliver corrective feedback until treatment integrity reached the mastery criterion.

Behavioral Skills Training was employed during telehealth sessions to teach a variety of protocols necessary to complete a therapy session, such as establishing rapport, procedures designed to increase compliance with instructions, and managing schedules of reinforcement. Parents were directly taught to implement these skills throughout the course of telehealth services using the following protocols: Time-in (TI), Effective Instruction Delivery (EID), Discrete Trial Training (DTT) with token economies, and Naturalistic Environment Teaching (NET). It should be noted that some caregivers had met mastery criteria for TI and EID in the clinic setting prior to telehealth services. Though the caregivers may have previously met mastery criteria for these protocols during contrived sessions in a clinic setting, data were not yet collected on the protocols in a less contrived, naturalistic home setting. At the time of clinic closure, it was unclear if the caregiver would generalize the targeted skills to the home setting. Thus, the implementation of TI and EID was evaluated through telemedicine following clinic closure to assess the generalization and maintenance of key components of the protocols (e.g., TI and EID) before training caregivers on implementing DTT and NET for specific language and skill acquisition protocols.

Time-In

Time-In (TI; Mandal et al., 2000), often identified in the literature as "pairing," is an evidence-based procedure used to establish rapport between caregivers and their children. Time-in has demonstrated effectiveness in decreasing inappropriate behavior and increasing the value of socially mediated attention provided by caregivers. Time-in consists of five skills, known as the acronym "PRIDE": Praise, Reflection, Imitation, Description, and Enthusiasm. Caregivers were taught to avoid general praise statements (i.e. "good job") and instead, provide enthusiastic praise for specific appropriate behaviors. For example, a caregiver may provide behavior-specific praise for the child cleaning up toys by saying, "Great job putting your cars back in the box!" Caregivers were also taught to reinforce their child's vocalizations by reflecting or rephrasing, sounds, words, or statements. For example, a child may say "Red!" and the caregiver would respond, "That is a red car!" In addition to praise and reflection, caregivers were taught to imitate what their child was doing. For example, if their child was stacking blocks, the caregiver would sit beside them, stacking a different set of blocks. While imitating the child's play, caregivers were also taught to verbally describe what the child was doing. For example, if the child was coloring, the caregiver would say, "It looks like you are drawing a star!" Caregivers were also taught to avoid presenting demands during time-in. For example, if a caregiver asked their child a question (e.g. "What color is this?") during TI, they were provided with in-vivo corrective feedback to rephrase their question into a description (e.g., "This is a red block!"). Caregivers were taught to gauge the effectiveness of their enthusiasm and genuine delivery of time-in by observing their child's approach behaviors, such as making eye contact with caregiver, smiling, and making physical contact.

Effective Instruction Delivery (EID)

Effective Instruction Delivery (EID; Mandal et al., 2000), often identified in the literature as three-step guided compliance, is an evidence-based approach to establishing consistent compliance from the child in the presence of demands. Guidelines of EID include: saying the child's name, gaining eye contact, delivering the demand within close proximity of the child, delivering the demand as a directive and descriptive statement (i.e. "Pick up the crayons" vs. "Can you pick up the crayons?"), and maintaining a 5-second wait period for the child's response between prompting. As a part of EID, caregivers were trained on how to implement a least-to-most prompting hierarchy to gain compliance from the child. Caregivers were trained to first present the demand. If the child complied with the demand within five seconds, caregivers were trained to provide enthusiastic behavior-specific praise (and sometimes access to a tangible reinforcer). If the child did not comply within five seconds, caregivers were trained to re-present the demand while also modeling the correct response. This was known as a gestural prompt. If the child complied within five seconds of the gestural prompt, caregivers were trained to provide praise alone (no tangible reinforcer) that was not as enthusiastic as if the participant provided independent compliance. If the child did not comply with the gestural prompt within 5 seconds of presentation, the caregivers were trained to re-present the command while also using gentle hand-over-hand guidance to complete the task. No praise was provided for this level of prompt.

Discrete Trial Training (DTT)

Discrete Trial Training (DTT; Anderson et al., 1996) is a structured approach to teaching new skills by directly reinforcing correct responses in the presence of an instruction. DTT is a method of teaching a targeted skill in simplified and structured steps, in which there is a clearly defined beginning and end to each trial. The primary technique used throughout the DTT method of instruction, regardless of target skill, consists of four parts: a) the caregiver's presentation of stimuli to which the participant responds, b) the participant's response, c) the consequence (i.e., various forms of reinforcement or error correction procedures), and d) an intertrial interval (i.e., short pause prior to the next command). Caregivers were initially trained to implement DTT protocols in the home setting that focused on skills from the foundational learning skills within the PEAK DT module (i.e., instructional control, eye contact, joint attention, and scanning a stimulus array). DTT protocols often utilized EID least-to-most prompting guidelines before more complex prompting procedures were utilized, to ensure that participants acquired targeted skills. Before implementing a token economy with their child, caregivers were instructed to provide reinforcement on a continuous reinforcement schedule using the EID least-to-most prompting guidelines (i.e., social praise and tangible reinforcer for independent correct responding, praise after prompted response, new teaching trial after fully guided response). Token Economies are based on behavior analytic principles that emphasize the use of generalized conditioned reinforcement to establish behavior change. Caregivers were trained on three components of the token economy: a) the target response, b) delivery of the token within one second of the participant independently providing the target response, and c) the backup reinforcer after receiving a pre-determined number of tokens according to their child's individualized scheduled of reinforcement. For example, contingent on a participant correctly responding "Red" in the presence of the instruction "What color is it?" the caregiver would provide the participant with a token. Thinning participant reinforcement schedules (i.e., increasing the number of tokens required before a backup reinforcer was provided) were determined by the behavior analyst.

Naturalistic Environment Teaching (NET)

Naturalistic Environment Teaching (NET; Rule, Losardo, Dinnebeil, Kaiser, & Rowland, 1998) is an evidence-based approach to instruction led by the child in the natural environment during naturally occurring activities (e.g., while the child is playing with preferred items). Caregivers were trained to follow several principles of NET: a) the caregiver follows the child's lead, b) the activities that provide the context for the intervention are child-led, and c) the language acquisition targets that are chosen address skills needed by the child (i.e., skill deficits), d) the caregiver is responsive to the participant's communicative attempts. For example, if the child is playing with toy blocks, the caregiver could contrive an opportunity to teach colors using the blocks. Similar to EID, NET protocols utilized least-to-most prompting guidelines to provide opportunities for skill acquisition to occur. NET skills were determined based on caregiver goals and skill previously targeted in the clinic setting (e.g. vocal mands).

Data Collection and Treatment Integrity

The PCA was administered by the BCBA responsible for the clinical care of each participant. The PCA includes a standardized method of presenting test items and directly testing the language skills located within the PEAK modules (e.g., PEAK-DT and PEAK-G). The pre-test PCA was administered prior to the onset of the COVID-19 pandemic, and the post-test PCA was administered before the participant returned to the clinic for therapy once the clinic was reopened. Data were collected via telemedicine for protocols that were implemented by caregivers. TI sessions were ten minutes in duration, and data were collected using a partial interval recording method with 10 second intervals. The mastery criterion for TI was 80-100% intervals with at least one of the five PRIDE skills across three consecutive sessions. An EID session consisted of ten discrete instructions provided by the caregiver. The mastery criterion for EID was a treatment integrity score of 80-100% correct across three consecutive sessions. The mastery criterion for DTT and NET was 80-100% treatment integrity across three consecutive sessions. Similar to EID sessions, DTT and NET sessions consisted of ten trials provided by the caregiver.

Data Analysis

Pre-Test and Post-Test PEAK PCA data were analyzed by examining the total number of skills that were acquired across each module of the assessment. In addition, a standardized mean difference (SMD) effect size was calculated for the pre-test and post-test scores for each of the PEAK modules within the PCA and the total PCA score. Effect size results were interpreted according to Lakens (2013): small ($d = 0.2$), medium ($d = 0.5$), and large ($d = 0.8$). Average treatment integrity scores were calculated for each protocol implemented during caregiver-led telemedicine sessions.

Results

PEAK Comprehensive Assessment (PCA)

Overall, the total score for each participant's PEAK PCA language assessment score increased following 12 weeks of telemedicine sessions completed by caregivers. The results of the total number of language skills that were acquired as measured by the PEAK PCA are presented in Table 1. On average, the participants acquired a total of 34 specific language skills (range: 18-58) outlined in the PEAK language curriculum. More specifically, participants acquired the highest number of language skills within the PEAK-DT module (*M* = 21, range: 13-42) and the lowest number of skills in the PEAK-E (*M* = 1, range: 1-5) and PEAK-T modules (*M* = 1, range 1-3). Claire, who had the highest pre-test PEAK PCA score, acquired 44 new language skills over the course of the caregiver-led telemedicine sessions. It may be important to note that Claire had the highest scores within the PEAK-E and PEAK-T modules relative to other participants. Cora acquired 58 new language skills over the course of telemedicine sessions, which was the greatest improvement in language skills relative to other participants in the study. It is important to note that Anna, Cora, and Sadie acquired enough skills within the PEAK-DT module that allowed for the beginning of the PEAK-G module over the course of telemedicine sessions. This module had not previously been introduced to any of these children. In contrast, Jack had the lowest pre-test PCA score with one skill in his repertoire prior to clinic closure, yet he acquired 19 new language skills over the course of caregiver-led telemedicine sessions.

The pre-test and post-test scores for each module are presented in Table 2, and the total PCA scores are presented in Table 2 and Figure1. On average, participants showed the greatest changes in scores within the PEAK-DT module. The average pre-test score for this module was 44, and the average post-test score was 65. This resulted in an effect size that is a small to medium effect (Cohen's *d* = 0.44). In addition, participants showed changes in the PEAK-G module with an average pre-test score of 18 and an average post-test score of 31. This resulted in a small to medium effect size (Cohen's *d* = 0.37). The PEAK-E and PEAK-T modules had an average change in score by 1. This resulted in small effect sizes for the PEAK-E module (Cohen's *d* = 0.17) and the PEAK-T module (Cohen's *d* = 0.16). Overall, the average pre-test total PEAK PCA score was 69 and the average post-test score was 104, which results in a small to medium effect size (Cohen's *d* = 0.36).

Table 1

Language Skills Acquired Following Caregiver-led Telemedicine Sessions

Participant	PEAK PCA Module				
	Direct Training	Generalization	Equivalence	Transformation	Total
Anna[a]	17	11	1	1	30
Cora[a]	42	8	5	3	58
Claire	16	26	1	1	44
Kayla	13	13	0	3	29
Jack	15	-	2	1	18
Nash	19	10	0	0	29
Sadie[a]	25	7	1	0	33
Average	21	13	1	1	34

[a] Reflects participants who began skill acquisition programs with their caregiver during telehealth due to the number of skills mastered within the Direct Training module.

Table 2

Participant Pre-Test and Post-Test PEAK scores

	PEAK PCA Module									
Participant	Direct Training		Generalization		Equivalence		Transformation		Total PCA Score	
	Pre-Test	Post-Test	Pre-Test	Post-Test	Pre-Test	Post-Test	Pre-Test	Post-Test	Pre-Test	Post-Test
Anna[a]	27	44	0	11	3	4	2	3	32	62
Cora[a]	12	54	0	8	0	5	0	3	12	70
Claire	146	162	78	104	24	25	23	24	271	315
Kayla	65	78	24	37	4	4	3	6	96	125
Jack	1	16	-	-	0	2	0	1	1	19
Nash	32	51	7	17	3	3	2	2	44	73
Sadie[a]	24	49	0	7	2	3	2	2	28	61
M	44	65	18	31	5	7	5	6	69	104
Range	1-146	16-162	0-78	7-104	0-24	2-25	0-23	1-24	1-271	19-315
SD	49	46	31	38	8	8	8	8	94	98
Cohen's *d*		0.44		0.37		0.17		0.16		0.36

Note. This table reflects each participant's PEAK score prior to clinic closure and upon reopening the clinic. Jack did not achieve a DT score to warrant assessment in the Generalization module.

[a] Reflects participants who began skill acquisition programs with their caregiver during telehealth due to the number of skills mastered within the Direct Training module.

Parent Treatment Integrity
Time In

The results for the implementation of TI with each caregiver are listed in Table 3. On average, all of the caregivers demonstrated correct implementation of TI skills for 94% of the observation across the 12 weeks of telemedicine sessions. Average treatment integrity scores for TI ranged from 82.76% - 100% of intervals in which caregivers demonstrated at least one of the PRIDE skills. Cora's caregiver received the lowest average treatment integrity score relative to other caregivers and often received corrective feedback from the BCBA to increase the rates of praise, reflection, and description components of TI.

EID

The results for the implementation of EID with each caregiver are listed in Table 3. On average, all of the caregivers correctly implemented EID procedures for 88% of the caregiver-implemented treatment sessions. Average treatment integrity scores for EID ranged from 66.87% - 100% correct. Kayla and Jack's caregivers demonstrated the lowest average treatment integrity, with scores of 66.87% correct for Kayla's caregiver and 66% correct for Jack's caregiver. Anecdotally, the lower scores were due to errors with delivering different instructions before following through with the least-to-most prompting hierarchy if the participant demonstrated challenging behavior.

DTT

The results for the implementation of DTT with each caregiver are listed in Table 3. On average, all caregivers correctly implemented the DTT protocols 99% of the time, the highest average treatment integrity relative to other treatment protocols. Average treatment integrity scores for DTT protocols ranged from 97.43% - 100% correct. Jack's family did not target DTT or token economies during telemedicine sessions. Thus, there is no score reported for Jack.

Table 3

Average Caregiver Treatment Integrity

Participant	Treatment Protocol			
	Time-In	EID	NET	DTT
Anna	100%	100%	99.43%	99.21%
Cora	82.76%	100%	85%	100%
Claire	100%	100%	-	100%
Kayla	91.11%	66.87%	-	99.36%
Jack	100%	66%	92.25%	-
Nash	89%	99.67%	84.70%	97.43%
Sadie	92.57%	85.24%	-	99.98%
Average	94%	88%	90%	99%

Note. This table demonstrates the average parent treatment integrity for TI, EID, NET, and DTT protocols with each participant over the course of 12 weeks of caregiver-led telemedicine sessions. Caregivers were not trained on protocols that were not targeted with the participant over the course of clinic closure.

Figure 1

Changes in Total PEAK PCA score

Note. The total PEAK PCA score for the Pre-Test (i.e., before clinic closure) and Post-Test (i.e., upon returning to the clinic) are shown for each participant.

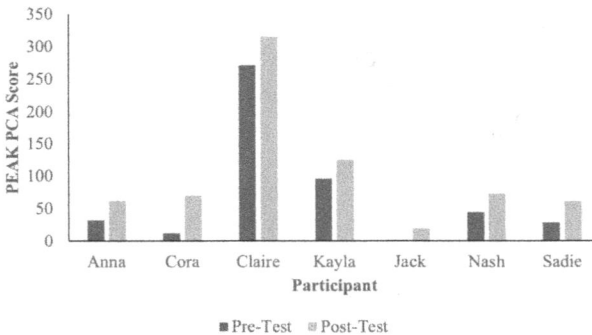

NET

The results for the implementation of NET protocols with each caregiver are listed in Table 3. On average, all caregivers participating in NET protocols with their children correctly implemented the protocols for 90% of the sessions. Average treatment integrity scores for NET protocols ranged from 84.70% - 100% correct. Claire, Kayla, and Sadie did not target language acquisition using NET protocols during telemedicine sessions. Thus, for these children there is no score to report.

Discussion

Access to care that utilizes methods rooted in Applied Behavior Analysis is important for families of children with ASD in rural communities. Without access to care early in their child's development, there may be persistent, pervasive barriers to learning that include delays in language development. For these families, the prohibitive cost of accessing care and the limited numbers of BCBAs distinguishes telemedicine as a lower-cost, evidence-based option for these services. However, a number of questions remain regarding language acquisition outcomes for children and families who participate in telemedicine programs in rural states.

The primary purpose of this study was to explore the effects of caregiver-led telemedicine sessions on the acquisition of language skills for children with ASD in rural, underserved areas. Overall, each of the participants made improvements in their total PCA score following caregiver-led telemedicine sessions, despite individual differences in the pre-test total PCA score and the number of hours of therapy delivered via telemedicine per week. The participants in this study represent children with a wide range of language skills represented by the total PCA score (Range = 1-271) and communication modalities (i.e., vocal speech, PECS®, and ASL). Although there was a low to moderate effect size for the total PCA score across all participants, it is possible that Claire's scores skewed those results due to her high pre-test PCA scores. Before telemedicine sessions began, Claire's PCA score was 271, with Kayla having the next highest score (i.e., 96) relative to other participants. Participants showed the greatest improvements within the PEAK-DT module. While this could have been due to a clinical focus on targeting skills within this module by caregivers, it is also possible that participants acquired a higher number of skills within this module once they acquired additional skills within the PEAK-E and PEAK-T modules. As suggested by Ming, Moran, and Stewart (2015), if a student can demonstrate derived relational responding of a particular type, then those skills may be used to program lessons for learning new vocabulary and academic skills more efficiently, in addition to rapidly expanding functional communication skills. For example, Cora acquired the most skills within PEAK-DT, PEAK-E, and PEAK-T. It is possible that the derived relational responding skills acquired within PEAK-E and PEAK-T over the course of telemedicine sessions helped to improve her PEAK-DT score beyond the improvements observed with other participants. Besides Cora, Claire acquired more skills than other participants which may have been due to the fact that she had the highest pre-test PCA score and higher pre-test scores in PEAK-E and PEAK-T. It is also possible that the level of parent participation in telemedicine sessions impacted the results. While five of the seven participants received at least 10 hours per week of telemedicine therapy, it is possible that fewer hours of telemedicine impacted the results for Jack. Jack received only 1 hour per week of therapy and acquired the fewest number of skills relative to other participants. In contrast, the five participants that received 10 hours or more of telemedicine therapy per week acquired 29 skills or more (e.g., Anna acquired 30 skills, Cora acquired 58 skills, Kayla acquired 29 skills, Nash acquired 29 skills, and Sadie acquired 33 skills, respectively). While this study did not determine the effects the dosage of telemedicine therapy has on language development in children with ASD, it is possible that these results could provide preliminary evidence that a higher dosage of caregiver-led therapy may provide higher rates of skill acquisition than one might expect in a clinical setting.

The clinical significance of the number of language skills acquired during caregiver-led telemedicine sessions may also be worth noting. These results may provide insight into the approximate number of skills that may be acquired over telemedicine in which parents receive training on the protocols included in this study, so that parents may serve as the primary interventionists. First, none of the participants experienced a lower total PCA score following the transition from clinic-based services to caregiver-led telemedicine sessions. It is possible that, in some cases, practitioners and caregivers will anticipate that skills do not maintain over time (i.e., skill regression) with children that transition from clinic-based services to caregiver-led sessions in the home, or when therapy hours are reduced from an early intervention program. Instead, the average number of skills acquired over 12 weeks of caregiver-led telemedicine sessions was 34 new skills (range = 18 – 58) for families that participated in the study. In addition to these gains in language development, three of the participants acquired a sufficient number of skills in the PEAK-DT module to warrant intervention within the PEAK-G module over the course of the caregiver-led telemedicine sessions. It is possible that without caregiver-led telemedicine sessions, the participants might not have had the opportunity to receive intervention within the PEAK-G module once they resumed services within the clinic setting. Further, the three participants who began intervention within the PEAK-G module during caregiver-led telemedicine sessions acquired between seven and 11 new skills within the module before returning to the clinic. For these three participants, not only did they begin treatment in the PEAK-G module, they continued to make progress within the module prior to returning to the clinic for the post-test assessment. This may provide initial evidence that participants in rural, underserved areas can progress through a curriculum designed to target language development, such as the PEAK curriculum, via caregiver-led telemedicine sessions.

This study also aimed to investigate the average integrity of each protocol the caregivers implemented over the course of caregiver-led telemedicine sessions. The caregivers who participated in telemedicine sessions were trained to implement multiple protocols that included TI (i.e., pairing), EID (i.e., Three-Step Guided Compliance), DTT, and NET (as clinically appropriate). Overall, the caregivers demonstrated the ability to implement a combination of these protocols with high, average treatment integrity over the course of an extended period of time, specifically 12 weeks. Anecdotally, Kayla and Jack's caregivers had the most difficulty with maintaining high average treatment integrity with the EID protocol, due to presenting different demands before moving through the prompt hierarchy in response to challenging behavior (e.g., stereotypy). Though Kayla and Jack's caregivers had difficulty with maintaining high levels of treatment integrity for the EID protocol, they were successful with maintaining high levels of treatment integrity for the DTT and NET protocols, which targeted specific language skills that could have contributed to the increase in PCA scores. It may also be worth noting that five of the seven caregivers implemented these protocols with high average treatment integrity for 10 hours or more per week for the duration the clinic was closed. This may provide some initial evidence that caregivers can provide a higher dosage of therapy with sufficient treatment integrity through telemedicine than previous studies have suggested. In addition, the protocols which were implemented by caregivers are different when compared to protocols found in other parent training programs. For example, programs similar to the RUBI program provide training to caregivers on ways to reduce problematic behaviors. While this is important for reducing problematic behaviors that could serve as barriers to learning, it may also be important for clinicians to provide caregivers with training on protocols that would be implemented to foster opportunities for language development beyond functional communication training. Similar to the procedures in this study, it may be beneficial for practitioners to first consider training caregivers on rapport building protocols, such as TI, and compliance training protocols, such as EID, prior to the implementation of more specific language acquisition protocols for children with ASD who do not demonstrate disruptive behaviors when delivering telemedicine services. Many ABA practitioners have adopted this approach for EIBI programs across the clinic, home, and community settings. Training parents to implement these interventions may promote a social approach and reduce avoidance behaviors prior to discrete-trial instruction (Shillingsburg, Hansen, & Wright, 2018). Since many children with ASD early in their development would require parent-led telemedicine sessions according to the recommendations outlined by The Council of Autism Service Providers (2021), taking this approach may not only lead to fewer problematic behaviors when access to ABA therapy providers are limited, but also to higher rates of language acquisition over the course of a telemedicine intervention.

There were numerous limitations to the study worth noting. First, the interpretation of the results is limited by a lack of experimental control. Since there was a small group of families who elected to participate in telemedicine therapy during the shelter-in-place orders, it is difficult to make comparisons across families who could have received lower or higher dosages of telemedicine treatment, or a control group that did not receive any telemedicine treatment prior to returning to the clinic. Though this study used a quasi-experimental design, it is possible that there were additional factors that might have influenced the results. For example, it is possible that participants with caregivers who had previously mastered protocols in the clinic setting acquired more language over the course of telemedicine sessions. While this is a limitation, the previously mastered protocols were mastered during controlled, contrived sessions within a clinic setting. Caregivers were encouraged to practice the protocols at home once they met the mastery criterion in the clinic setting, but it was unclear if they had implemented the previously mastered protocols with sufficient integrity in the less contrived, natural environment of the home setting. Since the telemedicine sessions were conducted in the home setting as a result of the shelter-in-place orders, BCBAs first conducted observations of the previously mastered protocols, such as TI and EID, to ensure that caregivers implemented the protocols with sufficient integrity in the home before training caregivers on additional protocols. In addition, caregivers may have continued to practice the skills targeted during telemedicine sessions beyond the observations by supervising BCBAs. This could have increased the rate of skill acquisition during telemedicine sessions resulting in higher PCA scores. An additional limitation of this study involves the discrepancy in amount of therapy provided: two families who received one hour per week of therapy and one family who received 20 hours per week of therapy were compared to four families who participated for 10 hours per week. Because there were participants who spent differing amounts of time receiving therapy, it is difficult to determine the effect higher or lower intensity telemedicine programs may have on language acquisition as measured by a standardized assessment like the PCA. The results from these participants were intentionally included to provide some initial evidence of the outcomes of the PCA. In addition, there were no IOA data collected due to the nature of the clinic closure over the course of the COVID-19 shelter-in-place orders. The BCBAs were solely responsible for the care of the participants and caregivers who received telemedicine services when the clinic closed. This study is also limited by the fact that participants were receiving clinic-based therapy prior to telemedicine. It is possible that the results for participants who received admission to an EIBI program before receiving telemedicine therapy alone would have different outcomes compared to participants who might have received telemedicine only. The participants' prior exposure to protocols such as EID, DTT, and NET from trained therapists in a clinic setting may have impacted their compliance with instructions delivered by their caregivers before telemedicine sessions began. Finally, there were individual differences across participants that limited the interpretation of the results. For example, three participants used PECS® as their primary mode of communication, while other participants used vocal communication. This could have limited the rate of individuals' language acquisition over the course of the caregiver-led telemedicine sessions and impacted their post-test PCA score. In addition, three of the caregivers in this study did not receive training on the NET protocol, which could have limited participant progress compared to other participants who received training on DTT and NET protocols.

Despite these limitations, the results may provide preliminary evidence for future directions of research. Though there were no notable differences based on the number of hours per week of telemedicine due to the sample size for this study, future studies may investigate the differential effects of the dosage of telemedicine and participant outcomes. The caregiver participation in telemedicine for the participants of this study varied over the course of the 12 weeks the early intervention clinic was closed; some caregivers participated as few as 1 hour per week while others participated 20 hours per week. While nearly half of the caregivers that participated for approximately 10 hours per week, it may be possible that more intensive telemedicine sessions may lead to larger increases in language skills over the course of admission. In addition, practitioners may want to consider the acceptability of higher dosages of caregiver-led telemedicine over the course of 12 weeks. While the clinic was closed due to shelter-in-place orders, some caregivers were available to deliver higher dosages of telemedicine therapy due to fewer or no work hours. Thus, it is possible that other caregivers will not have the ability or find it acceptable to deliver the same dosage of telemedicine therapy as the caregivers did in this study. In addition, future research may investigate the effects of individual differences in language skills, such as communication modality, on the outcomes of caregiver-led telemedicine sessions. Aside from differences across child participants, future research may also investigate the effects of individual caregiver differences, such as education level or occupation, on treatment integrity throughout the admission. While the participants in this study continued to make progress with their language development over the course of caregiver-led telemedicine sessions, the effects differences across participants and their caregivers might have on long-term outcomes remain unclear.

　　Families of children with ASD often experience limited availability of ABA providers in rural states, leaving many children without access to early intervention services. With nearly one-fifth of the United States living in rural areas (U.S. Census Bureau, 2010), telemedicine has become a viable, cost-effective option for addressing many of the barriers these families face when attempting to access ABA therapy (Pollard et al., 2017). And it is possible that a primary focus on high treatment integrity for protocols that focus on rapport building, instruction following, and effective teaching practices may lead to improved language development in early childhood. While these results may only provide preliminary evidence that caregiver-led telemedicine sessions in rural states could result in improvements in language development, practitioners may consider programs that provide a hybrid model whereby families initially attend clinic-based services with their child for an initial assessment and parent training, followed by telemedicine sessions once a treatment plan is developed and parents reach mastery of protocols similar to those included in this study. Thus, it is possible that families in areas with limited access to clinic-based or home-based ABA providers may observe progress in their child's language development with parent participation in a telemedicine program. These positive outcomes may be accomplished while simultaneously providing significant cost savings for the family, similar to other models for delivering telemedicine therapy.

References

Aishworiya, R. & Kang, Y. Q. (2020). Including children with developmental disabilities in the equation during this COVID-19 pandemic. *Journal of Autism and Developmental Disorders*. https://doi.org/10.1007/s10803-020-04670-6

Anderson S. R., Taras M., Cannon B. O'Malley (1996). Teaching new skills to young children with autism. In Maurice C., Green G., Luce S. C. (Eds.), *Behavioral intervention for young children with autism: A manual for parents and professionals.* (pp. 181–184).

Barretto, A., Wacker, D. P., Harding, J., Lee, J., & Berg, W. K. (2006). Using telemedicine to conduct behavioral assessments. *Journal of Applied Behavior Analysis, 39*(3), 333-340. https://doi.org/10.1901/jaba.2006.173-04

Bearss, K., Johnson, C. R., Handen, B. L., Butter, E., Lecavalier, L., Smith, T., & Scahill, L. (2018b). *Parent training for disruptive behavior: The RUBI autism network, clinician manual.* Oxford University Press.

Bearss, K. Burrell, T. L., Challa, S. A., Postorino, V., Gillespie, S. E., Crooks, C., & Scahill, L. (2018a). Feasibility of parent training via telehealth for children with autism spectrum disorder and disruptive behaviors: A demonstration pilot. *Journal of Autism and Developmental Disorders, 48*, 1020-1030. https://doi.org/10.1007/s10803-017-3363-2

Behavior Analyst Certification Board. (2021). Certificant Registry. https://www.bacb.com/services/o.php?page=101135

Belfer, M. L. & Saxena, S. (2006). WHO Child Atlas Project. *The Lancet, 367*(9510), 551-552. https://doi.org/10.1016/S0140-6736(06)68199-3

Bellipanni, K. D., Tingstrom, D. H., Olmi, D. J., & Roberts, D. S. (2013). The sequential introduction of positive antecedent and consequent components in a compliance training package with elementary students. *Behavior Modification, 37*(6), 768-789. DOI: 10.1177/0145445513501959

Boisvert, M., Russel, L., Andrianopoulos, M., & Boscardin, M. L. (2010). Telepractice in the assessment and treatment of individuals with autism spectrum disorders: A systematic review. *Developmental Neurorehabilitation, 13*(6), 423-432. https://doi.org/10.3109/17518423.2010.499889

Boutain, A. R., Sheldon, J. B., & Sherman, J. A. (2020). Evaluation of a telehealth parent training program in teaching self-care skills to children with autism. *Journal of Applied Behavior Analysis, 53*(3), 1259-1275. https://doi.org/10.1002/jaba.743

Brigance, A.H. *(2004). Inventory of Early Development—II.* North Billerica, MA: Curriculum Associates.

Brigance, A. H. (1999). *Brigance diagnostic comprehensive inventory of basic skills.* North Billerica, MA: Curriculum Associates.

Cidav, Z., Munson, J., Estes, A., Dawson, G., Rogers, S., & Mandell, D. (2017). Cost offset associated with Early Start Denver Model for children with autism. *Journal of the American Academy of Child Adolescent Psychiatry, 56*(9), 777-783. https://doi.org/10.1016/j.jaac.2017.06.007

Council of Autism Service Providers (2021). *Practice Parameters for Telehealth Implementation of Applied Behavior Analysis: Second Edition.* Wakefield, MA.

Dai, Y. G., Thomas, R. P., Brennan, L., Helt, M. S., Barton, M. L., Dumont-Mathieu, T., & Fein, D. A. (2020). Development and acceptability of a new program for caregivers of children with autism spectrum disorder: Online parent training in early behavioral intervention. *Journal of Autism and Developmental Disorders.* https://doi.org/10.1007/s10803-020-04863-z

Dixon, M. R., Whiting, S. W., Rowsey, K., & Belisle, J. (2014). Assessing the relationship between intelligence and the PEAK relational training system. *Research in Autism Spectrum Disorders, 8*(9), 1208-1213. https://doi.org/10.1016/j.rasd.2014.05.005

Fisher, W. W., Luczynski, K. C., Hood, S. A., Lesser, A. D., Machado, M. A., & Piazza, C. C. (2014). Preliminary findings of a randomized clinical trial of a virtual training program for applied behavior analysis technicians. *Research in Autism Spectrum Disorders, 8*, 1044-1054. https://doi.org/10.1016/j.rasd.2014.05.002

Ford, A. D., Olmi, D. J., Edward, R. P., & Tingstrom, D. H. (2001). The sequential introduction of compliance training components with elementary-aged children in general education classroom settings. *School Psychology Quarterly, 16*(2), 142-157. https://doi.org/10.1521/scpq.16.2.142.18702

Gerow, S., Radhakrishnan, S., Davis, T. N., Zambrano, J., Avery, S., Cosottile, D. W., & Exline, E. (2021). Parent-implemented brief functional analysis and treatment with coaching via telehealth. *Journal of Applied Behavior Analysis, 54*(1), 54-69. https://doi.org/10.1002/jaba.801

Gillis, J. M. & Pence, S. T. (2015). Token economy for individuals with autism spectrum disorder. In: DiGennaro Reed, F., Feed, D. (Eds.), *Autism Service Delivery and Child Psychopathology Series,* 257-277. Springer. https://doi.org/10.1007/978-1-4939-2656-5_9

Gould, E., Dixon, D. R., Najdowski, A. C., Smith, M. N., & Tarbox, J. (2011). A review of assessments for determining the content of early intensive behavioral intervention programs for autism spectrum disorders. *Research in Autism Spectrum Disorders, 5*(1), 990-1002. https://doi.org/10.1016/j.rasd.2011.01.012

Hao, Y., Franco, J. H., Sundarrajan, M., & Chen, Y. (2021). A pilot study comparing tele-therapy and in-person therapy: Perspectives from parent-mediated intervention for children with autism spectrum disorders. *Journal of Autism and Developmental Disorders, 51*, 129-143. https://doi.org/10.1007/s10803-020-04439-x

Ingersoll, B., Walner, A. L., Berger, N. I., Pickard, K. E., & Bonter, N. (2017). Comparison of a self-directed and therapist-assisted telehealth parent-mediated intervention for children with ASD: A pilot RCT. *Journal of Autism and Developmental Disorders, 46*, 2275-2284. https://doi.org/10.1007/s10803-016-2755-z

Klintwall, L. & Eikeseth, S. (2014). Early and intensive behavioral intervention (EIBI) in autism. In V, B. Patel, V. R. Preedy, & C, R. Martin (Eds.), *Comprehensive Guide to Autism*. Springer. https://doi.org/10.1007/978-1-4614-4788-7_129

LaBrot, Z. C., Kupzyk, S., Strong-Bak, W., Bates-Brantley, K., & Caserta, A. (2022). Generalization and maintenance of caregivers' effective instruction delivery following group behavioral skills training. *Behavioral Interventions, 37* (3), 640-659. https://doi.org/10.1002/bin.1866

Lakens, D. (2013). Calculating and reporting effect sizes to facilitate cumulative science: a practical primer for *t*-tests and ANOVAs. *Frontiers in Psychology, 4 (*863), 1-12. doi: 10.3389/fpsyg.2013.00863

LeBlanc, L. A., Lerman, D. C., & Normand, M. P. (2020). Behavior analytic contributions to public health and telehealth. *Journal of Applied Behavior Analysis, 53*(3), 1208-1218. https://doi.org/10.1002/jaba.749

Lindgren, S., Wacker, D., Schieltz, K., Suess, A., Pelzel, K., Kopelman, T., Lee, J., Romani, P., & O'Brien, M. (2020). A randomized controlled trial of functional communication training via telehealth for young children with autism spectrum disorder. *Journal of Autism and Developmental Disorders, 50*, 4449-4462. https://doi.org/10.1007/s10803-020-04451-1

Maenner, M. J., Shaw, K. A., Bakian, A. V., Bilder, D. A., Durkin, M. S., Esler, A., Furnier, S. M., Hallas, L., Hall-Lande, J., Hudson, A., Hughes, M. M., Patrick, M., Pierce, K., Poynter, J. N., Salinas, A., Shenouda, J., Vehorn, A., Warren, Z., Costantino, J. N., Cogswell, M. E. (2021). Prevalence and characteristics of autism spectrum disorder among children aged 8 years—Autism and developmental disabilities monitoring network, 11 sites, United States, 2018. *Morbidity and Mortality Weekly Report—Surveillance Summaries, 70*(11), 1-16. https://doi.org/10.15585/mmwr.ss7011a1

Mandal, R. L., Olmi, D. J., Edwards, R. P., Tingstrom, D. H., & Benoit, D. A. (2000). Effective instruction delivery and time-in: Positive procedures for achieving child compliance. *Child & Family Behavior Therapy, 22*(4), 1-12. https://doi.org/10.1300/j019v22n04_01

Ming, S., Moran, L., & Stewart, I. (2015). Derived relational responding and generative language: Applications and future directions for teaching individuals with autism spectrum disorders. *European Journal of Behavior Analysis, 15:2*, 199-224, DOI: 10.1080/15021149.2014.11434722.

Mississippi Autism Advisory Committee. (2020). *2020 report to legislature.* https://www.dmh.ms.gov/wp-content/uploads/2020/10/Final.-2020-MAAC-Report-to-the-Legislature.pdf

Mississippi Autism Board. (2021). *List of Active Licensees*. https://www.msautismboard. ms.gov/sites/autism/files/Licensee%20Lists/MAB%20Licensees%207.15.22.pdf

Mounzer, W. & Stenhoff, D. M. (2022). Early intensive behavioral intervention program for children with autism in Syria. *Focus on Autism and Other Developmental Disabilities*. https://doi.org/10.1177/10883576211073686

O'Handley, R. D., Dufrene, B. A., & Wimberly, J. (2021). Bug-in-the-ear training increases teachers' effective instruction delivery and student compliance. *Journal of Behavioral Education*. https://doi.org/10.1007/s10864-020-09429-8

Pollard, J. S., Karimi, K. A., & Ficcaglia, M. B. (2017). Ethical considerations in the design and implementation of a telehealth service delivery model. *Behavior Analysis: Research and Practice, 17*(4), 298-311. https://dx.doi.org/10.1037/bar0000053

Radley, K. C. & Dart, E. H. (2016). Antecedent strategies to promote children's and adolescents' compliance with adult requests: A review of the literature. *Clinical Child and Family Psychology Review, 19*, 39-54. https://doi.org/10.1007/s10567-015-0197-3

Rios, D., Schenk, Y. A., Eldrige, R. R., & Peterson, S. M. (2020). The effects of remote behavioral skills training on conducting functional analyses. *Journal of Behavioral Education, 29*, 449-468. https://doi.org/10.1007/s10864-020-09385-3

Roane, H. S., Fisher, W. W., & Carr, J. E. (2016). Applied behavior analysis as treatment for autism spectrum disorder. *The Journal of Pediatrics, 175*, 27-32. https://doi. org/10.1016/j.jpeds.2016.04.023

Roberts, C. A., Smith, K. C., & Sherman, A. K. (2019). Comparison of online and face-to-face parent education for children with autism and sleep problems. *Journal of Autism and Developmental Disorders, 49*, 1410-1422. https://doi.org/10.1007/s10803-018-3832-2

Rodgers, M., Marshall, D., Simmonds, M., Couteur, A., Biswas, M., Wright, K., Rai, D., Palmer, S., Stewart, L., & Hodgson, R. (2020). Interventions based on early intensive applied behaviour analysis for autistic children: A systematic review and cost-effectiveness analysis. *Health Technology Assessment, 35*, 1-306. https://doi.org/10.3310/hta24350

Rule, S., Losardo, A., Dinnebeil, L., Kaiser, A., & Rowland, C. (1998). Translating Research on Naturalistic Instruction into Practice. *Journal of Early Intervention, 21*(4), 283–293. https://doi.org/10.1177/105381519802100401

Shillingsburg, M. A., Hansen, B., & Wright, M. (2019). Rapport building and instructional fading prior to discrete trial instruction: Moving from child-led play to intensive teaching. *Behavior Modification, 43*(2), 288-306. https://doi.org/10.1177/0145445517751436

Sparrow, S.S., Cicchetti, D. V. & Saulnier, C. A. (2016). *Vineland Adaptive Behavior Scales*. (3rd ed.) Circle Pines, MN: American Guidance Service.

Speights-Roberts, D., Tingstrom, D. H., Olmi, D. J., & Bellipanni, K. D. (2008). Positive antecedent and consequent components in child compliance training. *Behavior Modification, 32*(1), 21-38. https://doi.org/10.1177/0145445507303838

Sundberg, M. L. (2014). *VB-MAPP Verbal Behavior Milestones Assessment and Placement Program, 2nd Ed: A Language and Social Skills Assessment Program for Children with Autism Or Other Intellectual Disabilities*. United States: AVB Press.

Thomson, K., Martin, G. L., Arnal, L., Fazzio, D., & Yu, C. T. (2009). Instructing individuals to deliver discrete-trials teaching to children with autism spectrum disorders: A review. *Research in Autism Spectrum Disorders, 3*(3), 590-606. https://doi.org/10.1016/j.rasd.2009.01.003

Tsami, L., Lerman, D., & Toper-Korkmaz, O. (2019). Effectiveness and acceptability of parent training via telehealth among families around the world. *Journal of Applied Behavior Analysis, 52*(4), 1113-1129. https://doi.org/10.1002/jaba.645

U.S. Census Bureau. (2010). *2010 Census Urban and Rural Classification and Urban Area Criteria*. Retrieved from http://www.census.gov/geo/reference/ua/urban-rural-2010.html

Vismara, L. A., Colombi, C., & Rogers, S. J. (2009). Can one hour per week of therapy lead to lasting changes in young children with autism? *Autism, 13*(1), 93-115. https://doi.org/10.1177/1362361307098516

Vismara, L. A., McCormick, C., Young, G. S., Nadhan, A., & Monlux, K. (2013). Preliminary findings of a telehealth approach to parent training in autism. *Journal of Autism and Developmental Disorders, 43*, 2953-2969. https://doi.org/10.1007/s10803-013-1841-8

Wacker, D. P., Lee, J. F., Padilla Dalmau, Y. C., Kopelman, T. G., Lindgren, S. D., Kuhle, J., Pelzel, K. E., Dyson, S., Schieltz, K. M., & Waldron, D. B. (2013). Conducting function communication training via telehealth to reduce the problem behavior of young children with autism. *Journal of Developmental and Physical Disabilities, 25*, 35-48. https://doi.org/10.1007/s10882-012-9314-0

Yi, Z. & Dixon, M. R. (2021). Developing and enhancing adherence to a telehealth ABA parent training curriculum for caregivers of children with autism. *Behavior Analysis in Practice, 14*, 58-74. https://10.1007/s40617-020-00464-5

An Alternating Treatment Design Comparing Small Group Reading Interventions Across Early Elementary Readers

Madison Billingsley-Ring, Kayla Bates-Brantley, Hailey Ripple, Mallie Donald, Daniel Gadke, and Sarah Wright Harry

Abstract

Learning how to read accurately and fluently is a critical component for a student's future academic success. Reading fluency is a skill that many students struggle to master. In addition, many students missed out on key skill development due to the loss of instruction from COVID-19. As schools begin to recover from these educational losses, small group reading interventions offer an efficient solution to service multiple students at once. Small group reading interventions such as Repeated Readings (RR), Listening Passage Preview (LPP) and LPP with RR (LPP+RR) have all been demonstrated to be effective methods for increasing reading fluency (Begeny et al., 2009; Begeny & Silber, 2006). Yet few studies have specifically examined the effectiveness of these interventions in comparison to each other in a group setting. The current study compared reading RR, LPP, and LPP+RR in a small group setting to determine which intervention yielded the largest gains in reading fluency.

Keywords: *Academic Intervention, Small Group, Reading Intervention, Elementary, Alternating Treatment Design*

An Alternating Treatment Design Comparing Small Group Reading Interventions Across Early Elementary Readers

Learning to read accurately and fluently is a critical learning component, with decades of literature documenting the correlation between reading ability and future academic outcomes (Koller, 2022). Unfortunately, a significant number of students face difficulty with reading and are not performing at an appropriate age or grade level (Begeny et al., 2009; Schreder et al., 2012). Foundational reading research completed in the late 1990's found that 74% of students who were identified as poor readers in the 3rd grade remained classified as poor readers in the 9th grade (Fletcher & Lyon, 1998). Over twenty years later, The Nation's Report Card (Institute of Education Sciences, 2019) found that across the United States, only 35% of fourth graders were proficient in reading. Taken together, this data indicate that the need for early intervention targeting students who are below proficiency in reading fluency is critical. Specifically, the importance of addressing foundational academic concerns before 3rd grade as prevention for a later academic crisis is imperative (Bates-Brantley et al., 2022). This critical need was further heightened by the COVID-19 pandemic. During the pandemic, schools across the world experienced shutdowns that led to prolonged loss of instruction (Kuhfeld et al., 2020). In the United States over 130,000 schools closed their doors impacting an estimated 57 million school aged children (Boa et al., 2021). With schools closing for a least three weeks and a majority closing for the remainder of 2019-2020 and parts of the 2020-2021 academic year, it is estimated that students lost at a minimum one month of literacy skills with many models predicting regressions larger than those seen when no instruction is provided during summer holiday (Hammerstein et al., 2021). Recent studies evaluating the effects of the pandemic on early learners (i.e. kindergarten students) estimated that early learners lost 67% of their literacy abilities due to school closure and lose of instruction (Bao et al., 2021). This global crisis further solidified not only the need for effective interventions, but also the need for efficient interventions during formative grades (i.e. kindergarten-3rd grade) (Kearney & Childs, 2021).

Evidence Based Reading Interventions

As a school-age child progresses, skills building is expected from one grade to the next with proficiency in reading expected by third grade (Musen, 2010). However, for some children this skill acquisition does not occur and therefore effective academic interventions are required. Research has focused on finding effective interventions to decrease the gap between a student's grade level and instructional level (Begeny et al., 2009; Bonfiglio et al., 2006; Lee et al., 2007). Repeated Reading (RR) and Listening Passage Preview (LPP) are two interventions which have been used most often to effectively target reading fluency, and they have high empirical support as evidence-based practice for elementary-age children (Begeny 2009; Skinner et al., 1997; Therrien, 2004). Through meta-analytic work and decades of published work, RR is one of the most utilized interventions in the literature to improve reading fluency (Powell & Gadke, 2018). RR has been demonstrated as an effective intervention for increasing a student's reading fluency, by having a participant read a passage multiple times until a predetermined number of words have been read or a fluency criterion is met (Szadokierski et al., 2017; Therrien, 2004). In a meta-analytic review, Stevens et al. (2016) found that RR was the most effective intervention for increasing fluency, specifically for students in grades kindergarten through fifth grade. While RR originated as an independent intervention targeting reading fluency, RR research has expanded and has been linked with generalization of other high order reading skills, including student gains in reading comprehension (Rogers & Ardoin, 2018).

In addition to RR, LPP is one of the most utilized reading interventions present in the literature, and often is compared to

RR (Powell & Gadke, 2018; Swain et al., 2017). LPP was historically utilized to help increase accuracy with reading while also addressing fluency deficits (Begeny et al., 2009; Daly & Martens, 1994). LPP involves the participant listening to a more skilled reader read a passage while following along silently. Following the modeled read, the learner is required to then read the passage independently (Begeny et al., 2009). In a study by Swain et al. (2017), LPP was found to be more effective at increasing the number of words read correctly per minute for an individual student when compared to RR.

Recent research has investigated the benefits of adding LPP before RR. Lee and Yoon (2017) hypothesized that adding the LPP component before the RR would increase accuracy and fluency during the RR. By adding the LPP to RR, the intervention would align with the Instructional Hierarchy that states a student must achieve accuracy before moving on to fluency (Roger & Ardoin, 2018). Rogers & Ardoin (2018) examined the effects of LPP+RR on individuals' reading fluency. Their study compared the effects of RR to LPP+RR and found that both interventions resulted in higher WCPM, but it wasn't until LPP+RR was introduced that those gains in reading fluency were observed.

The Need for Small Group Reading Interventions

Since COVID-19 hit the world in spring of 2020, schools have found themselves needing efficient resources to recover from lost instruction time (University of Virginia School of Education and Human Development, n.d.). The pandemic posed significant educational risks for students in early elementary school who were still learning to read. Specifically, research indicates that while a typical school year often results in the improvement of kindergarten reading scores by 13.8 points on an assessment of early literacy, students who experienced the disrupted 2020 school year were only predicted to increase by 9.5 points (Bao et al., 2020). Additionally, a recent study conducted in Virginia indicated a 13.6% increase in the number of children entering the 2021-2022 school year at high risk for reading difficulties when compared to pre-pandemic numbers (University of Virginia School of Education and Human Development, n.d.).

With the world entering a "post-pandemic" era, the need for efficient evidence-based interventions for schools to aid in the recovery of educational losses has never been more important. Small group reading interventions offer an efficient solution to service multiple students at once. Even before the pandemic, small group instruction was often used as the primary method for reading instruction and intervention (Foorman & Torgesen, 2001). A small group intervention is defined as an intervention delivered to a group of students who have common skill deficits in an area (Hall & Burns, 2018). Small group instruction is often preferred by educators due to the ability to assist multiple students at once (Elbaum et al., 2000). Small group instruction additionally maps on to the RTI model, which outlines Tier II for small group support (Begeny et al., 2018). Vaughn et al. (2003) found that interventions delivered in a 1:1 ratio and a 1:3 ratio were both effective at increasing reading fluency. However, when the ratio increased to 1:10, the effectiveness of the intervention decreased. Further, a recent meta-analysis by Hall & Burns (2018) found that, overall, small group interventions were effective for reading interventions. Specifically, they found that reading groups were most effective when groups had five participants or less. In a review of small group reading interventions by Begeny et al. (2018), small group interventions were found to be as effective or more effective than individual interventions 80% of the time.

While RR and LPP have historically been utilized as individualized student interventions, multiple studies have reported the success of these interventions in group settings (Begeny & Silber, 2006; Begeny et al., 2009; Chard et al., 2002; Swain et al., 2017). In a previous study by Begeny et al. (2009), the effects of RR, LPP, and Listening Only were compared in a small group setting. The results demonstrated that RR and LPP were more effective at increasing reading fluency than Listening Only. Additionally, there were no differences between the effects of RR and LPP (Begeny et al., 2009). Among group-based reading interventions, LPP is the most utilized intervention technique and has demonstrated effectiveness with group reading interventions (Begeny & Siber, 2006; Begeny et al., 2009; Begeny et al., 2018). Finally, Begeny & Silber (2006) found that adding LPP to RR resulted in greater improvement in reading fluency when compared to LPP with word list and RR with word list. This study was conducted in a small group setting, demonstrating the effectiveness for small group interventions of LPP+RR.

Current Study

The current study sought to expand the research on small group reading fluency interventions. Specifically, the study examined the effects of RR, LPP, and LPP+RR in a small group setting, using an alternating treatment design to compare interventions and determine which yielded the largest gains across reading fluency.

Method

Participants and Setting

Participants included four elementary-aged students enrolled at a rural public elementary school in the Southeastern part of the United States. All participants were enrolled in the first grade and placed in Tier III services for deficits across reading by their school's Tier III coordination team. All participants were enrolled in a general education curriculum and did not receive special education services. It should be noted that each of these participants was in the spring of their kindergarten year when COVID-19 shut down their school. Students returned in the fall of 2020 on a hybrid schedule and resumed 100% face-to-face schooling in the spring of 2021.

Participants were Clyde, an 8-year-old Caucasian male; Margot, a 7-year-old African American female; Livy, a 7-year-old Hispanic female; and Jade, a 7-year-old African American female. Pseudonyms were used across participates. All four of the participants were receiving Tier III intervention services 4 times per week and were enrolled in general education. The interventions were implemented in the Tier III classroom at the students' elementary school. The intervention took place twice a week for 30-minutes. Due to the number of students who qualified for Tier III supports and the limited number of resources available, this reading intervention was implemented in a group format. However, it should be noted that this is outside of normative practice for most Tier III interventions. A group reading intervention most closely aligns with the Tier II level of supports. The school which these children attended was in a rural district, with 74.9% of students receiving free and reduced lunches. The district also reported minimal supplemental academic support, with only one full time employee serving as the academic interventionist across 502 students K-5th grade. Academic intervention sessions were run by doctoral school psychology graduate students who served as academic support personal within the participants' school district.

Materials
Oral Reading Fluency Benchmarking Probes
To find the student's instructional level, easyCBM probes were administered (Alonzo et al., 2006). Students were administered the first grade easyCBM Passage Reading Fluency probes (Alonzo et al., 2006). Instructional level was determined based on Shapiro's (2011) recommendation that instructional level range is from the 25th to the 75th percentile. If a student scored below the 25th percentile, that student would fall in the frustrational category and would be administered the CBM probes of a grade level below (Shapiro, 2011). This process would be repeated until instructional level was found. The easyCBM probes are normed by grade level, and provide percentages relating a student's score to the national average scores for students in thatthe same grade (Alonzo et al., 2006).

Oral Reading Fluency Reading Probes

During the intervention phase, students read Dynamic Indicators of Basic Early Literacy Skills 8th Edition (DIBELS; University of Oregon, 2018) Oral Reading Fluency progress monitoring probes, which had been updated for 2021-2022. There are a total of 20 progress monitoring passages available, ensuring that that the students were exposed to a new passage with each read. Only the first 55 to 65 words were used for the reading passages, which is consistent with procedures in previous literature (Begeny et al. 2009). The passages were shortened to control for time constraints that might occur. The number of words in each passage were based on the students' easyCBM results. Median scores on the Passage Reading Fluency probes gave an estimated number of words that each student could read in one minute. These median scores were used to calculate the number of words a student could read for a passage that would take approximately 3 to 4 minutes. All passages were administered according to standard administration outlined by DIBELS 8th Edition Oral Reading Fluency instructions (University of Oregon, 2018).

Additional Materials

The researcher additionally utilized materials of a stopwatch and clipboard. The stopwatch was used to record both reading time and instructional time of the interventions. The researcher used a clipboard when implementing the intervention to prevent the students from seeing the data collection.

Experimental Design

An alternating treatment design was utilized to compare the effects of RR, LPP, LPP+RR, with a control condition in a small group setting. The control condition was utilized to compare the effects of the interventions to a condition of no implemented intervention. Alternating treatment designs are the preferred design for single-subject design research when examining the effectiveness of skill-building interventions (Riley-Tillman & Burns, 2009). Each participant received a total of 13 sessions including baseline (BL) across a nine-week time period. The participants received a total of ten trials of the different intervention conditions. The participants received three trials of the control condition, three trials of the RR condition, two trials of the LPP condition, and two trials of the LPP+RR condition. The order in which conditions were implemented was randomized using an internet-based list randomizer. The students were presented the intervention in a group format; therefore, all participants received the intervention at the same time. Due to the intervention being group-based, the order in which each participant read was randomized. Each participant randomly rotated between reading first, second, third, or fourth for every condition. By randomizing the order that the students read, it prevented one student from reading fourth during each trial and, as a result, having more exposure to the passages than the other students.

The dependent variable measured was words correct per minute (WCPM). To calculate WCPM, the researcher divided the number of words read correctly by the amount of time spent reading.

Data Analysis

Treatment effects were primarily analyzed through visual analysis of the graphed data. Visual analysis involves examining the graph's level of trend, variability, and changes in level from the BL conditions to intervention. (Kratochwill et al., 2010). Effect sizes were also calculated through nonoverlapping of all pairs (NAP) (Parker & Vannest, 2009). For the purpose of this study, NAP compared the different conditions to one another in order to quantify the effect sizes of each condition.

Procedures

Across all conditions, the researcher greeted the group of students with developmentally appropriate language. The researcher began each session by saying, "Today we are going to be reading some stories together. I want everyone to try their best when reading our stories. Remember that, during our reading, we all need to be on 'good behavior mode.'" Good behavior mode was a series of rules that the students had to follow while participating in the intervention. The first rule was to always do their best reading. The second rule was to listen to the directions given. The third rule was to follow along silently on their paper when the researcher or the other students were reading. The fourth rule was to respect their friends when they read by not speaking or distracting them. Before each session began, the researcher and students remembered the rules of 'good behavior mode,' and entered good behavior mode by swiping their hand in front of their face while saying, "Entering good behavior mode."

Before each session, the students also played "musical chairs." The musical chairs game arranged the students in the order that they would read for the day. The order of reading was prearranged by the researcher as explained above. Each student was told to sit in chair one, two, three, or four. The game of musical chairs made the process of determining who was reading easier for data collection and helped eliminate additional prompts for the next student to read.

Benchmarking

To determine the students' instructional level, easyCBM probes were administered according to the manualized procedures outlined by easyCBM (Alonzo et al., 2006). Students were administered the first grade easyCBM Passage Reading Fluency probe (Alonzo et al., 2006). The students' percentiles on the easyCBM passages were based on the winter national norms. Clyde, Margot, and Livvy all performed at the 25th to 50th percentiles for Passage Reading Fluency at first grade. Jade performed at the 25th percentile for Passage Reading Fluency at first grade.

Baseline

BL data were collected before the interventions were implemented. Three BL passages were utilized. The passages used for BL fell under the same guidelines as the intervention passages. BL probes were presented in isolation; each participant completed the BL reading probes separately. The researcher provided standard instructions. The researcher would not provide any corrections but would provide the word if the student hesitated longer than 5 seconds.

Repeated Readings

The RR condition was modeled after the procedures described in Begeny et al. (2009). Each student was provided with the reading passage before instructions were given. The researcher began by repeating the standardized instructions. The instructions explained that each student was going to read the passage once, and while the other students were reading, they should follow along silently on their own paper. The students were told to do their best reading and if they had trouble with a word, the researcher would help them with it. If the student misread a word, hesitated longer than 5 seconds, or skipped a word, the researcher would provide that word. Once the researcher finished with the instructions, the student in chair one was instructed to read the passage while the other students followed along silently. Once the first student finished reading, the same procedures were provided to the students in chairs two, three, and four. After each student finished reading, they were removed from the table to a separate area and were instructed to read the passage again. WCPM data were collected when the student was taken to the separate location.

Listening Passage Preview

For the LPP condition, the students were provided with their reading passage at the beginning of each session. The researcher began the session by outlining the standardized instructions, stating that students would silently follow along on their paper while listening to the researcher read the passage. Once the instructions were given, the researcher read the passage at a grade-level appropriate WCPM rate. The researcher then removed the students from the group and measured their WCPM similarly to the RR condition.

Repeated Readings with Listening Passage Preview

During the LPP+RR condition, the researcher provided each student with the reading passage. The researcher then explained the instructions to the students. The researcher instructed the students to follow along silently on their paper while the researcher read. The words were read at a grade-level appropriate WCPM rate. The researcher then explained that each student would read the passage once. If the student misread a word, skipped a word, or hesitated for longer than 5 seconds, the correct word would be provided by the researcher. The students who were not reading were instructed to read along silently while their peers read. Once all of the students read, they were removed from the table to read in a separate location for data collection. The procedures for data collection during RR were the same for the LPP+RR condition.

Control Condition

During the control condition, each student was provided with a reading passage. The control condition was not conducted in a group format but individually with each student. The students were taken to an area with only the researcher and the student. The students were instructed to read the passage by themselves. The student would only read the passage one time and no errors were corrected by the researcher. If the student hesitated longer than 5 seconds, the researcher provided the word.

Procedural Integrity

Interobserver agreement (IOA) was collected for 84% of the sessions. A trained specialist level or doctoral school psychology graduate student served as the second observer. The second observer had a second assessor's copy of the passage in order to collect data on each student's WCPM. IOA was collected by calculating the number of agreements divided by total agreements plus disagreements and dividing that number by 100. For Clyde, IOA was 99.21%. For Margot, IOA was 98.32%. For Livvy, IOA was 99.02%. For Jade, IOA was 98.31%.

To preserve treatment integrity, checklists for each condition were created for the researcher to follow. Treatment integrity was collected for 84% of the sessions. Treatment integrity was collected by the main researcher and a second observer who was a school psychology graduate student. Treatment integrity was measured by making checkmarks on a procedure sheet for each correct step followed by the researcher. To calculate treatment integrity, the total number of steps delivered was divided by the total number of steps and multiplied by 100. Treatment integrity was 100% for all sessions.

Results

Clyde

Clyde's results for WCPM during the alternating treatment design are presented in Figure 1. The preliminary results of the graph indicate that the LPP+RR condition resulted in the greatest change in level and highest WCPM. The LPP+RR condition demonstrated low variability between the two data points. The RR condition showed high variability; however, there was an increasing trend. Based on the last data point for RR, the results of the graph show similar effectiveness as LPP+RR. For the LPP condition, only one data point was collected due to an absence on that day of data collection. The LPP condition showed higher WCPM than both BL and the control condition; however, LPP was not as effective as RR and LPP+RR. Clyde's intervention data for the control condition showed an increasing trend for WCPM. NAP was computed to calculate the effect sizes and compare BL to the intervention conditions and the control condition to the intervention conditions. The NAP effect sizes are presented in Table 1.

Margot

Margot's WCPM data can be found in Figure 2. The graph showed immediate changes in level in WCPM for RR, LPP, and LPP+RR. There was no immediate change in level when comparing BL to the control condition. LPP, RR, and LPP+RR, all show increasing trends in WCPM, additionally with little variability. The control condition showed slight variability with a decreasing trend. Overall large effects were seen when baseline levels of WCPM were compared to baseline levels. Table 1 presents NAP scores across conditions.

Livvy

Livvy's intervention data is presented in Figure 3. NAP was calculated to determine the overall effect sizes between the different stages and conditions throughout the intervention and are presented in Table 1. Livvy had an immediate change in level from BL to intervention for both RR and LPP+RR. There was a slight change in level from BL to the control condition and LPP; however, the WCPM for the initial data points of LPP and the control condition were roughly the same. Both LPP and RR showed an increasing trend for WCPM, whereas LPP+RR exhibited a decreasing trend. Additionally, the control condition was increasing in trend.

Jade

Jade's WCPM can be found below in Figure 4. Jade's graph showed immediate changes in level when researchers compared BL to RR and BL to LPP+RR. There was a slight change in level from BL to LPP; however, BL to control conditions showed no change in level for WCPM. There was little variability in BL, control conditions, and the intervention conditions. LPP and the control conditions demonstrated an increasing trend for WCPM.

NAP was calculated to obtain the effect sizes comparing the different intervention components. These results are displayed across Table 1.

Table 1
NAP Results

	BL-C	BL-RR	BL-LPP	BL-LPP+ RR	C-RR	C-LPP	C-LPP +RR	RR-LPP	RR-LPP +RR	LPP-RR +LPP
	NAP	NAP	NAP	NAP	NAP	NAP	NAP	NAP	NAP	NAP
Clyde	0.67*	1.0**	1.0**	1.0**	0.89*	1.0**	1.0**	0.33	0.83*	1.0**
Margot	1.0**	1.0**	1.0**	1.0**	1.0**	1.0**	1.0**	0.67*	0.67*	0.75*
Livvy	1.0**	1.0**	1.0**	1.0**	1.0**	0.67*	1.0**	0.25	0.75*	0.75*
Jade	0.78*	1.0**	1.0**	1.0**	1.0**	0.83*	1.0**	0.50	1.0**	1.0**

Note: BL: baseline; C: control; RR: repeated readings; LPP: listening passage preview; LPP+RR: listening passage preview with repeated readings; NAP: nonoverlapping of all pairs. Large effect sizes**, Medium effect sizes*, all other effect sizes: small effect sizes.

Figure 1

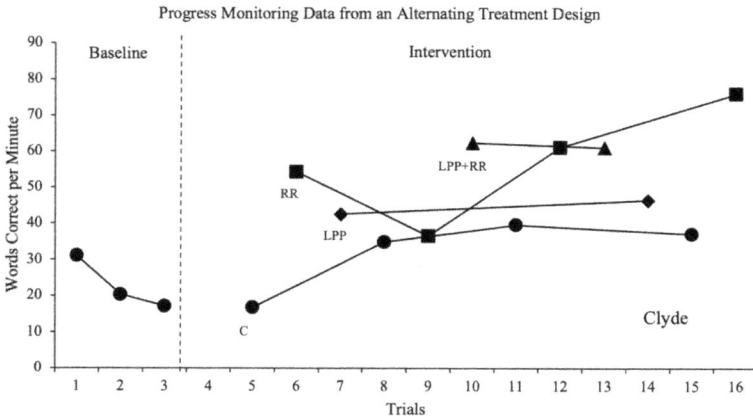

Progress Monitoring Data from an Alternating Treatment Design

Figure 2

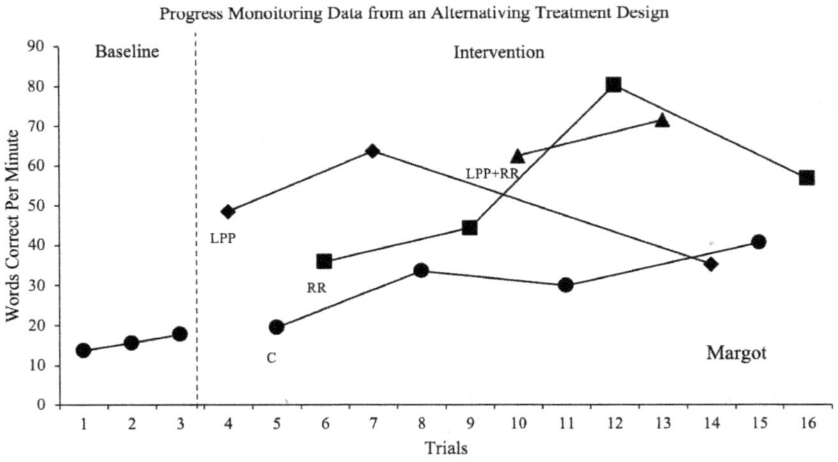

Progress Monoitoring Data from an Alternativing Treatment Design

Figure 3

Progress Monitoring Data from an Alternating Treatment Design

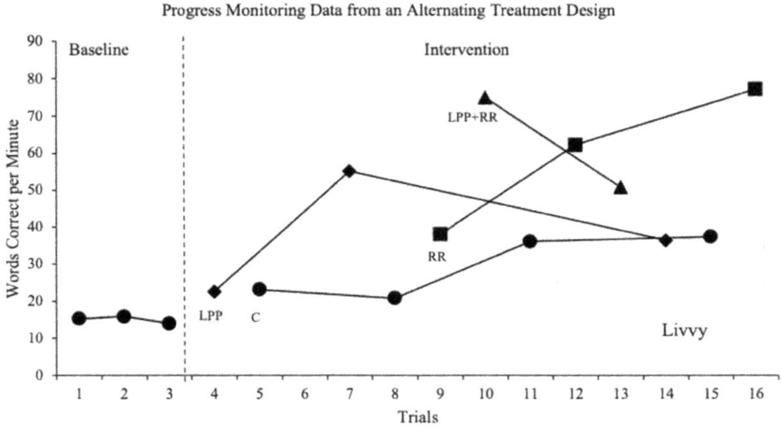

Figure 4

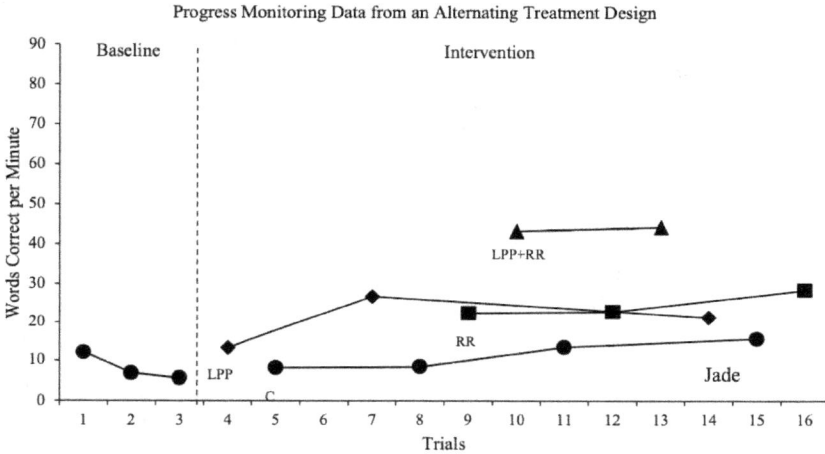

Progress Monitoring Data from an Alternating Treatment Design

Discussion

As professionals in the field of education begin to address the needs of young students who experienced a significant disruption in their curriculum due to the COVID-19 pandemic, the need has never been more dire for effective, efficient reading interventions that can be delivered at the group level. In fact, a recent study has identified a significant increase in students at high risk for reading difficulties from pre-pandemic to the present (University of Virginia School of Education and Human Development, n.d.). This study was designed to determine the effectiveness of a small group reading intervention, comparing the interventions of RR, LPP, and LPP+RR. Although research has shown that small group reading interventions utilizing RR, LPP, and LPP+RR are effective, no study has compared the interventions using an alternating treatment design (Begeny & Silber, 2006; Begeny et al., 2009). The current study expands on research done by Begeny et al. (2009) which found that RR and LPP are effective in a small group setting for increasing reading fluency. LPP+RR was added as a comparison intervention due to its effectiveness at increasing fluency and accuracy, as well as findings from previous research that showed that LPP+RR was more effective than RR and LPP alone (Begeny & Silber, 2006; Rogers & Ardoin, 2018). LPP+RR may be a more effective intervention to use with younger readers who are trying to gain accuracy and fluency quickly. The results of this study demonstrate that all conditions (RR, LPP, and LPP+RR) resulted in higher WCPM for each student when compared to the control conditions and BL conditions.

For Clyde, the LPP+RR condition proved to be the most effective intervention, as demonstrated by NAP and visual analysis. Specifically, LPP+RR showed the largest change in level from BL and exhibited the lowest variability. However, both LPP and RR were effective at increasing WCPM when compared to BL and control conditions. For Margot, LPP+RR and RR both resulted in large increases for WCPM when compared to BL and control conditions. RR resulted in the largest WCPM and had significant effect sizes when compared to BL and control conditions. Additionally, LPP was effective at increasing WCPM, but it did not show as substantial gains as RR and LPP+RR. Overall, RR was the most effective at increasing Margot's WCPM. For Livvy, there was high variability in each intervention condition. LPP+RR demonstrated moderate effect sizes when compared to RR and LPP, whereas the comparison between LPP and RR yielded weak effect sizes. For Jade, LPP+RR proved to result in the largest gains in WCPM when compared to the other interventions. Jade demonstrated the lowest accuracy when compared to the other participants at the beginning of the study. The fact that LPP+RR demonstrated the greatest gains in WCPM adds to the research that supports the effectiveness of LPP+RR at increasing accuracy and fluency (Lee & Yoon, 2017). Although all of the interventions in this study increased WCPM, LPP+RR proved to be the most effective at increasing reading fluency for most participants. RR was more effective than LPP at increasing WCPM, but RR's increases were not at the same level as LPP+RR.

Limitations

Because of factors occurring during the implementation of this intervention, the increases in reading fluency cannot be solely attributed to the intervention. Several other environmental factors could have affected the participants' increases in reading fluency. Environmental factors that could have affected the internal validity include general classroom instruction and curriculum, as well as other services received in the Tier III classroom when the researcher was not present. Another noteworthy limitation is the process of data collection. Due to the intervention being delivered in a small group format, the researcher had to control for data collection by having data collection occur in a separate area of the room. This resulted in a time gap between when students were provided the intervention and when the students' data was collected. The delay between the intervention's delivery and data collection could have resulted in lower WCPM. Although this effect was considered and the students read in a randomized order, the researcher cannot determine what effect this delay had on WCPM. Future research should examine if a time delay between intervention and independent reading affects students' WCPM. Lastly, due to time constraints, this intervention took place over a 9-week period. Therefore, each intervention could only be provided a maximum of three times; however, the interventions were most commonly implemented twice. Future research should aim to collect more data points for each intervention to ascertain whether different or novel patterns in responding may emerge. Finally, this research study only included four participants. Replication and verification of findings are encouraged with future projects that include additional participants.

In conclusion, this study examined the effects of different reading interventions on WCPM in a small group setting. All four of the participants were chosen due to their difficulties in reading fluency, and were shown to have improvements in their WCPM. The improvements in WCPM were evident during intervention and generalized to novel passages, as evident in the control conditions and in progress monitoring. Three out of the four participants reached instructional level in reading fluency for spring first grade norms. Results indicated that these reading interventions are additionally effective when provided in a small group format. The small group format could prove useful for Tier II interventions in the classroom and for students who are experiencing difficulty after missing instruction due to COVID-19.

References

Alonzo, J., Tindal, G., Ulmer, K., & Glasgow, A. (2006). *easyCBM® online progress monitoring assessment system.* Behavioral Research and Teaching.

Bao, X., Qu, H., Zhang, R., & Hogan, T. P. (2020). Modeling reading ability gain in kindergarten children during COVID-19 school closures. *International Journal of Environmental Research and Public Health, 17*(17). https://doi.org/10.3390/ijerph17176371

Bates-Brantley, K., Donald, M., Sorrell, J., Huff, M., McHenry, R., & Harry, S. W. (2022). An early childhood intervention targeting academic and behavioral skill deficits. *Perspectives on Early Childhood Psychology and Education. 7(1), 35-57.*

Begeny, J. C., Krouse, H. E., Ross, S. G., & Mitchell, R. C. (2009). Increasing elementary-aged students' reading fluency with small-group interventions: A comparison of repeated reading, listening passage preview, and listening only strategies. *Journal of Behavioral Education, 18*(3), 211–228. https://doi.org/10.1007/s10864-009-9090-9

Begeny, J. C., Levy, R. A., & Field, S. A. (2018). Using small-group instruction to improve students' reading fluency: An evaluation of the existing research. *Journal of Applied School Psychology, 34(1),* 36–64. https://doi.org/10.1080/15377903.2017.1328628

Begeny, J. C., & Silber, J. M. (2006). An examination of group-based treatment packages for increasing elementary-aged students' reading fluency. *Psychology in the Schools, 43(2),* 183–195. https://doi.org/10.1002/pits.20138

Bonfiglio, C. M., Daly, E. J., III, Persampieri, M., & Andersen, M. (2006). An Experimental Analysis of the Effects of Reading Interventions in a Small Group Reading Instruction Context. *Journal of Behavioral Education, 15(2),* 93–109. https://doi.org/10.1007/s10864-006-9009-7

Chard, D. J., Vaughn, S., & Tyler, B.J. (2002). A synthesis of research on effective interventions for building reading fluency with elementary students with learning disabilities. *Journal of Learning Disabilities, 35*(5), 386–406. https://doi.org/10.1177/00222194020350050101

Daly, E. J., & Martens, B. K. (1994). A comparison of three interventions for increasing oral reading performance: Application of the instructional hierarchy. *Journal of Applied Behavior Analysis, 27*(3), 459–469. https://doi.org/10.1901/jaba.1994.27-459

Elbaum, B., Vaughn, S., Tejero Hughes, M., & Watson Moody, S. (2000). How effective are one-to-one tutoring programs in reading for elementary students at risk for reading failure? A meta-analysis of the intervention research. *Journal of Educational Psychology, 92*(4), 605–619. https://doi.org/10.1037/0022-0663.92.4.605

Fletcher, J. M., & Lyon, G. R. (1998). Reading: A research-based approach. In W. M. Evers (Ed.), *What's gone wrong in America's classrooms* (pp. 49–90). Hoover Institution Press.

Foorman, B. R., & Torgesen, J. (2001). Critical elements of classroom and small-group instruction promote reading success in all children. *Learning Disabilities Research & Practice, 16(4)*, 203–212. https://doi.org/10.1111/0938-8982.00020

Hall, M. S., & Burns, M. K. (2018). Meta-analysis of targeted small-group reading interventions. *Journal of School Psychology, 66*, 54–66. https://doi.org/10.1016/j.jsp.2017.11.002

Hammerstein, S., König, C., Dreisörner, T., & Frey, A. (2021). Effects of COVID-19-related school closures on student achievement-a systematic review. *Frontiers in Psychology*, 4020. https://doi.org/10.3389/fpsyg.2021.746289

Institute of Education Sciences. (2019). *The Nation's Report Card: 2019 Mathematics and Reading Assessments.* U.S. Department of Education, https://www.nationsreportcard.gov/highlights/reading/2019/

Kearney, C. A., & Childs, J. (2021). A multi-tiered systems of support blueprint for re-opening schools following COVID-19 shutdown. *Children and Youth Services Review 122 (105919)*. https://doi.org/10.1016/j.childyouth.2020.105919

Koller, K. A., Hojnoski, R. L., & Van Norman, E. R. (2022). Classification accuracy of early literacy assessments: Linking preschool and kindergarten performance. *Assessment for Effective Intervention, 48*(1), 13–22. https://doi.org/10.1177%2F15345084221081091

Kratochwill, T. R., Hitchcock, J., Horner, R. H., Levin, J. R., Odom, S. L., Rindskopf, D. M & Shadish, W. R. (2010). Single-case designs technical documentation. Retrieved from *What Works Clearinghouse.* http://ies.ed.gov/ncee/wwc/pdf/wwc_scd.pdf.

Kuhfeld, M., Soland, J., Tarasawa, B., Johnson, A., Ruzek, E., & Liu, J. (2020). Projecting the potential impact of COVID-19 school closures on academic achievement. *Educational Researcher, 49*(8), 549–565. http://dx.doi.org/10.3102/0013189X20965918

Lee, J., Grigg, W., and Donahue, P. (2007). *The Nation's Report Card: Reading 2007.* National Center for Education Statistics. https://nces.ed.gov/nationsreportcard/pubs/main2007/2007496.asp

Lee, J., & Yoon, S. Y. (2017). The effects of repeated reading on reading fluency for students with reading disabilities: A meta-analysis. *Journal of Learning Disabilities, 50*(2), 213–224. https://doi.org/10.1177/0022219415605194

Parker, R. I., & Vannest, K. (2009). An improved effect size for single-case research: Nonoverlap of all pairs. *Behavior Therapy, 40*, 357–367.

Powell, M. B., & Gadke, D. L. (2018). Improving oral reading fluency in middle-school students: A comparison of repeated reading and listening passage preview. *Psychology in the Schools, 55*(10), 1274–1286. https://doi.org/10.1002/pits.22184

Riley-Tillman, T. C., & Burns, M. K. (2009). *Evaluating educational interventions: Single-case design for measuring response to intervention.* The Guilford Press.

Rogers, L. S., & Ardoin, S. P. (2018). Investigating the benefit of adding listening passage preview to repeated readings. *School Psychology Quarterly, 33*(3), 439–447. https://doi.org/10.1037/spq0000227

Schreder, S. J., Hupp, S. D. A., Everett, G. E., & Krohn, E. (2012). Targeting reading fluency through brief experimental analysis and parental intervention over the summer. *Journal of Applied School Psychology, 28*(2), 200–220. https://doi.org/10.1080/15377903.2012.670047

Shapiro, E. S. (2011). *Academic skills problems: Direct assessment and intervention. Fourth Edition.* The Guilford Press.

Skinner, C. H., Cooper, L., & Cole, C. L. (1997). The effects of oral presentation previewing rates on reading performance. *Journal of Applied Behavior Analysis, 30*(2), 331–333. https://doi.org/10.1901/jaba.1997.30-331

Stevens, E. A., Walker, M. A., & Vaughn, S. (2017). The effects of reading fluency interventions on the reading fluency and reading comprehension performance of elementary students with learning disabilities: A synthesis of the research from 2001 to 2014. *Journal of Learning Disabilities, 50*(5), 576–590. https://doi.org/10.1177/0022219416638028

Swain, K. D., Leader-Janssen, E. M., & Conley, P. (2017). Effects of repeated reading and listening passage preview on oral reading fluency. *Reading Improvement, 54*(3), 105–111.

Szadokierski, I., Burns, M. K., & McComas, J. J. (2017). Predicting intervention effectiveness from reading accuracy and rate measures through the instructional hierarchy: Evidence for a skill-by-treatment interaction. *School Psychology Review, 46(2)*, 190–200. https://doi.org/10.17105/SPR-2017-0013.V46-2

Therrien, W. J. (2004). Fluency and comprehension gains as a result of repeated reading: A meta-analysis. *Remedial and Special Education, 25*(4), 252–261. https://doi.org/10.1177/07419325040250040801

University of Oregon (2018). *Dynamic Indicators of Basic Early Literacy Skills (DIBELS)*, 8th edition. https://dibels.uoregon.edu/

University of Virginia School of Education and Human Development. (n.d.). *Examining the impact of COVID-19 on the identification of at-risk students: Fall 2021 literacy screenings*. http://pals.virginia.edu/data-reports

Vaughn, S., Linan-Thompson, S., Kouzekanani, K., Bryant, D. P., Dickson, S., & Blozis, S. A. (2003). Reading instruction grouping for students with reading difficulties. *Remedial and Special Education, 24*, 301–315.

List of Contibutors

Indicates corresponding author and inclusion of contact information.

*Kayla Bates-Brantley, PhD, is an assistant professor in the school psychology program at Mississippi State University. She is a Licensed Board-Certified Behavior Analyst, Doctoral as well as a National Certified School Psychologist. Her research interests include academic and behavioral consultation in applied settings, applied behavior analysis and early intervention for developmental disabilities. *email: keb240@msstate.edu*

Kathleen M. Baggett, PhD, is the Director of the Mark Chaffin Center for Healthy Development, and Associate Professor of Health Policy and Behavioral Sciences in the School of Public Health at Georgia State University. She is trained as an applied developmental psychologist and is a licensed psychologist health service provider.

Brian Barger, PhD, is a Research Associate Professor of Population Health Sciences (Biostatistics) in the School of Public Health at Georgia State University. Dr. Barger's research program focuses on understanding how young children with disabilities are identified in their communities so they may receive early intervention and community-based treatments.

Laura Katherine Barker, M.S., BCBA, LBA, Laura-Katherine serves as a Behavior Analyst at Canopy Children's Autism Early Intervention Clinic where she provides clinical care to autistic children between the ages of 2-8. Laura-Katherine's clinical interests include: reduction of problematic behaviors, such as self-injurious behaviors and aggression towards others, and language and skill acquisition goals.

Brenda Bassingthwaite, PhD, BCBA, is an Associate Professor in the Psychology Department at the Munroe-Meyer Institute at the University of Nebraska Medical Center. She provides training to master's, pre-doctoral, and post-doctoral level trainees in school-based behavior consultation for students with intellectual and developmental disabilities who engage in challenging behaviors.

*Chloe Beacham, M.Ed., is a doctoral candidate in School Psychology at Georgia State University. She is currently a Bridging the Word Gap Research Network Emerging Scholar and is completing her doctoral internship in Health Service Psychology at Children's Healthcare of Atlanta and Emory University School of Medicine, Department of Pediatrics. *Email: cbeacham2@student.gsu.edu*

Madison Billingsley-Ring is a fourth year doctoral student in the school psychology program at Mississippi State University. Her research interest include academic and behavioral interventions in rural and applied settings, developmental disabilities, and behavioral interventions to increase transition based skills such as communication, functional academics, and driving.

Robyn Brewer, M.S., BCBA, LBA, serves as a Behavior Analyst for Canopy Children's Solutions working in the Autism Early Intervention Clinic in Jackson. She provides clinical to autistic children between the ages of 2-8. Robyn attained her accreditation as a BCBA and her License as a Behavior Analyst in 2018.

Alexandra G. Brunner, M.A., is a graduate of Mississippi State University where she earned her master's degree in Educational Psychology with an emphasis in Applied Behavior Analysis. While a student, she was a graduate assistant with Canopy Autism Solutions where she worked under the supervision of multiple Board-Certified Behavior Analysts.

Emily R. DeFouw, PhD, BCBA is an Assistant Professor of Psychology at the University of Southern Mississippi. Her research focuses on evaluating treatment intensity and implementation for research-based math interventions delivered within a Response-to-Intervention (RtI) framework and school-based consultation.

*Cara Dillon, PhD, completed her doctorate degree at University of Cincinnati's School Psychology program. She will be continuing her work in implementation science to support school psychologists and teachers. *Email: dilloncr@mail.uc.edu*

Mallie Donald is a second-year doctoral candidate in the school psychology program at Mississippi State University. While at

Mississippi State, she has worked in both the school and clinic setting using academic and behavioral evidenced-based interventions. Her research interests include academic and behavioral interventions for autism or related disorders, pediatric feeding disorders, and parent consultation involving behavior analytic principles.

Claire Donehower, PhD, is an assistant professor in the Department of Learning Sciences. She received her doctorate from the University of Central Florida in the Exceptional Education Program. Her research focuses on improving academic, social and behavioral outcomes for students with autism spectrum disorders (ASD) using innovative technology.

Brad A. Dufrene, PhD, is a Professor of Psychology at The University of Southern Mississippi. He is primarily interested in increasing access to evidence-based practices for underserved populations. In particular, Dr. Dufrene is interested in the treatment integrity of evidence-based interventions for preschoolers at-risk for emotional and behavioral disorders.

*Christopher M. Furlow, PhD, BCBA-D, LBA, is the Director of Autism Solutions for Canopy Children's Solutions' Autism Early Intervention Clinics in Jackson. As Director, Chris is involved with the supervision of clinical staff, strategizing appropriate interventions with behavior analysts, and guiding therapeutic innovation and research initiatives for the Autism Solutions team.

Email: christopher.furlow@mycanopy.org

Daniel L. Gadke, PhD, NCSP, BCBA, LP, is professor of school psychology at Mississippi State University, Mississippi State, Mississippi. His primary research interests include the examination academic and behavioral interventions from an applied behavioral analytic model using single subject design research methodology.

*Sarah Wright Harry, PhD, is an assistant professor in the educational psychology department at Ball State University. She functions as a core faculty member in the School Psychology program. Dr. Harry is a licensed clinical psychologist in the state of Indiana, board certified behavior analyst at the doctoral level and a nationally certified school psychologist. She focuses her research in areas of academic assessment and intervention as well as class-wide behavior interventions. *email: swharry@bsu.edu*

Frances K. Huff is a graduate student at Florida Institute of Technology where she is pursuing a master's degree in Applied Behavior Analysis. While a training to become a BCBA, she works as a Registered Behavior Technician with Canopy Autism Solutions under the supervision of multiple Board-Certified Behavior Analysts.

*__Jessica M. Kemp,__ PhD, is a Licensed Psychologist in Massachusetts and Nationally Certified School Psychologist. She is currently at Devereux Advanced Behavioral Health, Massachusetts as a school psychologist and specializes in systems-level consultation, positive behavior interventions and supports, social-emotional learning, and trauma-informed care for students.
Email: jkemp@devereux.org

*__Sara Kupzyk,__ PhD, LP, BCBA-D, is an Assistant Professor in Psychology at the University of Nebraska at Omaha. She teaches courses in the Applied Behavior Analysis Master's Program. Her research interests include home-school collaboration, consultation, and treatment integrity. She previously provided outpatient behavioral health services to children and families in integrated primary care settings. *Email: skupzyk@unomaha.edu*

*__Zachary C. LaBrot,__ PhD, is an Assistant Professor of School Psychology at the University of Southern Mississippi. Dr. LaBrot's research interests include consultation in early childhood education settings, class wide interventions, and behavioral parent training. Additionally, Dr. LaBrot is proudly a practicing licensed psychologist.
Email: zachary.labrot@usm.edu

Abigail Lawson is a third-year graduate student in the University of Southern Mississippi School Psychology Doctoral Program. She received her B.S. in Psychology at Mississippi State University. Her primary research interests focus on implementing effective classroom intervention strategies and academic interventions.

Marshall Lundy received his Masters in Applied Behavior Analysis from the University of Southern Mississippi. He is a board certfied behavior analyst (BCBA). Marshall's work has focused on children with autism and related neurodevelopmental disorders in both school and clinical settings.

Emily Maxime is a third-year graduate student in the University of Southern Mississippi School Psychology Doctoral Program. Emily's research interest examine the implementation of intervention and consultation strategies that can be generalized by students and teachers to help further their overall success at school and home.

Lauren McKinley is a Licensed Specialist in School Psychology in Klein Independent School District in Texas, where her role focuses on assessment and consultation for students receiving special education services. She received her doctoral degree in School Psychology from the University of Cincinnati and is a Nationally Certified School Psychologist.

Kayla McVay is a 2nd year student in the University of Southern Mississippi School Psychology Doctorate Program. Kayla received her bachelor's degree from Tougaloo College. Her primary research interests include implementing technology to improve academic outcomes and applying/ adapting academic interventions to aid in better outcomes among racial and ethnic minorities.

Daniel Newman, PhD, NCSP, is an Associate Professor in the School Psychology Program in the College of Education, Criminal Justice, and Human Services at the University of Cincinnati. His research interests include school consultation practice and training, clinical supervision, and professional issues in school psychology.

Philip D. Nordness, PhD, is a Peter Kiewit Distinguished Professor in the Department of Special Education and Communication Disorders at the University of Nebraska Omaha. In addition to his research on interdisciplinary collaboration, Professor Nordness teaches courses related to behavior modification and children with emotional and behavioral disorders.

Catherine Perkins, PhD, is the Coordinator of the Educational Specialist Program in School Psychology at Georgia State University and a research fellow with the Center for Research on School Safety, School Climate, and Classroom Management. Dr. Perkins consults nationally and internationally on assessment and intervention in early childhood.

Hailey Ripple, PhD, BCBA-D, is an assistant professor in the school psychology program at Mississippi State University. She is a Board-Certified Behavior Analyst, Doctoral and her research interests include pediatric feeding disorders, functional analysis of problem behavior in individuals with sensory impairments, the effectiveness of interventions rooted in applied behavior analysis, and CHARGE Syndrome.

Andrew Roach, PhD, is a Professor and the Coordinator of the School Psychology PhD Program in the Department of Counseling & Psychological Services at Georgia State University. Dr. Roach is a facilitator with the Center for Courage & Renewal and a certified mindfulness educator with Mindfulness Without Borders.

Andrew Rozsa is a school psychology doctoral student currently on predoctoral internship in the Tucson Unified School District. Professional interests include parent management training, neurodevelopmental disabilities in children and adolescents, applied behavior analysis, and third wave cognitive behavioral therapies.

*Tyler E. Smith, PhD, is an Assistant Professor of School Psychology in the Department of Educational, School, and Counseling Psychology at the University of Missouri. Dr. Smith's research focuses on family engagement in education, school-based consultation, and systematic review/meta-analysis.
Email: smithtyle@missouri.edu

Mary "Nicole" Thomason, M. Ed., BCBA, LBA, currently serves as a Behavior Analyst for Canopy Children's Solutions Early Intervention Autism Clinic in Jackson, MS. With more than a decade of experience working with children with autism, Nicole attained her accreditation as a BCBA in 2017 and has experience in both school and outpatient clinical settings.

Adam D. Weaver, PhD, BCBA, is an Associate Professor at the University of Nebraska at Omaha. He teaches the behavioral sequence of courses in the School Psychology graduate training program, and formerly worked as a practitioner in public schools for nine years.

Sara A. Whitcomb, PhD, is Associate Professor and Director of Clinical Training in the School Psychology Program at the University of Massachusetts Amherst. Dr. Whitcomb has written several books, peer-reviewed articles, and given numerous presentations on behavioral, social, and emotional assessment, as well as social and emotional learning.

Breya L. Whitefield, M.A., is a fourth-year doctoral student at Ball State University. Her research interests include the implementation of behavioral interventions across settings to support individuals diagnosed with neurodevelopmental disorders. Upon graduation, Breya plans to become a licensed psychologist working with pediatric clients and their families in behavior management strategies.

Perspectives on Early Childhood Psychology and Education

PECPE publishes twice a year, in the fall and spring. These two issues on specific focuses are typically guest-edited and can also include a few general articles.

Editorial Policy and Submission Guidelines

Perspectives on Early Childhood Psychology and Education focuses on publishing original contributions from a broad range of psychological and educational perspectives relevant to infants, young children (to age 8 years), families, and caregivers. Manuscripts incorporating evidence-based research, theory, and practice within clinical, community, developmental, neurological, and school psychology perspectives are considered. In addition, the journal accepts test and book reviews, literature reviews, program descriptions and evaluations, clinical studies, and other professional materials of interest to psychologists and educators working with young children. Proposals for special focus topics may be made to the Editor.

Format: Manuscripts should be original work not currently submitted for publication to other journals. Authors must follow the guidelines of the Publication Manual of the American Psychological Association (Sixth Edition). Manuscripts may not exceed 35 double-spaced pages in length, including the cover page, abstract, references, tables, and figures.

Submission: Submit an electronic copy of the manuscript for editorial review. Avoid including any identifying author information in the text. Selection of manuscripts is based on blind peer review. Include a cover page with the following information: the title of article, author(s) full name(s), title(s), institution or professional affiliations, and mailing and email address of primary author. The cover page will not be sent to reviewers.

Selection Criteria:

- Importance of topic in early childhood psychology and education
- Theory and research related to content
- Contribution to professional practice in early childhood psychology and education
- Clear and concise writing

Submit manuscripts to the Editor electronically at the following email address: PECPE@bsu.edu.

Volume 7, Issue 2 of
Perspectives on Early Childhood Psychology and Education
was published in Fall 2022
by Pace University Press

Cover and interior layout by Adjei Kwesi Boateng
The journal was typeset in Minion and Myriad
and printed by Lightning Source

Pace University Press
Director: Manuela Soares
Associate Director: Erica Johnson
Design Consultant: Joseph Caserto
Marketing Consultant: Tina McIntyre
Production Associate: Lucely Garcia

Graduate Assistants: Adjei Kwesi Boateng and Ariel Stevenson
Graduate Student Aide: Harper Elizabeth Bullard

www.ingramcontent.com/pod-product-compliance
Lightning Source LLC
Chambersburg PA
CBHW061003280326
41935CB00009B/816